ALEXANDER IN INDIA

A PORTION OF THE HISTORY

OF

QUINTUS CURTIUS

ALEXANDER IN INDIA
A PORTION OF THE HISTORY
OF
QUINTUS CURTIUS

EDITED BY

W. E. HEITLAND, M. A.

AND

T. E. RAVEN, B. A.

GYAN

Published by

GYAN

Gyan Publishing House
5, Ansari Road
Daryaganj, New Delhi-110002
Phone: 011-47034999, 9811692060
E-mail: books@gyanbooks.com

Distribution Network
gyanbooks.com
India, USA, Canada, UK, Australia, France

ISBN : 978-81-212-9086-9 (PB)
First Published, 1879

2nd Impression 2023

Printed at: Gyan Press, Delhi.

ALEXANDER IN INDIA A PORTION OF THE HISTORY OF QUITUS CURTIUS

EDITORS: W. E. HEITLAND AND T. E. RAVEN

A PORTION OF THE HISTORY

OF

QUINTUS CURTIUS

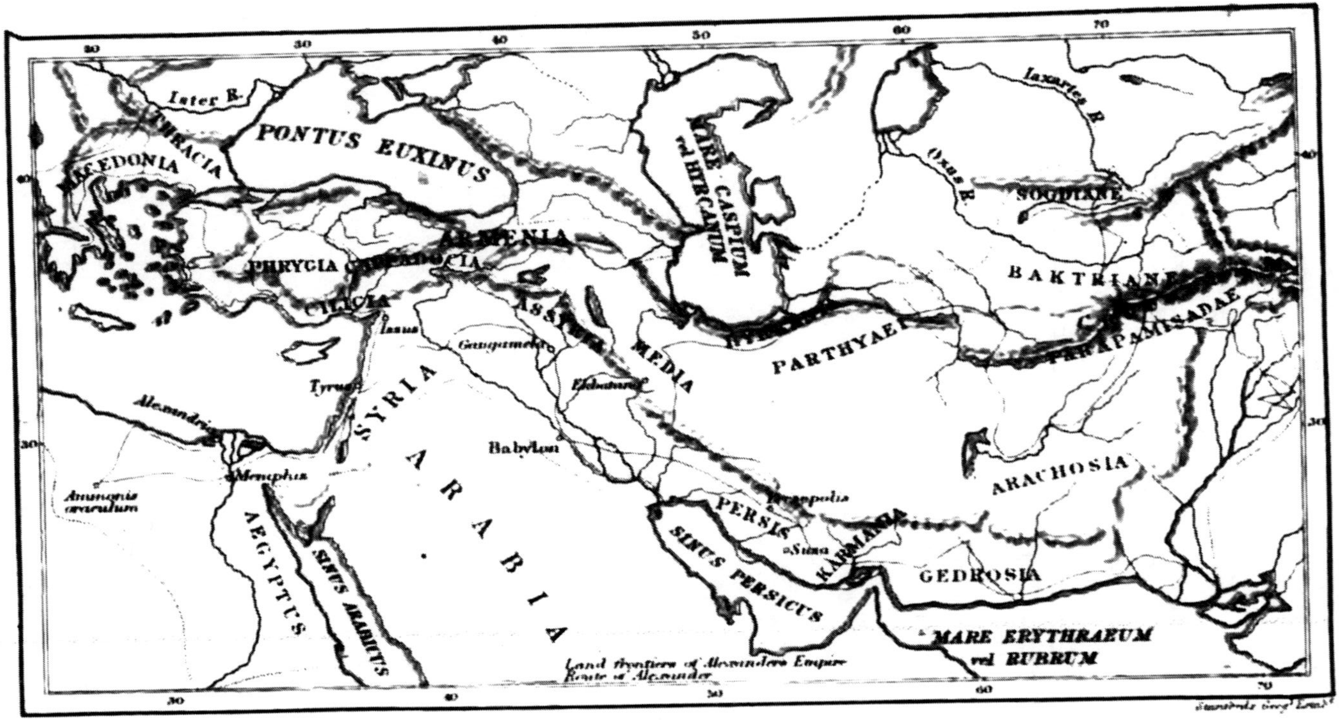

Cambridge University Press

Pitt Press Series.

ALEXANDER IN INDIA.

A PORTION OF THE HISTORY

OF

QUINTUS CURTIUS

EDITED FOR SCHOOLS AND COLLEGES

BY

W E HEITLAND M A,

FELLOW AND LECTURER OF ST JOHN'S COLLEGE CAMBRIDGE,

AND

T E RAVEN B A,

ASSISTANT MASTER IN SHERBORNE SCHOOL, LATE SCHOLAR OF
GONVILLE AND CAIUS COLLEGE CAMBRIDGE.

EDITED FOR THE SYNDICS OF THE UNIVERSITY PRESS.

Cambridge:
AT THE UNIVERSITY PRESS.

London: CAMBRIDGE WAREHOUSE, 17, PATERNOSTER ROW.
Cambridge: DEIGHTON, BELL, AND CO.
Leipzig: F A BROCKHAUS.
1879

[On mention of the tomb of Alexander at Alexandria.]

illic Pellaei proles uesana Philippi,
felix praedo, iacet terrarum uindice fato
raptus: sacratis totum spargenda per orbem
membra uiri posuere adytis: fortuna pepercit
manibus, et regni durauit ad ultima fatum.
nam sibi libertas unquam si redderet orbem,
ludibrio seruatus erat, non utile mundo
editus exemplum, terras tot posse sub uno
esse uiro. Macetum fines, latebrasque suorum
deseruit, uictasque patri despexit Athenas:
perque Asiae populos, fatis urgentibus actus,
humana cum strage ruit, gladiumque per omnes
exegit gentes: ignotos miscuit amnes,
Persarum Euphraten, Indorum sanguine Gangen:
terrarum fatale malum, fulmenque quod omnes
percuteret pariter populos, et sidus iniquum
gentibus. oceano classes inferre parabat
exteriore mari. non illi flamma, nec undae,
nec sterilis Libye, nec Syrticus obstitit Ammon.
isset in occasus, mundi deuexa secutus,
ambissetque polos, Nilumque a fonte bibisset:
occurrit suprema dies naturaque solum
hunc potuit finem uesano ponere regi,
qui secum inuidia, qua totum ceperat orbem,
abstulit imperium; nulloque haerede relicto
totius fati, lacerandas praebuit urbes.
sed cecidit Babylone sua, Parthoque uerendus.
pro pudor! eoi propius timuere sarissas
quam nunc pila timent populi. licet usque sub Arcton
regnemus, Zephyrique domos, terrasque premamus
flagrantis post terga Noti; cedemus in ortus
Arsacidum domino. non felix Parthia Crassis
exiguae secura fuit prouincia Pellae.

LUCAN *Pharsalia* X 20—52.

PREFACE.

In attempting to bring before English classical students a portion of the work of an author once widely read both elsewhere and in this country, but now used seldom—at least in England—, we hope that we have not undertaken a thankless task. The want of variety in Latin prose authors read in schools has often been felt by schoolmasters; and, if none but the writers of the purest Latin are to be studied, we are at once thrown back upon Caesar and Cicero alone. And it may with reason be held that University students would not lose by reading portions of a wider range of authors than they now usually do. The claims of Curtius are dealt with in the introduction.

As we are not preparing this book with the view of furnishing candidates for some particular examination with a short and simple means to mark-getting, but seek to help and instruct several different classes of students, we have not thought fit to restrict our notes to the clearing up of difficulties in each separate sentence,—in fact to the repeating of things that 'every fourth form boy' ought to know and does not. On the contrary, while dealing with grammatical questions of an even elementary nature, we have freely illustrated the matter by quotation and reference. The notes on the first chapter are mainly of an illustrative character, as the nature of the subject required.

In the spelling of Indian names we have generally followed the best *modern* authorities; but in citing authorities we have used the spelling adopted by the several writers. Thus we write *Brahman*, but in citing Elphinstone *Bramin*, and so forth.

A copious index will make up for some deficiencies in cross reference, and appendix D will help in understanding the plan of Alexander's Indian expedition generally.

The notes on the first chapter are the work of Mr Heitland: the rest are all written in common. Mr Raven has supplied the index and list of names, Mr Heitland the introductions and appendices.

When quotations from Greek writers seemed not to require to be left in the original for some good cause, we have generally given an English translation or abstract. Mr Heitland is responsible for the text, which is based on that of Hedicke; also for the maps, which depend mainly on General Cunningham's *Ancient Geography of India*.

Elphinstone's *History of India* has been cited from the fifth (Cowell's) edition, and Thirlwall's *History of Greece* from the first edition in Lardner's Cabinet Cyclopaedia. Perhaps the most specially useful book to us has been Otto Eichert's lexicon to Curtius (Hanover 1870). The help got from other books is acknowledged on occasion in the notes.

W E H
T E R.

March 1879

TABLE OF CONTENTS

	PAGES
Introduction	9—31
Analysis of the Narrative	32
Text	33—83
Variations from Hedicke's text	85, 86
Notes	87—179
Appendices	180—189
Short list of names	190—194
Index	195—204

INTRODUCTION.

A. *Curtius and his book.*

(1) Of Quintus Curtius Rufus the author of the work before us we know perhaps less than of any other writer ancient or modern whose name has come down to us with his book. We know nothing whatever as to who he was, unless indeed we identify him with the adventurer spoken of[1] by Tacitus and the younger Pliny under the same name. But this has been so gravely questioned by Orelli Nipperdey and Teuffel[2] that it would not be safe to assume it here. This however is not all: we are not certain even as to the time at which he wrote, and shall have to content ourselves with probabilities. On the very meagre and obscure evidence of a passage in the tenth book (9 §§ 3—6) the date of the com-

[1] Tac ann XI 20, 21, Plin epp VII 27. It is argued that Tacitus would have mentioned his writings, had he been speaking of the present Curtius. But he seems not to have mentioned those of Corbulo and Frontinus, of whom he speaks; and here there is no question as to the personal identity. Again it is said that our writer in describing battles shews ignorance of military matters, and so cannot have been the man who was proconsul of Africa. Is this inference so very certain? It might further be asked, would so mean-born a man as the proconsul have had the rhetorical training that our author clearly had? Might this not have been the very means whereby he gained the praetorship which he held before the proconsulate?

[2] Geschichte der Römischen literatur § 292.

position of his history has been fixed variously by different critics; some find therein an allusion to Augustus, others to Claudius, to Vespasian, or even to Septimius Severus. Of these interpretations that which refers the words to the accession of Claudius seems the most plausible. And with this view, which would place him between Velleius and Petronius, his Latin style agrees well. He is perhaps to be identified with the rhetorician mentioned by Suetonius in his treatise *de rhetoribus*, for that Q Curtius Rufus must have flourished in this period.

(2) In forming our judgment as to the merits of his work it is most necessary first to arrive at some notion of the object with which it was composed. One of the first things that strikes the reader is the unevenness of the writer. Like Tigellius in Horace, *nil fuit umquam sic impar sibi.* In the many well-wrought speeches with which his work is after the manner of ancient writers[1] copiously adorned, and in the picturesque and telling descriptions of important or striking incidents, we are conscious that our author is doing his best to equal the dignity of the subject and fix the attention of his readers. But in the ordinary course of the narrative, when the matter has no striking interest of its own to take the common fancy, we find him generally meagre and occasionally dull. This seems to indicate that his purpose was to present his readers with a series of interesting pictures, and by a quiet and compressed narrative to bind them into a whole: so that we should fairly judge him not by the bare and lifeless passages which serve to make transition, but rather by the more effective scenes[2] which he has set himself specially to pourtray. This view of his purpose suits well with the probable opinion that he followed

[1] See the remarks of Diodorus XX 1, 2. Voltaire in the preface to his history of Russia under Peter the Great § 7 says well '*Les harangues sont une autre espèce de mensonge oratoire que les historiens se sont permis autrefois. On faisait dire à ses héros ce qu'ils auraient pu dire.*' The Curtian speeches, like those in Livy and Lucan, are good but rather wanting in distinctive character.

[2] Such as VIII 13, 14, IX 4, 5, 9.

mainly the authority of Klitarchus[1], an Alexandrine historian who wrote about 300 B C, and is said to have sacrificed truth to effect; not trusting to the solid merits of his work (which were considerable) but seeking to render it attractive by fabulous and exaggerated[2] descriptions. Probably Curtius, whether drawing direct from Klitarchus or not, dressed up or recast many of his exaggerations as he saw fit at the time, but was too sober to load his book with recounting other marvels which were most likely at once dreary and incredible. There is also reason to think that Curtius, though in the main a reporter rather than a historian, did sometimes[3] check the statements of his guide by those of more trustworthy authors such as Ptolemy, who with Aristobulus is the writer most relied upon by the judicious Arrian[4]. While therefore we must conclude that much in the work before us is overdrawn, the singular accuracy observable in many small points[5] and in some descriptions of places[6] forbids us to regard it as a mere romance to be ranked with Xenophon's *Cyropaedia* or Johnson's *Rasselas*. That Curtius is above all things a rhetorician we may readily admit; but looking to the close con-

[1] Quintilian X 1 § 74 *Clitarchi probatur ingenium, fides infamatur.* Pliny the elder reports some of his marvels in the 'Natural History,' and Strabo in his Geography. See in particular Strabo VII 2 § 1. From Diodorus II 7 and Strabo XI 5 § 4 it has been wrongly inferred that he had been with Alexander on his expedition. See also Plut Alex 46, and our notes below on VIII 9 §§ 21, 25, 22, IX 10 § 10.

[2] Voltaire well says in his preface to the history of Russia under Peter the Great § 7 '*une troisième espèce de mensonge, et la plus grossière de toutes, mais qui fut longtemps la plus séduisante, c'est le merveilleux: il domine dans toutes les histoires anciennes, sans en excepter une seule.*' The last sentence is a little too sweeping, but not much. Lucian's papers called 'A true history' and 'How to write history' are not quite so sweeping in their denunciation but to the full as severe.

[3] See on IX 1 § 34, 5 § 21.

[4] See the preface to his *anabasis*.

[5] See on VIII 9 § 4 *gelidior* etc, 12 § 14 *Taxilen*.

[6] Such as in the passage of the Hydaspes VIII 13, and the adventure with the fleet in the Indus estuary IX 9.

nexion maintained by Roman writers between rhetoric and history[1]—particularly in the days of the empire—this is only what we should expect. The same may be said in various degrees of Sallust Livy and Tacitus. This, as well as the epigrammatic sentences with which his work is studded, is nothing but the natural result of an age of recitations[2], when books were composed rather with a view to afford a choice of extracts fit to tickle the ears of a lecture-room audience than to supply solid information to the student in his closet. So too, if not critical, he is to some extent imaginative[3]: he is seldom at a loss to infer the motive for an action, or draw a bold and appropriate moral.

(3) It has often been remarked that Curtius was an imitator of Livy, and this is an indubitable fact. It has also been well pointed out by Vogel that, if we suppose him to have published his book in 41 or 42 A D, it is quite credible that he may in his youth have seen and even been a pupil of that eminent master. All that has been said above of his merits and defects as a writer in respect of manner and matter will apply with slight modification to Livy also; and the two

[1] Quintilian X I §§ 31—34 allows the oratorical student to read history, but sparingly, as it is a sort of poetry in prose, *et scribitur ad narrandum non ad probandum*. It has a sort of poetic license in expression, so as to enliven the narrative. The conciseness of Sallust is wasted on a jury, *neque illa Livii lactea ubertas satis docebit eum qui non speciem expositionis sed fidem quaerit*. In digressions the orator may now and then allow himself the sleek plumpness of historical style. In fact the orator must be content generally with a tamer style than the historian. So too Pliny epp V 8 §§ 9—11, though VII 17 § 3 has another sound. The pretensions of Livy in his preface are not to be taken as meaning the same as we now should by the same words. Style had in fact with all ancient historians an undue prominence. So Tacitus Agr 10 refers to Livy and Rusticus as *eloquentissimi auctores* when merely citing a statement of theirs.

[2] See Mayor on Juvenal III 9, particularly pp 180, 181, where their effect in causing the whole of a book to be sacrificed to the parts is clearly and fully detailed.

[3] See Thirlwall chapter 49 p 154 note, chapter 52 p 304.

have this further trait in common with the mass of Roman writers, that they utterly miss the high aims and far-sightedness which give its true grandeur to the character of Alexander. To them—whether from national jealousy or imperfect information—the Macedonian youth is merely the brilliant conqueror of insatiate ambition, Fortune's very darling. To us the partial view of Plutarch seems nearer the truth, that he was ever at odds with Fortune and became great in spite of her.

(4) The Latin of Curtius is probably a good average specimen of the Latin of the early Empire, the so-called silver-age. Inferior in vigour to the balanced sermon style of Seneca or the painful and muscular energy of the Tacitean Annals, it reminds us in descriptive passages of the elder Pliny, and generally (both in the speeches and elsewhere) of the earlier writings of Tacitus. His imitation of Livy is sufficiently transparent, and in common with most writers of his day he betrays frequently an attentive study of Virgil. To enter into minute details concerning the peculiarities of his diction and syntax is beyond the scope of the present edition. It may be remarked in general that his vocabulary is a limited and commonplace one, containing few strange words but many familiar words in strange senses. His habit of using the very same construction and even the same phrase over and over again has a tiresome effect; but this is a common fault in the later Greek and Latin writers. Still with all its defects the style of Curtius has the merit of being terse and generally clear; if he now and then strains too hard after antithesis, at least he succeeds in bringing his point home to the reader. A few of his more notable usages may perhaps be recorded with advantage here.

(*a*) the continual use of *quippe* (='you see') as an equivalent for *nam*, *enim*, *scilicet*.

(*b*) the equally frequent use of *ceterum*, as = *sed*, *autem*.

(*c*) *ipsum*, *ipsos*, *ipsius*, *ipsorum*, *ipsi*, *ipsis*, where *se*, *sibi*, *suus* would have been used in the best Latin. This is very characteristic of Curtius. See note on VIII 10 § 1.

(*d*) the misplacement of *quoque*, very common in Livy.

(*e*) the omission of the demonstrative before the relative (*qui*=*ei qui* and so on), even where some obscurity is caused thereby.

(*f*) the frequent ending of a sentence with a participle or adjective.

(*g*) the sudden change (or omission) of the subject of the sentence.

(*h*) the frequent use of the future participle active (*usurus* etc) to express a purpose.

(*i*) a certain looseness in the use of the ablative absolute, where a parenthetic or additional clause would have been better for both sound and sense.

(*k*) the use of the pluperfect=perfect with an adverb (such as *paullisper* etc). See VIII 12 § 17, 13 § 11, 14 § 23, IX 6 § 22, 7 § 20, 8 § 6, 9 §§ 14, 23.

(*l*) the preference shewn for the construction with the pluperfect active over the simpler passive construction. So VIII 13 § 10 *quam compleverant* etc rather than *quae completa erat* etc. See also IX 1 §§ 29, 33, 4 § 30, 7 § 15, 8 § 22, 9 § 19. In some cases the effect is thus rather more vivid, in others the usage is inappropriate and affected.

(*m*) the occasionally strange order of words. See VIII 12 § 10, 14 §§ 13, 14.

(*n*) the use of poetical language.

It must not be supposed that these usages are peculiar to Curtius. On the contrary they are for the most part mannerisms common to him with Livy and other writers, and only take the attention as they do from the want of Livian brilliancy to carry them off. And if he is less pleasant than Livy to read he is also less difficult.

(5) Curtius has since the revival of learning down to recent times been a popular author, and has been repeatedly edited by scholars on the continent. But so entirely has he passed out of the notice of our schools that this will possibly be

news to many modern English schoolmasters. His popularity was probably owing in the first instance to the deep interest felt in the subject of his book. Men got their first impressions[1] of the Macedonian hero from the account of Curtius. Four English translations of him deserve mention,

John Brende[2]	London	1553
Robert Codrington	"	1652
John Digby	"	1747
Peter Pratt	"	1809, 2nd ed 1821,

while Arrian remained untranslated in English till he was taken in hand by John Rooke[3] (1729, 2nd ed 1821). The controversy which had long been on foot respecting the merits of the two writers had then been finally decided in Arrian's favour. That there should ever have been a dispute as to their relative historical values shews well what a strong hold Curtius once had as a historian. But he had other claims on the readers and teachers of the age of revival. Before the rise of historical criticism, when wisdom was sought directly[4] from 'the ancients,' his moral sentences and epigrammatic phrases would be certain to find favour. A narrative of stirring events sprinkled with neat expressions of elevated sentiment was at once a quarry for the moralist and a fit model for the schoolboy. Voltaire[5] has

[1] It is well known that there was a legendary history of Alexander current in the Middle Ages (see Col Yule's Marco Polo introd p 110) which took the place of the true one. But it seems to have been quite distinct from the latter, with which alone we are here concerned. See appendix C.

[2] A specimen of this fine old English version is given in appendix B.

[3] A poor version, but it has prefixed to it the dissertation of Le Clerc on Curtius.

[4] Witness the authority long assigned to Aristotle's explanations of phenomena and Pliny's statements taken for fact. The appetite for proverbs and sayings is shewn by the popularity of such books as the Adagies and Apophthegms of Erasmus. So Hamlet will (I v 100) wipe from his memory 'all saws of books.'

[5] History of Charles XII book I '*Dès qu'il eut quelque connaissance*

told us how 'Swedish Charles' was in his boyhood fascinated by the story—by the matter even more than the manner. And if the conditions of school teaching are now so far changed that these claims would in themselves hardly suffice to restore Curtius to favour, we have now a further one to urge—that it is desirable that the habit of reading critically, without light unreasoning belief, should be acquired early, and that Curtius is eminently adapted for this purpose. However little we may know of the author's personality, we soon feel that he was a real man with human weaknesses and vanities, one on whom the temptation to self-display had a constant influence, and whose statements require continual checking and correction.

(6) It is to be hoped that the portion of his work which we have here striven to explain will be found to have a special interest from its connexion with India. It is not necessary to enter here into a detailed examination of the knowledge of that country possessed by Greek and Roman writers. We now know that the companions of Alexander and other early travellers (such as Megasthenes[1]) were mistaken in some of their impressions of the Hindus, and that the stories set afloat by some of them concerning the country and its inhabitants were absurd and fabulous. But making every allowance it must be admitted that the best of them reported what they saw with scrupulous accuracy and that their geographical knowledge—obtained no doubt mainly from native informants—was marvellously correct. That the tendency to romance, observable in the narratives of Alexander's campaigns, corrupted also the

de la langue latine, on lui fit traduire Quinte-Curce: il prit pour ce livre un goût que le sujet lui inspirait beaucoup plus encore que le style.'

[1] A translation of the fragments of this valuable author has just appeared under the title 'Ancient India as described by Megasthenes and Arrian', by J W McCrindle, Principal of the Government College Patna (London, Trübner and Co). It is always to be remembered that the accounts of the early Greek travellers, referring to widely distant parts of India, were confused and mingled by later writers who used them. There is a collection of the *Alexandri Magni historiarum scriptores aetate suppares* by R Geier (Leipsic 1844).

accounts of the country and products, was remarked by Strabo. But this applies to some of the accounts far more strongly than to others; particularly to that of the notorious[1] Onesikritus. It therefore was of the first importance to later writers that they should use the best authorities and use them with judgment. In this regard it must be admitted that Curtius on the whole has acquitted himself very creditably. It is plain throughout the digression on India (viii 9) that he is rather looking for points of contrast[2] to the state of things with which he and his readers were familiar, than composing the best and fullest account in his power. So did Tacitus in his 'Germany', a book written in a very similar spirit. But, with all this temptation to adopt the most striking and exaggerated accounts, he has kept himself singularly free from such blame: so far as it goes, there is little in his description that calls for censure on the ground of levity or loose writing.

[1] See note on IX 10 § 3.

[2] This defect seems to be (in various degrees) common to all the ancient Greek and Roman writers who speak of India.

B. *A sketch of Alexander's career.*

(1) How the Greek states wore themselves out in struggles for the first place, and brought themselves down to one dead level of weariness and exhaustion, while the Macedonians rested in strength unimpaired though as yet not organized: how Philip on ascending the Macedonian throne devoted himself to the consolidation of the power and development of the resources of

Macedonia, and the formation of a national army; how he took advantage of the weakness and mutual jealousies of the Greek states to win for himself a place among them; how he then by various arts overcame them one by one and made himself lord of Hellas:—all this is well known to the readers of Grecian history[1], and needs not to be here further dealt with than by way of allusion. Being now at the height of his power in Europe, Philip purposed to invade Asia and assail and perhaps overthrow the Persian monarchy. But he fell in B C 336 by the sword of an assassin[2], and Alexander, his son by Olympias, reigned in his stead.

(2) This youth, born to be the ruler of a people just emerging from barbarism, newly conscious of their strength and proud of their recent conquests, had received a training perhaps more complete in its kind than has fallen to the lot of any other great king or conqueror. From Leonidas[3] he acquired the spare habits and bodily hardihood which carried him through so many long and severe campaigns; from Lysimachus[4] he learnt to know and love the Homeric poems, and so his naturally ambitious spirit was fostered by emulation of the hero Achilles, whom indeed he claimed as a mythical ancestor of his race. Under these influences, backed only by his early experience of warfare, he might indeed have become a great conqueror, but not Alexander the Great. It is only fair[5] in accordance with the testimony of antiquity to assign the greatest weight in the matter of his education to the teaching of Aristotle[6]. Had not the prince studied under the first of living philosophers—one unrivalled in the extent of his learning as in clearness of thought—he could hardly have attained that intellectual development which made conspicuous for true judgment and wise forecast a youth who came suddenly to the throne at the age of twenty and died before he was thirty-three.

[1] Thirlwall cc 41—46, Grote cc 86—90.

[2] See on IX 6 § 25.

[3] Plut Alex 5, 22, 25.

[4] Plut Alex 5.

[5] Thirlwall c 47.

[6] Plut Alex 7, 8. Diog Laert V § 4.

(3) On his father's death he became king of the Macedonians, and found himself in possession of no inheritance of ease. The Greeks were looking to the recovery of their lost freedom; there were risings in Illyria and Thrace; and the young king's power was not yet safely established in his own kingdom of Macedonia. But by the time he had been a year and a half on the throne all was quiet again. By rapid campaigns in the Illyrian mountains and on the Danube he had pacified the North; the Greeks had once more submitted to his yoke, and Thebes had paid the penalty of her rebellion by being destroyed utterly; and all domestic disaffection had been suppressed[1]. He now made preparations[2] for carrying out on a grander scale the darling project of his father, the invasion of Asia.

(4) The Persian empire[3] had long been falling into decay. Extending as it did from the western coast of Asia Minor to the Jaxartes and the Indus, it comprised within its borders many races speaking divers tongues and widely differing from one another in their feelings and modes of life. Some of these races had never been thoroughly subdued: indeed of the hill tribes nominally included in the empire, while some professed allegiance to the Great King but set his commands at nought, others openly refused to make a show of submission, and even levied black-mail on the monarch and his officers for safe conduct through their passes. The only way in which it was possible to rule such a vast domain was by parcelling it out among governors and making them severally responsible for their districts. Thus the Persian empire was divided into satrapies[4] each under the rule of a governor called the Satrap, somewhat resembling a Turkish Pacha. But such governors could do little unless entrusted with ample powers: and accordingly we find that in practice little notice was taken of the proceedings of a satrap or the condition of affairs in his satrapy, so long as he did not rebel against the Great King and regularly sent up to the royal treasury the amount of tribute with which

[1] Thirlwall c 47.
[2] Thirlwall c 48, Grote c 92.
[3] Thirlwall c 48.
[4] Grote c 72.

his district stood charged[1] in the imperial registers at Susa. Under such circumstances it was impossible that the central power should remain strong and efficient. The satrapies in many cases became by custom hereditary governments: the cohesion of the empire was weakened, and the Great King, happy if not troubled by local rebellions, was forced to look helplessly on while the jealousies of the satraps led them into quarrels and intrigues or even into open war. But the imperial treasuries were known[2] to be filled with hoards of untold wealth: and, though since the days of Plataea and Salamis the Greeks had made light of the prowess of the Persians in open fight, none seriously thought of assailing in his own dominions a prince who could set in motion at will the fleets of Tyre and Sidon and the clouds of nomad horsemen from the plains of Asia. It seemed easy to penetrate into the Persian empire, but hard to retreat. But the successful retreat of the 10,000 Greeks from the field of Kunaxa, in spite of all that force or guile could do to stop them, shewed plainly for all to see the inner weakness of that empire, and Philip and his son had both learnt the lesson well. So too had the Persian kings, who now ceased to rely on their Asiatic infantry, and more and more used their stores of gold in hiring mercenary Greeks to give some steadiness to their huge ill-trained armies.

(5) Early in 334 B C Alexander crossed over into Asia with 30,000 foot and 5000 horse. He now began a course of conquest which it is impossible to describe adequately in this short sketch[3]. After defeating the Persians in three great battles, and taking Tyre by siege—one of the most famous sieges of history—he entered Susa as a conqueror in 331. The Great King

[1] Grote c 45 note on the convention between Athens and Persia.

[2] Grote c 93 note on the imperial treasures.

[3] Granikus 334, Issus 333, siege of Tyre 332, Gaugamela or Arbela 331 B C. The expedition to Egypt in 332—1 B C, though important as including the foundation of Alexandria and the visit to the oracle of Ammon, does not affect the narrative of his military progress. Read the story in Thirlwall c 50.

Darius[1] was now a fugitive, yet not without some hopes of better fortune. But Alexander left him no rest. He pushed on at once to Persepolis, and early in the following year (330) entered Ekbatana, the ancient capital of the Medes. Four years had thus sufficed to drive Darius from his throne and put the Macedonian king in possession of all the chief seats of government. His object now was to secure by rapid pursuit the person of Darius, and in this he nearly succeeded: but Bessus the Satrap of Baktria and the other traitors who had accompanied the Great King in his flight[2] slew their master themselves when he refused to fly further; for they feared lest he should fall alive into the hands of Alexander.

(6) The throne of the great Medo-Persian empire was now vacant, and Alexander saw that he must at once ascend it[3]. He would thus appear to the nations of the East not only as a great conqueror but also as the successor of the great Cyrus by whom the empire lately held by the Persians had of old been wrested from the Medes. He saw too with the clear discernment which distinguished him that as Great King he could no longer remain Macedonian: he must adopt somewhat of the Oriental pomp and splendour which the subjects of the Persian government looked for in their ruler: if he would continue to conquer he must not cease to be an Alexander; if he would rule over the conquered peoples he must put on something of a Darius. His Macedonian generals might take it ill that their young king, with whom they had lived almost as equals in the camp and by whose side they had fought at Issus and Gaugamela, should now withdraw himself from them as a being apart, and surround himself with the circumstantial formalities of an Eastern court; nay more, that he should even clothe his person in a mongrel dress, wherein a Macedonian eye jealously marked the Persian garments. But so it must needs be, for the king had made up his mind on the point and the common soldiers were not deeply moved by the change: so

1 Codomannus, who on his accession had taken the name of Darius.

2 Thirlwall c 51, Grote c 94.

3 See Thirlwall c 51, Grote c 94.

the murmuring generals sullenly gave way. It was of far greater moment that in taking on himself the outward semblance of the Great King Alexander seemed to have caught something of the arbitrary and suspicious bearing of an Eastern despot. The readiness with which he accepted informations against Parmenion and Philotas, the murder of Kleitus in a fit of drunken rage, the unjust execution of the sophist Kallisthenes, all[1] seem to shew that he was to some extent at least undergoing a moral deterioration at this time.

(7) But none the less[2] he went on from victory to victory, putting down rebellions, founding colonies, and extending his conquests. The year 329 found him on the Jaxartes[3]; and, after much severe fighting on his march thence towards the south, he reached[4] the Indus by about the end of 327. He had made great preparations for this Indian expedition, which had for some time been one of his most cherished schemes. He rightly judged that the undertaking would prove an arduous one, and was resolved not to fail in it: he must not be foiled in the attempt to learn the truth concerning the things that he had heard[5] of the wealth and wonders of the distant East. So, taking advantage of the jealousies of the Indian rajas to form useful alliances[6], he passed the Indus early in 326 and entered the Panjab. By dexterous strategy he succeeded in passing the Hydaspes, and in the ensuing battle defeated and secured

[1] For these see Thirlwall c 52.

[2] Mr Wheeler well says 'his oriental indulgences had perverted his moral sense, but had not vitiated his military and political culture.'

[3] The *Syr Darya* or river Syr, for which see Schuyler's *Turkistan*.

[4] Through the Khaiber or Khuram. Authorities differ as to the identification of the pass, and the question must be settled by the experts.

[5] Wondrous tales had been current concerning India before the time of Herodotus. See Rawlinson on Herod III 98—106, and Wheeler's Geography of Herodotus, Asia c 5. Also 'The commerce and navigation of the ancients in the Indian Ocean, by William Vincent DD, Dean of Westminster'. London 1807.

[6] See appendix D.

the submission of king Porus. In this interesting campaign Alexander got as far as the river Hyphasis[1], beyond which his army refused to advance: so, getting over his disappointment as best he might, he retraced his steps to the Hydaspes, which he prepared to descend with a fleet in order to reach the Indus and whatever sea might lie beyond.

(8) This eventful voyage, in the course of which Alexander established his supremacy in the part of India now known as Sindh, brought him to Patala (at the head of the Indus delta) early in 325. He now sent some of his army home by an inland route under Kraterus, and occupied the time while the nautical preparations were going on at Patala in exploring the branches of the river and in other excursions with a view to render more easy the homeward passage of his forces by sea and land. The hardships endured by the fleet under Nearchus in its voyage[2] from the mouth of the Indus to the Persian Gulf, and the still greater sufferings of the land force under the king himself in their march through the deserts of Gedrosia[3], are famous in the records of antiquity, and presented beyond doubt a memorable example of what is possible to unflinching unrelenting determination. In the hour of their triumph the survivors strove to forget what they had endured in that terrible journey.

(9) But Alexander soon tore himself from revelry and went up into the heart of his vast empire, giving earnest attention to administrative reforms and more than ever bent on accomplishing that fusion of the races beneath his sway to which he had long looked as the only sure tie by which he could bind together[4]

[1] Now Bias, at a point south of its present junction with the Hesudrus (Satlej). But it seems probable that in the time of Alexander these two rivers did not meet at all before joining the Akesines (Chenab). See General Cunningham p 222 and map 5.

[2] See 'The voyage of Nearchus, and the Periplus of the Erythraean sea, translated from the Greek by William Vincent DD, Dean of Westminster'. Oxford 1809.

[3] See 'Travels in Beloochistan and Sinde, accompanied by a geographical and historical account of those countries' etc. By Lieut Henry Pottinger. London 1816.

[4] Thirlwall c 55.

such a motley throng of subjects. His frontiers were advanced up to the Jaxartes and the Danube and beyond the Indus and the Nile. A serious rising in Greece (B C 330) had been crushed by his lieutenant Antipater; other risings in the East had been put down effectually, at least for the present: all seemed to be going well when the conqueror held his great marriage feast at Susa in the year 324. On this occasion he himself and many of his generals had taken wives of the conquered peoples; the West was holding out hands to the East[1]. What might have been the result, had the hero lived to carry on his work, it would now be vain to enquire. His days were numbered, and at the height of his power and glory he died at Babylon[2] in 323. His empire at once fell to pieces, and out of the fragments his generals carved out kingdoms and founded great dynasties of their own. The most noteworthy of these was that of the Ptolemies[3] in Egypt, founded by Ptolemy Lagus one of Alexander's best generals, who when king wrote the history of his great master's campaigns. It was natural that Ptolemy more than any other man should recall the memories of those conquests, having ever before him one of Alexander's master-strokes of genius,—the new port of Alexandria rising into wealth and greatness day by day. To this city[4] he artfully contrived to transport the remains of its royal founder, and laid them in a fitting sepulchre.

(10) Posterity has assigned to Alexander the title of Great. And we must admit that on many distinct grounds he

[1] Arrian VII 4 §§ 4—8, Curtius X 3 §§ 10—14.

[2] See Mayor on Juvenal X 171—2. According to some accounts he was buried there.

[3] For the Ptolemies see Strabo XVII 1 § 11 beginning Πτολεμαῖος γὰρ ὁ Λάγου διεδέξατο Ἀλέξανδρον etc.

[4] See Diodorus XVIII 28, Herodian IV 8 § 9, Lucan X 20, 21, Dion Cassius LI 16 § 5, Lucian dial mort 13 § 5, Aelian var hist XII 64, Suet Aug 18, Cal 52, and Curtius X 10 § 20. Also 'The tomb of Alexander, a dissertation on the sarcophagus brought from Alexandria and now in the British Museum', by Edward Daniel Clarke LLD, Fellow of Jesus College Cambridge.

fully deserved this title, if ever man did. As a warrior, he rivalled the finest soldiers of his army in endurance of toil and hardship and in reckless bravery on the battle-field; while few even of the greatest generals have equalled him in the patient and skilful forethought with which his plans were laid, or in the speed and vigour with which he carried them out. Even plans of doubtful wisdom succeeded by reason of his rapidity of movement. The confidence he inspired in his soldiers under the most trying circumstances produced a ready obedience to discipline even in the hour of victory. The power—indispensable in a general—of rapidly taking advantage of his adversary's mistakes and correcting his own was possessed by him in a very high degree. As a king, though his designs were crude and though with the hopefulness of youth he fondly deemed that the possible work of centuries might be surely accomplished in years, there was in him a grandeur of conception, a liberal breadth of view, which places him in the first rank among the rulers of mankind. His freedom from prejudice and readiness to do justice to the merits of others are wonderful, if we consider his age and circumstances: his ambition and occasional acts of cruelty have had their parallels in all ages not excepting our own. With a true kindliness of heart and manner and a benevolent zeal[1] for the welfare of his subjects he united a love of order and a capacity for affairs[2] which would bear comparison with the coldest and most calculating ministers of modern times. When he had to choose between two great difficulties, the risk of offending Macedonian pride on the one hand or of trying to hold down so many nations by sheer force

[1] He even made provision for soldiers' orphan children. Plut Alex 71.

[2] Plut Alex 42 notes the wonderful extent and minuteness of his correspondence among his manifold other occupations. To his mother and his lieutenants (Antipater and others) he wrote constantly, and also to Aristotle and Leonidas his teachers, to Pausanias the doctor, to Phokion at Athens, to the Athenians etc, and also kept journals of his doings (ἐφημερίδες).

on the other, his 'clear spirit' never faltered in the choice[1]: so they would be his good obedient subjects, Macedonian Greek Indian and Baktrian to him were all alike. But if he approached more nearly than any other man has done to his own ideal, the Homeric Agamemnon[2]

ἀμφότερον βασιλεύς τ' ἀγαθὸς κρατερός τ' αἰχμητής,

yet this was not all; as an explorer he must stand high, eager as he was for discovery and never losing an opportunity of extending the knowledge of the geography and products of foreign lands and of the laws customs and ideas of their inhabitants. Not only was he in general an encourager of all research, but we are credibly informed[3] in particular that Aristotle's studies in natural history were materially assisted by the magnificent and judicious help of his former pupil.

(11) His defects were mainly of a kind that it is at this distance of time most difficult to judge fairly. They were failings of temper, excusable in a quick-witted and warm-hearted youth, but annoying and even alarming to his companions, particularly when he had conquered the East and when life or death hung upon his smile or frown. It must be admitted that his temper did not improve with years. His marshals and literary courtiers must often have drawn a sigh of relief when released safely from a banquet which they could not refuse to attend and at which they had been sitting within a few feet of a fiery and capricious despot who became every moment more drunk and therefore more dangerous. In connexion with this social defect we may mention other weak points upon which the judgment of his contemporaries was probably too lenient, at least from our point of view. We should think his magnificence

[1] Plut de Alex fort I 6 says that Aristotle had advised him to rule Greeks as subjects and barbarians as slaves (τοῖς μὲν Ἕλλησιν ἡγεμονικῶς τοῖς δὲ βαρβάροις δεσποτικῶς): but Alexander knew better, and brought the nations together as an impartial ruler, and blended various elements, ὥσπερ ἐν κρατῆρι φιλοτησίῳ, μίξας τοὺς βίους καὶ τὰ ἤθη.

[2] Iliad III 179.

[3] Plin nat hist VIII § 44, Plut Alex 8, de Alex fort I 10, Athenaeus IX p 398 e.

and generosity too ostentatious, and his clemency too exclusively the result of calculation: but judged by the standard of his own day these would pass for unmixed heroic virtues. His ambition seems to us somewhat deformed by a too ready acceptance of flattery and by the vanity which led him to claim a divine origin. But to find fault with such weaknesses[1] in a young conqueror situated as he was is merely saying that he was a man. His tender affection for Hephaestion, and the unwavering love he bore to the high-spirited mother[2] from whom he inherited his self-willed and ambitious temperament, shew that he remained inwardly sound and amiable to the last.

(12) If we try Alexander by a test commonly applied to great kings—the permanence of their work—we shall not find him wanting. That his vast empire, won as it was by only ten years of conquest, should have fallen to pieces when the master's hand[3] was so untimely withdrawn, is no blot on his fame: it could not have held together. But that any of his work, performed in such haste, should have stood the test of time is indeed a marvel. Yet not only did the kingdoms of his successors in the West attain to great strength, but there was formed in the East a kingdom of Baktria[4] which lasted for centuries and long retained the traces of its Greek or Macedonian origin. The Greeks at home had long lost the power[5] of combining to form a really powerful state; and it

[1] See Arrian VII 29 §§ 1, 3, Curtius X 5 §§ 29, 33.

[2] Curtius X 5 § 30, Plut Alex 39.

[3] Plutarch has preserved a neat remark made at the time, that the Macedonian army on losing its leader resembled the Cyclops with his one eye put out.

[4] For the long vivid and still enduring memory of the great Iskender or Sekander in Asia, and for the Baktrian kingdom, see Marco Polo I 29 and Col Yule's note, also on III 15, IV 21, Schuyler's Turkistan c 3 (vol I p 115), c II (vol II p 142), app II (vol I p 366), note on c 9 (vol II p 50), D'Herbelot's bibliothèque orientale vol I p 640, Elphinstone app IV, Wheeler vol III p 177. There has just appeared a treatise on Alexander's successors in Baktria and India by A von Sallet.

[5] The general decay of Greek life and feeling at this time is vividly described by Mommsen in his History of Rome bk III c 14.

was perhaps well that they should bear the Macedonian yoke for a while and learn—some of them at least—to seek a humbler road to freedom in the unambitious federation of the Achaean League. The spread of Greek civilization[1] in Asia Minor and Syria was due in the first instance to the conquests of Alexander; but of all that he did nothing is so truly a monument of his greatness as the city[2] of Alexandria. He knew that he had found a site for a great and wealthy port, and the result more than fulfilled his expectation. Under the wise care of the Ptolemies there arose in this great mart of commerce such a system of libraries museums observatories lecture-rooms and other means of learning as the world had never yet seen and of which it did not, after their destruction, see the like for many centuries. Here were wrought out the most solid achievements of the Greek mind, those of the mathematicians[3] whose astonishing progress in many sciences formed a starting-point for the great advances of modern times. Here too in the days of the Roman Empire was one of the chief seats of the theologistic Christianity[4] of the East. We see then that what he had done left it possible for smaller men to found smaller kingdoms of a Greekish character in Asia and Africa; and that a hybrid race was to a great extent produced on his very plan, by the fusion[5] of the Oriental and the Greek.

(13) Such a test is however hardly necessary in the case

[1] *τὴν Ἑλλάδα σπεῖραι*, as Plut de Alex fort I 10 makes him say. See also c 5 of the same work.

[2] See the description of the city in Strabo XVII 1 § 13. He calls it *μέγιστον ἐμπόριον τῆς οἰκουμένης*, writing in the time of Augustus. Also Gibbon c 10.

[3] For instance Euclid, Konon, Hero, Ktesibius, Eratosthenes, Apollonius, Hipparchus, Ptolemy (the astronomer and geographer), and Pappus. The great Archimedes studied there.

[4] See Gibbon cc 15, 21, 28.

[5] Whether this Hellenizing of the East produced a desirable type of character, is a different question, and may well be doubted from our point of view. See Juvenal III 58—125.

of Alexander. The mere fact of the general interest that so many generations have taken in his career shews that he must have had in him something to distinguish him from the ordinary run of kings and conquerors. He became the favourite theme[1] of the rhetoricians. Imagination revelled in the fancy of all he might have thought or said at the critical moments of his life. The vocabulary of praise was exhausted[2] in finding names of attributes sufficient to pourtray the perfection of his character. There is at the same time some reason to suspect that, in order to account for the misdeeds of a hero so apparently faultless, his tendency to drunkenness has been exaggerated. We have good authority[3] for believing that he drank sparingly and rather by way of good-fellowship than from a liquorish appetite; while we know that he was naturally quick-tempered and passionate. There are still extant, chiefly in Plutarch, a number of tales of his boyhood and youth shewing him to have been a daring and wayward but generous lad, swelling with pride and ambition, of quick wit, active and inquisitive. These anecdotes are probably true enough in the main; at all events he grew up such as these glimpses of his early years would lead us to expect. Among the most interesting stories of his manhood are those describing his interview[4] with the Greek Cynic philosopher Diogenes and his curiosity concerning the Indian Brahmans[5]. He saw that

[1] See Cic de orat II § 341, de fin II § 116, Mayor on Juv X 168, and appendix A at end of our notes.

[2] Plutarch in his two orations or pamphlets *περὶ τῆς Ἀλεξάνδρου τύχης ἢ ἀρετῆς* assigns him the following qualities; *εὐβουλία, καρτερία, ἀνδρεία, σωφροσύνη, μεγαλοψυχία, σύνεσις, ἀνδραγαθία, δικαιοσύνη, πρᾳότης, κόσμος, εὐσέβεια, πίστις, εὐτέλεια, ἐγκράτεια, εὐποιΐα, ἀφοβία, εὐψυχία, φιλανθρωπία, ὁμιλία εὐάρμοστος, ἀψευδὲς ἦθος, εὐστάθεια ἐν βουλαῖς, τάχος ἐν πράξεσι, ἔρως δόξης, προαίρεσις ἐν τῷ καλῷ τελεσιουργός*, and speaks of him as *φιλόσοφος, ἡγεμὼν κοινός, βασιλεὺς φιλάνθρωπος, νήφοντι καὶ πεπνυμένῳ τῷ λογισμῷ πάντα πράττων.*

[3] See Arrian VII 29 § 4, Plutarch Alex 4, 23. [4] Plut Alex 14.

[5] See Arrian VII 1 § 5—3 § 6, Strabo XV 1 §§ 61—65, Plut Alex 64, 65, de Alex fort I 10, Thirlwall c 53, Wheeler vol III p 169.

to be content with a little was merely another way of achieving the satisfaction which he himself sought by vast labour; were he not Alexander the conqueror, he would rather live the life of a recluse or ascetic than be vexed by the vain unfulfilled desires that torment ordinary men and send them disappointed to their graves. In later times the name of Alexander became[1] a proverbial expression for ambition, and was constantly used to point the moral[2] that great and small alike must 'come to dust'. As to his personal appearance we are told[3] that his well-grown figure indicated great strength and activity; his countenance was fair and ruddy, his eyes soft and pleasing. His profile on coins and gems shews the marked prominence of the lower part of the forehead which we often notice in men of an eager and pushing temperament. He was blessed with a good digestion, and, in spite of all the trials to which he subjected his constitution, he enjoyed on the whole excellent health. It is certain that he died leaving the execution of many even of his prepared schemes wholly unattempted. Whether the papers found in his cabinet after his death relating to several such schemes were all or in part genuine cannot be determined. But he seems not to have conceived any definite plan[4] for attacking the Roman republic now growing into a formidable power in the West. If however he had lived twenty years longer there would probably have been a collision between

[1] Everywhere. See in particular Seneca epp 119 § 7 *numquam parum est quod satis est, et numquam multum est quod satis non est: post Dareum et Indos pauper est Alexander*, and de benef I 13.

[2] Juvenal X 168—173, Statius silv II 7 93—5, and epigram 437 in Riese's anthology *quisquis adhuc nondum fortunae mobile regnum nec sortem varias credis habere vices, aspice Alexandri positum memorabile corpus: abscondit tantum putris harena virum*. See Hamlet V i 191—200.

[3] Plut Alex 4, Curtius X 5 § 27.

[4] Unless we are to believe the statement of some writers whom Arrian VII 1 § 3 quotes without naming and evidently does not believe. See however Plin nat hist III § 57 and Dante *de monarchia* II 9.

them. It was this consideration that led the Greeks to say[1] in after times that Rome never had a greater stroke of luck than in the early death of Alexander. Roman writers were not at a loss for answers to the sneer. But their main argument, the taking of Hannibal's failure as a case in point, is utterly worthless. Not only was the destructive Hannibal far inferior to the constructive Alexander, but Rome in the fourth century B C had not that solid organization of power throughout Italy which foiled the genius of the Phoenician adventurer in the third. The controversy is interesting to us as shewing the interest felt not only in what Alexander actually did but in what he might have done.

(14) Here then we take our leave of our hero, perhaps the most striking figure in all antiquity; one who roused even to despair the widely different ambitions[2] of Caesar and Julian, and is perhaps only commensurable with one other character in history—the emperor Charles the Great.

1 Plutarch περὶ τῆς Ῥωμαίων τύχης chapter 13. Weissenborn thinks that the remark had been already made by Timagenes, and that the retort of Livy IX 17—19 is very likely directed against this writer.

2 See Suet Jul 7, and Julian p 253 a, b.

[*Note.* It may be well to remark that the name Panjab, the land of the 'five streams', is well explained and illustrated by Mr Isaac Taylor in 'Words and Places' c 9 pp 131—133. The five are Jhelam, Chenab, Ravi, Bias, Satlej.]

ANALYSIS OF THE NARRATIVE.

VIII 9 Description of India.

10, 11 Alexander's operations in the country to the west of the Indus.

12, 13 Passage of the Indus, and submission of certain rajas. Alexander brought face to face with Porus on the Jhelam. Strategic movements and passage of the river.

14 Battle on the Eastern bank, and defeat of the Hindu army.

IX 1 Alexander's advance through the Panjab. Submission of rajas. Products and customs described.

2 Schemes and enquiries of Alexander. He tries in a speech to induce his army to advance further.

3 Answer of Coenus on behalf of the army. March back to the Jhelam and descent of the river.

4, 5 Operations in descending the Jhelam and Chenab. Great danger of Alexander.

6 Descent of the Indus. Remonstrances of the generals through Craterus. Reply of Alexander.

7, 8 A meeting in Bactria quelled. Submission of the Sudracae and Malli. Banquet and remarkable duel. Further operations in descending the Indus. Danger of Ptolemy. Arrival at Patala.

9 Alexander explores the mouths of the Indus. The fleet in great danger from the rise and fall of the tide.

10 The homeward march.

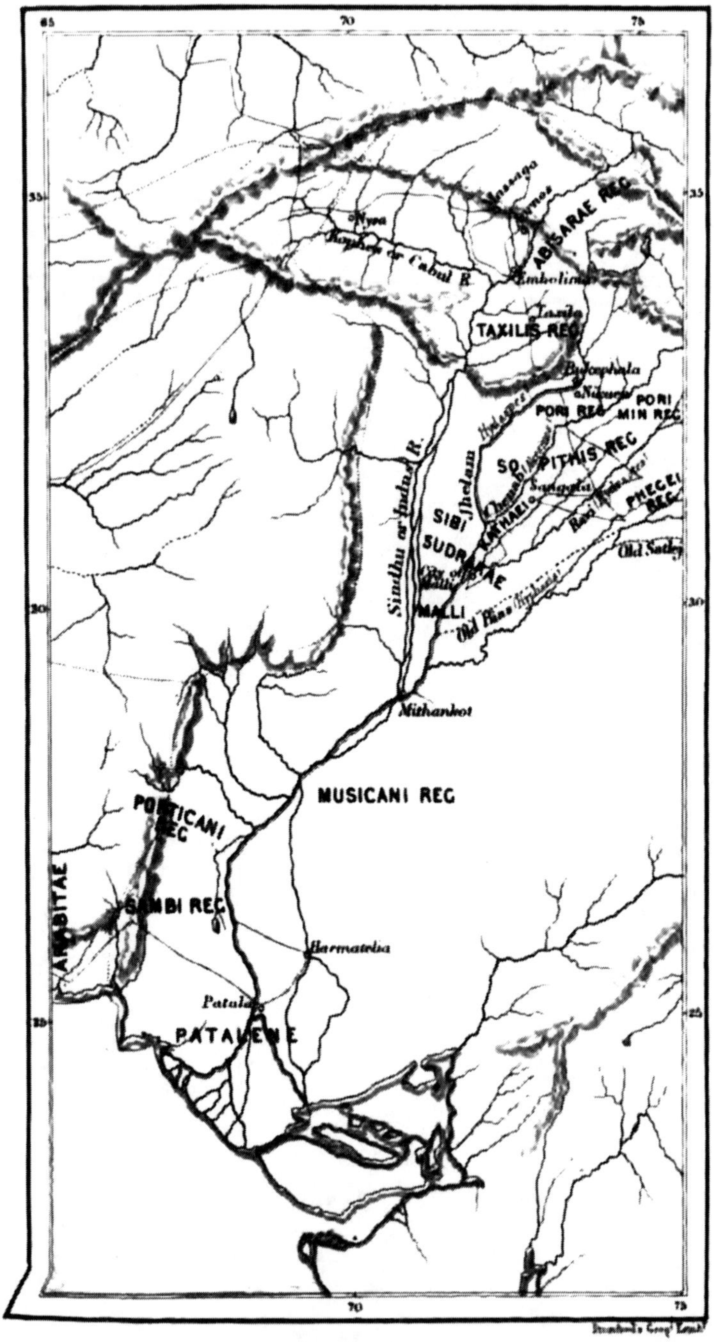

Stanford's Geog[l] Estab[t]

Cambridge University Press.

QUINTI CURTI RUFI HISTORIARUM ALEXANDRI MAGNI MACEDONIS LIBER VIII AB INITIO CAPITIS IX.

Sed ne otium serendis rumoribus natum aleret, in 9
Indiam movit, semper bello quam post victoriam clarior.
India tota ferme spectat orientem, minus in latitudinem, 2
quam recta regione spatiosa. quae austrum accipiunt, in 3
altius terrae fastigium excedunt: plana sunt cetera multisque
inclitis amnibus Caucaso monte ortis placidum per campos
iter praebent. Indus gelidior est, quam ceteri: aquas vehit 4
a colore maris haud multum abhorrentes. Ganges, om- 5
nium ab Oriente fluvius eximius, ad meridianam regionem
decurrit et magnorum montium iuga recto alveo stringit:
inde eum obiectae rupes inclinant ad orientem. uterque 6
rubro mari accipitur. Indus ripas multasque arbores cum
magna soli parte exsorbet, saxis quoque inpeditus, quis 7
crebro reverberatur: ubi mollius solum reperit, stagnat in-
sulasque molitur. Acesines eum auget. Ganges decur- 8
surum in mare *Iomanen* intercipit, magnoque motu amnis
uterque colliditur: quippe Ganges asperum os influenti
obicit, nec repercussae aquae cedunt. Dyardenes minus 9
celeber auditu est, quia per ultima Indiae currit: ceterum
non crocodilos modo, uti Nilus, sed etiam delphinos igno-
tasque aliis gentibus beluas alit. Ethimantus, crebris 10
flexibus subinde curvatus, ab accolis rigantibus carpitur:
ea causa est, cur tenues reliquias iam sine nomine in mare

11 emittat. multis praeter hos amnibus tota regio dividitur,
12 sed ignobilibus, quia non adeo interfluunt. ceterum quae
propiora sunt mari, aquilone maxime deuruntur: is cohibi-
tus iugis montium ad interiora non penetrat, ita alendis
13 frugibus mitia. sed adeo in illa plaga mundus statas tem-
porum vices mutat, ut, cum alia fervore solis exaestuant,
Indiam nives obruant, rursusque, ubi cetera rigent, illic
intolerandus aestus existat. nec, cur inverterit se natura,
14 causa. mare certe, quo adluitur, ne colore quidem ab-
horret a ceteris. ab Erythro rege inditum est nomen:
15 propter quod ignari rubere aquas credunt. terra lini ferax:
inde plerisque sunt vestes. libri arborum teneri haud secus
16 quam chartae litterarum notas capiunt. aves ad imitan-
dum humanae vocis sonum dociles sunt. animalia invisi-
tata ceteris gentibus nisi invecta. eadem terra rhinocerotas
17 alit, non generat. elephantorum maior est vis, quam quos
18 in Africa domitant, et viribus magnitudo respondet. aurum
flumina vehunt, quae leni modicoque lapsu segnes aquas
19 ducunt. gemmas margaritasque mare litoribus infundit:
neque alia illis maior opulentiae causa est, utique postquam
vitiorum commercium vulgavere in exteras gentes: quippe
aestimantur purgamenta exaestuantis freti pretio, quod
20 libido constituit. ingenia hominum, sicut ubique, apud
21 illos locorum quoque situs format. corpora usque pedes
carbaso velant, soleis pedes, capita linteis vinciunt, lapilli ex
auribus pendent, brachia quoque et lacertos auro colunt,
22 quibus inter populares aut nobilitas aut opes eminent. ca-
pillum pectunt saepius, quam tondent, mentum semper
intonsum est, reliquam oris cutem ad speciem levitatis exae-
23 quant. regum tamen luxuria, quam ipsi magnificentiam
appellant, super omnium gentium vitia. cum rex semet in
publico conspici patitur, turibula argentea ministri ferunt
totumque iter, per quod ferri destinavit, odoribus conplent.

aurea lectica margaritis circumpendentibus recubat: dis- 24
tincta sunt auro et purpura carbasa, quae indutus est: lecti-
cam sequuntur armati corporisque custodes, inter quos 25
ramis aves pendent, quas cantu seriis rebus obstrepere
docuerunt. regia auratas columnas habet: totas eas vitis 26
auro caelata percurrit, aviumque, quarum visu maxime
gaudent, argenteae effigies opera distinguunt. regia ad- 27
euntibus patet, cum capillum pectit atque ornat: tunc
responsa legationibus, tunc iura popularibus reddit. demp-
tis soleis odoribus inlinuntur pedes. venatus maximus 28
labor est inclusa vivario animalia inter vota cantusque peli-
cum figere. binum cubitorum sagittae sunt, quas emittunt
maiore nisu quam effectu: quippe telum, cuius in levitate
vis omnis est, inhabili pondere oneratur. breviora itinera 29
equo conficit: longior ubi expeditio est, elephanti vehunt
currum, et tantarum beluarum corpora tota contegunt auro.
ac ne quid perditis moribus desit, lecticis aureis pelicum
longus ordo sequitur: separatum a reginae ordine agmen
est aequatque luxuriam. feminae epulas parant. ab isdem 30
vinum ministratur, cuius omnibus Indis largus est usus.
regem mero somnoque sopitum in cubiculum pelices refe-
runt, patrio carmine noctium invocantes deos. quis credat 31
inter haec vitia curam esse sapientiae? unum agreste et
horridum genus est, quod sapientes vocant. apud hos 32
occupare fati diem pulchrum, et vivos se cremari iubent,
quibus aut segnis aetas aut incommoda valitudo est: ex-
pectatam mortem pro dedecore vitae habent, nec ullus cor-
poribus, quae senectus solvit, honos redditur: inquinari
putant ignem, nisi qui spirantes recipit. illi, qui in urbibus 33
publicis moribus degunt, siderum motus scite spectare
dicuntur et futura praedicere. nec quemquam admovere
leti diem credunt, cui expectare interrito liceat. deos pu- 34
tant, quidquid colere coeperunt, arbores maxime, quas vio-

35 lare capital est. menses in quinos denos discripserunt dies,
36 anni plena spatia servantur. lunae cursu notant tempora,
non, ut plerique, cum orbem sidus inplevit, sed cum se
curvare coepit in cornua, et idcirco breviores habent menses,
37 qui spatium eorum ad hunc lunae modum dirigunt. multa
et alia traduntur, quibus morari ordinem rerum haud sane
operae videbatur.

10 Igitur Alexandro fines Indiae ingresso gentium suarum
reguli occurrerunt, imperata facturi, illum tertium Iove
genitum ad ipsos pervenisse memorantes: patrem Liberum
atque Herculem fama cognitos esse, ipsum coram adesse
2 cernique. rex benigne exceptos sequi iussit, isdem itinerum
ducibus usurus. ceterum cum amplius nemo occurreret,
Hephaestionem et Perdiccan cum copiarum parte praemisit
ad subigendos, qui aversarentur imperium: iussitque ad
flumen Indum procedere et navigia facere, quis in ulteriora
3 transportari posset exercitus. illi, quia plura flumina supe-
randa erant, sic iunxere naves, ut solutae plaustris vehi
4 possent rursusque coniungi. post se Cratero cum phalange
iusso sequi equitatum ac levem armaturam eduxit eosque,
qui occurrerunt, levi proelio in urbem proximam conpulit.
5 iam supervenerat Craterus. itaque ut principio terrorem
incuteret genti nondum arma Macedonum expertae, prae-
cipit, ne cui parceretur, munimentis urbis, quam obsidebat,
6 incensis. ceterum, dum obequitat moenibus, sagitta ictus
cepit tamen oppidum, et omnibus incolis eius trucidatis
etiam in tecta saevitum est.

7 Inde domita ignobili gente ad Nysam urbem pervenit.
forte castris ante ipsa moenia in silvestri loco positis noc-
turnum frigus vehementius quam alias horrore corpora
8 adfecit, opportunumque remedium ignis oblatum est. caesis
quippe silvis flammam excitaverunt, quae igni alita oppida-
norum sepulcra comprehendit. vetusta cedro erant facta

conceptumque ignem late fudere, donec omnia solo aequata
sunt. et ex urbe primum canum latratus, deinde etiam 9
hominum fremitus auditus est. tum et oppidani hostem,
et Macedones ad urbem ipsos venisse cognoscunt. iamque 10
rex eduxerat copias et moenia obsidebat, cum hostium, qui
discrimen temptaverant, obruti telis sunt. aliis ergo dedi-
tionem, aliis pugnam experiri placebat: quorum dubitatione
conperta circumsideri tantum eos et abstineri caedibus iussit:
tandemque obsidionis malis fatigati dedidere se. a Libero 11
patre conditos se esse dicebant: et vera haec origo erat.
sita est sub radicibus montis, quem Meron incolae appellant. 12
inde Graeci mentiendi traxere licentiam, Iovis femine Libe-
rum patrem esse celatum. rex situ montis cognito ex 13
incolis cum toto exercitu praemissis commeatibus verticem
eius ascendit. multa hedera vitisque toto gignitur monte,
multae perennes aquae manant. pomorum quoque varii 14
salubresque suci sunt sua sponte fortuitorum seminum
fruges humo nutriente. lauri baccarisque multa in illis
rupibus agrestis est silva. credo equidem non divino in- 15
stinctu, sed lascivia esse provectos, ut passim hederae ac
vitium folia decerperent redimitique fronde toto nemore
similes bacchantibus vagarentur. vocibus ergo tot milium 16
praesidem nemoris eius deum adorantium iuga montis col-
lesque resonabant, cum orta licentia a paucis, ut fere fit, in
omnes se repente vulgasset. quippe velut in media pace 17
per herbas adgestamque frondem prostravere corpora. et
rex fortuitam laetitiam non aversatus large ad epulas omni-
bus praebitis per x dies Libero patri operatum habuit exerci-
tum. quis neget eximiam quoque gloriam saepius fortunae 18
quam virtutis esse beneficium? quippe ne epulantes quidem
et sopitos mero adgredi ausus est hostis, haud secus bac-
chantium ululantiumque fremitu perterritus, quam si proeli-
antium clamor esset auditus. eadem felicitas ab oceano

revertentes temulentos comissantesque inter ora hostium
texit.

19 Hinc ad regionem, quae Daedala vocatur, perventum
est. deseruerant incolae sedes et in avios silvestresque
montes confugerant. ergo Acadira transit, aeque usta et des-
20 tituta incolentium fuga. itaque rationem belli necessitas
mutavit. divisis enim copiis pluribus simul locis arma
ostendit, oppressique, ubi non expectaverant hostem, omni
21 clade perdomiti sunt. Ptolomaeus plurimas urbes, Alexander
maximas cepit: rursusque, quas distribuerat, copias iunxit.
22 superato deinde Choaspe amne Coenon in obsidione urbis
opulentae—Beiram incolae vocant—reliquit: ipse ad Maza-
gas venit. nuper Assacano, cuius regnum fuerat, demortuo
23 regioni urbique praeerat mater eius Cleophis. XXXVIII milia
peditum tuebantur urbem non situ solum, sed etiam opere
munitam. nam qua spectat orientem, cingitur amne tor-
renti, qui praeruptis utrimque ripis aditum ad urbem inpedit.
24 ad occidentem et a meridie velut de industria rupes prae-
altas admolita natura est, infra quas cavernae et voragines
longa vetustate in altum cavatae iacent, quaque desinunt,
25 fossa ingentis operis obiecta est. XXXV stadium murus
urbem conplectitur, cuius inferiora saxo, superiora crudo
latere sunt structa. lateri vinculum lapides sunt, quos inter-
posuere, ut duriori materiae fragilis incumberet, simulque
26 terra humore diluta. ne tamen universa consideret, inpositae
erant trabes validae, quibus iniecta tabulata muros et tege-
27 bant et pervios fecerant. haec munimenta contemplantem
Alexandrum consiliique incertum, quia nec cavernas nisi
aggere poterat inplere nec tormenta aliter muris admovere,
28 quidam e muro sagitta percussit. tum forte in suram
incidit telum: cuius spiculo evolso admoveri equum iussit:
quo vectus ne obligato quidem vulnere haud segnius desti-
29 nata exequebatur. ceterum cum crus saucium penderet, et

cruore siccato frigescens vulnus adgravaret dolorem, dixisse
fertur se quidem Iovis filium dici, sed corporis aegri vitia
sentire. non tamen ante se recepit in castra, quam cuncta 30
perspexit, et, quae fieri vellet, edixit. ergo, sicut imperatum
erat, alii extra urbem tecta moliebantur ingentemque vim
materiae faciendo aggeri detrahebant, alii magnarum arborum
stipites cum ramis ac moles saxorum in cavernas deiciebant.
iamque agger aequaverat summae fastigium terrae: itaque 31
turres erigebant, quae opera ingenti militum ardore intra
nonum diem absoluta sunt. ad ea visenda rex nondum
obducta vulneri cicatrice processit laudatisque militibus
admoveri machinas iussit, e quibus ingens vis telorum in
propugnatores effusa est. praecipue rudes talium operum 32
terrebant mobiles turres, tantasque moles nulla ope, quae
cerneretur, adiutas deorum numine agi credebant: pila
quoque muralia et excussas tormentis praegraves hastas
negabant convenire mortalibus. itaque desperata urbis tutela 33
concessere in arcem. inde, quia nihil obsessis praeter dedi-
tionem patebat, legati ad regem descenderunt veniam peti-
turi. qua inpetrata regina venit cum magno nobilium 34
feminarum grege aureis pateris vina libantium. ipsa genibus 35
regis parvo filio admoto non veniam modo, sed etiam pris-
tinae fortunae inpetravit decus. quippe appellata regina
est: et credidere quidam plus formae quam miserationi
datum. puero quoque certe postea ex ea utcumque genito 36
Alexandro fuit nomen.

Hinc Polypercon ad urbem Noram cum exercitu missus 11
inconditos oppidanos proelio vicit: intra munimenta con-
pulsos secutus urbem in dicionem redegit. multa ignobilia 2
oppida deserta a suis venere in regis potestatem. quorum
incolae armati petram Aornim nomine occupaverunt. hanc
ab Hercule frustra obsessam esse terraeque motu coactum
absistere fama vulgaverat. inopem consilii Alexandrum, quia 3

undique praeceps et abrupta rupes erat, senior quidam peritus
locorum cum duobus filiis adiit, si pretium operae esset,
4 aditum se monstraturum esse promittens. LXXX talenta
constituit daturum Alexander et altero ex iuvenibus obside
5 retento ipsum ad exequenda, quae obtulerat, dimisit. leviter
armatis dux datus est Mullinus, scriba regis. hos enim
circuitu, quo fallerent hostem, in summum iugum placebat
6 evadere. petra non, ut pleraeque, modicis ac mollibus clivis
in sublime fastigium crescit, sed in metae maxime modum
erecta est, cuius ima spatiosiora sunt, altiora in artius coeunt,
7 summa in acutum cacumen exurgunt. radices eius Indus
amnis subit, praealtus, utrimque asperis ripis: ab altera parte
voragines eluviesque praeruptae sunt. nec alia expugnandi
8 patebat via, quam ut replerentur. ad manum silva erat,
quam rex ita caedi iussit, ut nudi stipites iacerentur: quippe
rami fronde vestiti inpedissent ferentes. ipse primus trun-
cam arborem iecit, clamorque exercitus, index alacritatis,
secutus est nullo detrectante munus, quod rex occupavis-
9 set. intra septimum diem cavernas expleverant, cum rex
sagittarios et Agrianos iubet per ardua niti: iuvenesque
10 promptissimos ex sua cohorte XXX delegit. duces his dati
sunt Charus et Alexander, quem rex nominis, quod sibi cum
eo commune esset, admonuit. ac primo, quia tam mani-
festum periculum erat, ipsum regem discrimen subire non
11 placuit: sed ut signum tuba datum est, vir audaciae promp-
tae conversus ad corporis custodes sequi se iubet primusque
invadit in rupem. nec deinde quisquam Macedonum sub-
stitit, relictisque stationibus sua sponte regem sequebantur.
12 multorum miserabilis fuit casus, quos ex praerupta rupe lap-
sos amnis praeterfluens hausit, triste spectaculum etiam non
periclitantibus: cum vero alieno exitio, quid ipsis timendum
foret, admonerentur, in metum misericordia versa non ex-
13 tinctos, sed semetipsos deflebant. et iam eo perventum

erat, unde sine pernicie nisi victores redire non possent, in-
gentia saxa in subeuntes provolventibus barbaris, quis per-
culsi instabili et lubrico gradu praecipites recidebant.
evaserant tamen Alexander et Charus, quos cum xxx 14
delectis praemiserat rex, et iam pugnare comminus coepe-
rant: sed cum superne tela barbari ingererent, saepius ipsi
feriebantur, quam vulnerabant. ergo Alexander et nominis 15
sui et promissi memor, dum acrius quam cautius dimicat,
confossus undique obruitur. quem ut Charus iacentem 16
conspexit, ruere in hostem omnium praeter ultionem in-
memor coepit multosque hasta, quosdam gladio interemit:
sed cum tot unum incesserent manus, super amici corpus
procubuit exanimis. haud secus, quam par erat, promptissi- 17
morum iuvenum ceterorumque militum interitu commotus
rex signum receptui dedit. saluti fuit, quod sensim et in- 18
trepidi se receperunt, et barbari hostem depulisse contenti
non institere cedentibus. ceterum Alexander cum statuisset 19
desistere incepto—quippe nulla spes potiundae petrae
offerebatur—tamen speciem ostendit in obsidione perseve-
rantis. nam et itinera obsideri iussit et turres admoveri et
fatigatis alios succedere. cuius pertinacia cognita Indi per 20
biduum quidem ac duas noctes cum ostentatione non
fiduciae modo, sed etiam victoriae, epulati sunt, tympana suo
more pulsantes. tertia vero nocte tympanorum quidem 21
strepitus desierat audiri, ceterum ex tota petra faces refulge-
bant, quas accenderant barbari, ut tutior esset ipsis fuga,
obscura nocte per invia saxa cursuris. rex Balacro, qui 22
specularetur, praemisso cognoscit petram fuga Indorum esse
desertam. tum dato signo, ut universi conclamarent, in-
conposite fugientibus metum incussit: multique, tamquam 23
adesset hostis, per lubrica saxa perque invias cotes praecipi-
tati occiderunt, plures aliqua membrorum parte mulcati ab
integris deserti sunt. rex locorum magis quam hostium 24

victor tamen magnae victoriae *speciem* sacrificiis et cultu
25 deum fecit. arae in petra locatae sunt Minervae Victoriaeque. ducibus itineris, quo subire iusserat leviter armatos, etsi promissis minora praestiterant, pretium cum fide redditum est. petrae regionisque ei adiunctae Sisocosto tutela permissa.

12 Inde processit Ecbolima: et cum angustias itineris obsideri XX milibus armatorum ab Erice quodam conperisset, gravius agmen exercitus Coeno ducendum modicis itineribus
2 tradidit: ipse praegressus *per* funditores ac sagittarios deturbatis, qui obsederant saltum, sequentibus se copiis viam fecit.
3 Indi sive odio ducis, sive gratiam victoris inituri Ericen fugientem adorti interemerunt caputque eius atque arma ad Alexandrum detulerunt. ille facto inpunitatem dedit, honorem denegavit exemplo.

4 Hinc ad flumen Indum sextisdecumis castris pervenit omniaque, ut praeceperat, ad traiciendum praeparata ab Hephaestione repperit. regnabat in ea regione Omphis,
5 qui patri quoque fuerat auctor dedendi regnum Alexandro et post mortem parentis legatos miserat, qui consulerent eum, regnare se interim vellet, an privatum opperiri eius adven-
6 tum. permissoque ut regnaret, non tamen ius datum usurpare sustinuit. is benigne quidem exceperat Hephaestionem, gratuitum frumentum copiis eius admensus, non tamen ei
7 occurrerat, ne fidem ullius nisi regis experiretur. itaque venienti obviam cum armato exercitu egressus est; elephanti quoque per modica intervalla militum agmini inmixti procul
8 castellorum fecerant speciem. ac primo Alexander non socium, sed hostem adventare credebat, iamque et ipse arma milites capere et equites discedere in cornua iusserat, paratus ad pugnam. at Indus cognito Macedonum errore iussis
9 subsistere ceteris ipse concitat equum, quo vehebatur: idem *Alexander* quoque fecit, sive hostis sive amicus occurreret,

vel sua virtute vel illius fide tutus. coivere, quod ex utri-
usque vultu posset intellegi, amicis animis: ceterum sine
interprete non poterat conseri sermo. itaque adhibito eo
barbarus occurrisse se dixit cum exercitu totas imperii vires
protinus traditurum nec expectasse, dum per nuntios daretur
fides. corpus suum et regnum permittere illi, quem sciret 10
gloriae militantem nihil magis quam famam timere perfidiae.
laetus simplicitate barbari rex et dexteram, fidei suae pig-
nus, dedit et regnum restituit. LVI elephanti erant, quos 11
tradidit Alexandro, multaque pecora eximiae magnitudinis,
tauros ad III milia, pretiosum in ea regione acceptumque
animis regnantium armentum. quaerenti Alexandro, plures 12
agricultores haberet, an milites, cum duobus regibus bellanti
sibi maiore militum quam agrestium manu opus esse respon-
dit. Abisares et Porus erant, sed in Poro eminebat auctori- 13
tas. uterque ultra Hydaspen amnem regnabat et belli fortu-
nam, quisquis arma inferret, experiri decreverat. Omphis 14
permittente Alexandro et regium insigne sumpsit et more
gentis suae nomen, quod patris fuerat: Taxilen appellavere
populares, sequente nomine imperium, in quemcumque
transiret. igitur cum per triduum hospitaliter Alexandrum 15
accepisset, quarto die et, quantum frumenti copiis, quas
Hephaestion duxerat, praebitum a se esset, ostendit et aureas
coronas ipsi amicisque omnibus, praeter haec signati argenti
LXXX talenta dono dedit. qua benignitate eius Alexander 16
mire laetus et, quae is dederat, remisit et mille talenta ex
praeda, quam vehebat, adiecit multaque convivalia ex auro
et argento vasa, plurimum Persicae vestis, XXX equos ex suis
cum isdem insignibus, quis adsueverant, cum ipsum veherent.
quae liberalitas sicut barbarum obstrinxerat, ita amicos ipsius 17
vehementer offendit. e quibus Meleager super cenam largiore
vino usus gratulari se Alexandro dixit, quod saltem in India
repperisset dignum talentis mille. rex haud oblitus, quam 18

aegre tulisset, quod Clitum ob linguae temeritatem occidisset,
iram quidem tenuit, sed dixit invidos homines nihil aliud
quam ipsorum esse tormenta.

13 Postero die legati Abisarae adiere regem. omnia dicioni
eius, ita ut mandatum erat, permittebant: firmataque invicem
2 fide remittuntur ad regem. Porum quoque nominis sui fama
ratus ad deditionem posse conpelli, misit ad eum Cleo-
charen, qui denuntiaret ei, ut stipendium penderet et in
primo suorum finium aditu occurreret regi. Porus alterum
ex his facturum sese respondit, ut intranti regnum suum
3 praesto esset, sed armatus. iam Hydaspen Alexander
superare decreverat, cum Barzaentes, defectionis Arachosiis
auctor, vinctus trigintaque elephanti simul capti perducuntur,
opportunum adversus Indos auxilium; quippe plus in beluis,
4 quam in exercitu spei ac virium illis erat. Samaxus quoque,
rex exiguae partis Indorum, qui Barzaenti se coniunxerat,
5 vinctus adductus est. igitur transfuga et regulo in custodiam,
elephantis autem Taxili traditis ad amnem Hydaspen per-
venit, in cuius ulteriore ripa Porus consederat transitu pro-
6 hibiturus hostem. LXXX et V elephantos obiecerat eximio
corporum robore ultraque eos currus CCC et peditum XXX
fere milia, in quis erant sagittarii, sicuti ante dictum est,
7 gravioribus telis, quam ut apte excuti possent. ipsum ve-
hebat elephantus super ceteras beluas eminens, armaque auro
et argento distincta corpus rarae magnitudinis honestabant.
par animus robori corporis, et quanta inter rudes poterat
8 esse sapientia. Macedonas non conspectus hostium solum,
sed etiam fluminis, quod transeundum erat, magnitudo terre-
bat. IIII in latitudinem stadia diffusus profundo alveo et
9 nusquam vada aperiente speciem vasti maris fecerat. nec
pro spatio aquarum late stagnantium impetum coercebat, sed
quasi in artum coeuntibus ripis torrens et elisus ferebatur,
occultaque saxa inesse ostendebant pluribus locis undae re-

percussae. terribilior erat facies ripae, quam equi virique 10
conpleverant. stabant ingentes vastorum corporum moles
et de industria inritatae horrendo stridore aures fatigabant.
hinc amnis, hinc hostis capacia quidem bonae spei pectora 11
et saepe se experta inproviso tamen pavore percusserant.
quippe inhabiles rates nec dirigi ad ripam, nec tuto adplicari
posse credebant. erant in medio amne insulae crebrae, in 12
quas et Indi et Macedones nantes levatis super capita armis
transibant. ibi levia proelia conserebantur, et uterque rex
parvae rei discrimine summae experiebatur eventum. ceterum 13
in Macedonum exercitu temeritate atque audacia insignes
fuere Symmachus et Nicanor, nobiles iuvenes et perpetua
partium felicitate ad spernendum omne periculum accensi.
quis ducibus promptissimi iuvenum lanceis modo armati trans- 14
navere in insulam, quam frequens hostis tenebat, multosque
Indorum, nulla re melius quam audacia armati, interemerunt.
abire cum gloria poterant, si umquam temeritas felix inveniret 15
modum: sed dum supervenientes contemptim et superbe
quoque expectant, circumventi ab iis, qui occulti enaverant,
eminus obruti telis sunt. qui effugerant hostem, aut impetu 16
amnis ablati sunt aut verticibus impliciti. eaque pugna mul-
tum Pori fiduciam erexit cuncta cernentis e ripa. Alexander 17
inops consilii tandem ad fallendum hostem talem dolum
intendit. erat insula in flumine amplior ceteris, silvestris
eadem et tegendis insidiis apta. fossa quoque praealta haud
procul ripa, quam tenebat ipse, non pedites modo, sed etiam
cum equis viros poterat abscondere. igitur ut a custodia 18
huius opportunitatis oculos hostium averteret, Ptolomaeum
omnibus turmis obequitare iussit procul insula et subinde
Indos clamore terrere, quasi flumen transnaturus foret. per 19
conplures dies Ptolomaeus id fecit eoque consilio Porum
quoque agmen suum ei parti, quam se petere simulabat,
coegit advertere. iam extra conspectum hostis insula erat. 20

Alexander in diversa parte ripae statui suum tabernaculum
iussit adsuetamque comitari ipsum cohortem ante id taber-
naculum stare et omnem apparatum regiae magnificentiae
21 hostium oculis de industria ostendi. Attalum etiam, aequalem
sibi et haud disparem habitu oris et corporis, utique cum
procul viseretur, veste regia exornat, praebiturum speciem,
ipsum regem illi ripae praesidere nec agitare de transitu.
22 huius consilii effectum primo morata tempestas est, mox
adiuvit, incommoda quoque ad bonos eventus vertente
23 fortuna. traicere amnem cum ceteris copiis in regionem in-
sulae, de qua ante dictum est, parabat, averso hoste in eos,
qui cum Ptolomaeo inferiorem obsederant ripam, cum pro-
cella imbrem vix sub tectis tolerabilem effundit. obrutique
milites nimbo in terram refugerunt navigiis ratibusque de-
sertis. sed tumultuantium fremitus obstrepentibus ventis ab
24 hoste non poterat audiri. deinde momento temporis repres-
sus est imber: ceterum adeo spissae intendere se nubes, ut
conderent lucem, vixque conloquentium inter ipsos facies
25 noscitarentur. terruisset alium obducta nox caelo, cum ig-
noto amne navigandum esset, forsitan hoste eam ipsam
26 ripam, quam caeci atque inprovidi *petebant*, *tenente*. at rex
periculo gloriam accersens et obscuritatem, quae ceteros
terrebat, suam occasionem ratus dato signo, ut omnes silentio
ascenderent in rates, eam, qua ipse vehebatur, primam iussit
27 expelli. vacua erat ab hostibus ripa, quae petebatur: quippe
adhuc Porus Ptolomaeum tantum intuebatur. una ergo navi,
quam petrae fluctus inliserat, haerente ceterae evadunt:
armaque capere milites et ire in ordines iussit.

14 Iamque agmen in cornua divisum ipse ducebat, cum
Poro nuntiatur armis virisque ripam obtineri et rerum adesse
discrimen. ac primo humani ingenii vitio spei suae indul-
gens Abisaren belli socium—et ita convenerat—adventare
2 credebat. mox liquidiore luce aperiente aciem hostium c

quadrigas et IIII milia equitum venienti agmini obiecit. dux
erat copiarum, quas praemisit, Hages, frater ipsius, summa
virium in curribus: senos viros singuli vehebant, duos clipe- 3
atos, duos sagittarios, ab utroque latere dispositos: aurigae
erant ceteri, haud sane inermes; quippe iacula conplura, ubi
comminus proeliandum erat, omissis habenis in hostem in-
gerebant. ceterum vix ullus usus huius auxilii eo die fuit. 4
namque, ut supra dictum est, imber violentius quam alias
fusus campos lubricos et inequitabiles fecerat, gravesque et
propemodum inmobiles currus inluvie ac voraginibus haere-
bant. contra Alexander expedito ac levi agmine strenue 5
invectus est. Scythae et Dahae primi omnium invasere
Indos: Perdiccam deinde cum equitibus in dextrum cornu
hostium emisit. iam undique pugna se moverat, cum ii, qui 6
currus agebant, illud ultimum auxilium suorum rati effusis
habenis in medium discrimen ruere coeperunt. anceps id 7
malum utrisque erat: nam et Macedonum pedites primo
impetu obterebantur et per lubrica atque invia inmissi currus
excutiebant eos, a quibus regebantur: aliorum turbati equi 8
non in voragines modo lacunasque, sed etiam in amnem
praecipitavere curricula: pauci telis hostium exacti penetra- 9
vere ad Porum acerrime pugnam cientem. is, ut dissipatos
tota acie currus vagari sine rectoribus vidit, proximis ami-
corum distribuit elephantos. post eos posuerat peditem ac 10
sagittarios *et* tympana pulsare solitos. id pro cantu tubarum
Indis erat, nec strepitu eorum movebantur, olim ad notum
sonum auribus mitigatis. Herculis simulacrum agmini 11
peditum praeferebatur. id maximum erat bellantibus in-
citamentum, et deseruisse gestantes militare flagitium habe-
batur. capitis etiam sanxerant poenam iis, qui ex acie non 12
rettulissent, metu, quem ex illo hoste quondam conceperant,
etiam in religionem venerationemque converso. Macedonas
non beluarum modo, sed etiam ipsius regis aspectus parum-

13 per inhibuit. beluae dispositae inter armatos speciem turrium procul fecerant. ipse Porus humanae magnitudinis propemodum excesserat formam. magnitudinem corpori adicere videbatur belua, qua vehebatur, tantum inter ceteras eminens,
14 quanto aliis ipse praestabat. itaque Alexander contemplatus et regem et agmen Indorum, 'tandem', inquit, 'par animo meo periculum video. cum bestiis simul et cum egregiis
15 viris res est.' intuensque Coenon, 'cum ego', inquit, 'Ptolomaeo Perdiccaque et Hephaestione comitatus in laevum hostium cornu impetum fecero, viderisque me in medio ardore certaminis, ipse dextrum move et turbatis signa infer. tu, Antigene, et tu, Leonnate, et Tauron, invehemini in
16 mediam aciem et urgebitis frontem. hastae nostrae praelongae et validae non alias magis quam adversus beluas rectoresque earum usui esse poterunt: deturbate eos, qui vehuntur, et ipsas confodite. anceps genus auxilii est et in suos acrius furit. in hostem enim imperio, in suos pavore
17 agitur.' haec elocutus concitat equum primus: iamque, ut destinatum erat, invaserat ordines hostium, cum Coenus in-
18 genti vi in laevum cornu invehitur. phalanx quoque mediam Indorum aciem uno impetu perrupit. at Porus, qua equitem invehi senserat, beluas agi iussit: sed tardum et paene in-
19 mobile animal equorum velocitatem aequare non poterat. ne sagittarum quidem ullus erat barbaris usus: quippe longas et praegraves, nisi prius in terra statuerent arcum, haud satis apte et commode inponunt: tum humo lubrica et ob id inpediente conatum molientes ictus celeritate hostium occu-
20 pantur. ergo spreto regis imperio—quod fere fit, ubi turbatis acrius metus quam dux imperare coepit—totidem erant im-
21 peratores, quot agmina errabant. alius iungere aciem, alius dividere, stare quidam et nonnulli circumvehi terga hostium
22 iubebant. nihil in medium consulebatur. Porus tamen cum paucis, quibus metu potior fuerat pudor, colligere dispersos,

obvius hosti ire pergit elephantosque ante agmen suorum
agi iubet. magnum beluae iniecere terrorem, insolitusque 23
stridor non equos modo, tam pavidum ad omnia animal,
sed viros quoque ordinesque turbaverat. iam fugae circum- 24
spiciebant locum paulo ante victores, cum Alexander
Agrianos et Thracas leviter armatos, meliorem concursatione
quam comminus militem, emisit in beluas. ingentem hi vim 25
telorum iniecere et elephantis et regentibus eos. phalanx
quoque instare constanter territis coepit. sed quidam 26
avidius persecuti beluas in semet inritavere vulneribus.
obtriti ergo pedibus earum ceteris, ut parcius instarent, fuere
documentum. praecipue terribilis illa facies erat, cum manu 27
arma virosque corriperent et super se regentibus traderent.
anceps ergo pugna nunc sequentium, nunc fugientium ele- 28
phantos in multum diei varium certamen extraxit: donec
securibus—id namque genus auxilii praeparatum erat—pedes
amputare coeperunt. copidas vocabant gladios leviter cur- 29
vatos, falcibus similes, quis adpetebant beluarum manus. nec
quicquam inexpertum non mortis modo, sed etiam in ipsa
morte novi supplicii timor omittebat. ergo elephanti vul- 30
neribus tandem fatigati suos impetu sternunt, et, qui rexerant
eos, praecipitati in terram ab ipsis obterebantur. itaque
pecorum modo magis pavidi quam infesti ultra aciem exige-
bantur, cum Porus, destitutus a pluribus, tela multo ante 31
praeparata in circumfusos ex elephanto suo coepit ingerere
multisque eminus vulneratis expositus ipse ad ictus undique
petebatur. novem iam vulnera hinc tergo, illinc pectore ex- 32
ceperat multoque sanguine profuso languidis manibus magis
elapsa quam excussa tela mittebat. nec segnius belua in- 33
stincta rabie, nondum saucia, invehebatur ordinibus, donec
rector beluae regem conspexit fluentibus membris omissisque
armis vix compotem mentis. Tum beluam in fugam con- 34
citat sequente Alexandro: sed equus eius multis vulneribus

confossus deficiensque procubuit posito magis rege, quam
effuso. itaque dum equum mutat, tardius insecutus est.
35 interim frater Taxilis, regis Indorum, praemissus ab Alex-
andro monere coepit Porum, ne ultima experiri perseveraret
36 dederetque se victori. at ille, quamquam exhaustae erant
vires, deficiebatque sanguis, tamen ad notam vocem excita-
tus, 'adgnosco', inquit, 'Taxilis fratrem, imperii regnique
sui proditoris': et telum, quod unum forte non effluxerat,
contorsit in eum: quod per medium pectus penetravit
37 ad tergum. hoc ultimo virtutis opere edito fugere acrius
coepit: sed elephantus quoque, qui multa exceperat tela,
deficiebat. itaque sistit fugam peditemque sequenti hosti
38 obiecit. iam Alexander consecutus erat et pertinacia Pori
cognita vetabat resistentibus parci. ergo undique et in
pedites et in ipsum Porum tela congesta sunt: quis tandem
39 gravatus labi ex belua coepit. Indus, qui elephantum regebat,
descendere eum ratus more solito elephantum procumbere
iussit in genua: qui ut se submisit, ceteri quoque—ita enim
instituti erant—demisere corpora in terram. ea res et Porum
40 et ceteros victoribus tradidit. rex spoliari corpus Pori,
interemptum esse credens, iubet, et, qui detraherent loricam
vestemque, concurrere: cum belua dominum tueri et spoli-
antes coepit adpetere levatumque corpus eius rursus dorso
suo inponere. ergo telis undique obruitur, confossoque eo
41 in vehiculum Porus inponitur. quem rex ut vidit adlevan-
tem oculos, non odio, sed miseratione commotus, 'quae,
malum', inquit, 'amentia te coegit rerum mearum cognita
fama belli fortunam experiri, cum Taxilis esset in deditos
42 clementiae meae tam propinquum tibi exemplum?' at ille,
'quoniam', inquit, 'percontaris, respondebo ea libertate,
quam interrogando fecisti. neminem me fortiorem esse cen-
sebam. meas enim noveram vires, nondum expertus tuas:
fortiorem esse te belli docuit eventus. sed ne sic quidem

parum felix sum, secundus tibi.' rursus interrogatus, quid 43
ipse victorem statuere debere censeret, 'quod hic', inquit,
'dies tibi suadet, quo expertus es, quam caduca felicitas
esset.' plus monendo profecit, quam si precatus esset: 44
quippe magnitudinem animi eius interritam ac ne fortuna
quidem infractam non misericordia modo, sed etiam honore
excipere dignatus est. aegrum curavit haud secus, quam si 45
pro ipso pugnasset: confirmatum contra spem omnium in
amicorum numerum recepit, mox donavit ampliore regno,
quam tenuit. nec sane quicquam ingenium eius solidius aut 46
constantius habuit, quam admirationem verae laudis et
gloriae: simplicius tamen famam aestimabat in hoste, quam
in cive. quippe a suis credebat magnitudinem suam destrui
posse, eandem clariorem fore, quo maiores fuissent, quos
ipse vicisset.

LIBER IX.

1 Alexander, tam memorabili victoria laetus, qua sibi
orientis finis apertos esse censebat, Soli victimis caesis mili-
tes quoque, quo promptioribus animis reliqua belli obirent,
pro contione laudatos docuit, quidquid Indis virium fuisset,
2 illa dimicatione prostratum: cetera opimam praedam fore
celebratasque opes in ea regione eminere, quam peterent.
proinde iam vilia et obsoleta esse spolia de Persis: gemmis
margaritisque et auro atque ebore Macedoniam Graeciam-
3 que, non suas tantum domos repletum ire. avidi milites et
pecuniae et gloriae, simul quia numquam eos adfirmatio eius
fefellerat, pollicentur operam: dimissisque cum bona spe
navigia exaedificari iubet, ut, cum totam Asiam percucurris-
4 set, finem terrarum, mare, inviseret. multa materia navalis
in proximis montibus erat: quam caedere adgressi magnitu-
5 dinis inuisitatae repperere serpentes. rhinocerotes quoque,
rarum alibi animal, in isdem montibus erant. ceterum hoc
nomen beluis inditum a Graecis: sermonis eius ignari aliud
6 lingua sua usurpant. rex duabus urbibus conditis in utra-
que fluminis, quod superaverat, ripa copiarum duces coronis
et mille aureis singulos donat: ceteris quoque pro portione
aut gradus, quem in amicitia obtinebant, aut navatae operae
7 honos habitus est. Abisares, qui prius, quam cum Poro
dimicaretur, legatos ad Alexandrum miserat, rursus alios
misit pollicentes, omnia facturum, quae imperasset, modo
ne cogeretur corpus suum dedere: neque enim aut sine
8 *regio* imperio victurum, aut regnaturum esse captivum. cui

Alexander nuntiari iussit, si gravaretur ad se venire, ipsum
ad eum esse venturum.

Hinc porro amne superato ad interiora Indiae processit.
silvae erant prope in inmensum spatium diffusae proceris- 9
que et in eximiam altitudinem editis arboribus umbrosae.
plerique rami instar ingentium stipitum flexi in humum rur- 10
sus, qua se curvaverant, erigebantur, adeo ut species esset
non rami resurgentis, sed arboris ex sua radice generatae.
caeli temperies salubris: quippe et vim solis umbrae levant 11
et aquae large manant e fontibus. ceterum hic quoque 12
serpentium magna vis erat squamis fulgorem auri redden-
tibus. virus haud ullum magis noxium est: quippe morsum
praesens mors sequebatur, donec ab incolis remedium obla-
tum est. hinc per deserta ventum est ad flumen Hyarotim. 13
iunctum erat flumini nemus, opacum arboribus alibi inuisi-
tatis agrestiumque pavonum multitudine frequens. castris 14
inde motis oppidum haud procul positum corona capit obsi-
dibusque acceptis stipendium inponit.

Ad magnam deinde, ut in ea regione, urbem pervenit,
non muro solum, sed etiam palude munitam. ceterum bar- 15
bari vehiculis inter se iunctis dimicaturi occurrerunt: tela
aliis hastae, aliis secures erant, transiliebantque in vehicula
strenuo saltu, cum succurrere laborantibus suis vellent. ac 16
primo insolitum genus pugnae Macedonas terruit, cum
eminus vulnerarentur: deinde spreto tam incondito auxilio
ab utroque latere vehiculis circumfusi repugnantes fodere
coeperunt. et vincula, quis conserta erant, iussit incidi, 17
quo facilius singula circumvenirentur. itaque VIII milibus
suorum amissis in oppidum refugerunt. postero die scalis 18
undique admotis muri occupantur: paucis pernicitas saluti
fuit. qui cognito urbis excidio paludem transnavere, in
vicina oppida ingentem intulere terrorem, invictum exerci-
tum et deorum profecto advenisse memorantes.

19 Alexander ad vastandam eam regionem Perdicca cum
expedita manu misso partem copiarum Eumeni tradidit, ut
is quoque barbaros ad deditionem conpelleret: ipse ceteros
ad urbem validam, in quam aliarum quoque confugerant
20 incolae, duxit. oppidani missis, qui regem deprecarentur,
nihilo minus bellum parabant. quippe orta seditio in diversa
consilia diduxerat vulgum: alii omnia deditione potiora,
21 quidam nullam opem in ipsis esse ducebant. sed dum nihil
in commune consulitur, qui deditioni inminebant, apertis
22 portis hostem recipiunt. Alexander quamquam belli aucto-
ribus iure poterat irasci, tamen omnibus venia data et obsi-
dibus acceptis ad proximam deinde urbem castra movit.
23 obsides ducebantur ante agmen. quos cum ex muris adgno-
vissent, utpote gentis eiusdem, in conloquium convocaverunt.
illi clementiam regis simulque vim commemorando ad de-
ditionem eos conpulere: ceterasque urbes simili modo
domitas in fidem accepit.

24 Hinc in regnum Sopithis perventum est. gens, ut bar-
bari credunt, sapientia excellet bonisque moribus regitur.
25 genitos liberos non parentum arbitrio tollunt aluntque, sed
eorum, quibus spectandi infantum habitum cura mandata
est. si quos insignes aut aliqua parte membrorum inutiles
26 notaverunt, necari iubent. nuptiis coeunt non genere ac
nobilitate coniunctis, sed electa corporum specie, quia
27 eadem aestimatur in liberis. huius gentis oppidum, cui
Alexander admoverat copias, ab ipso Sopithe obtinebatur.
clausae erant portae, sed nulli in muris turribusque se
armati ostendebant, dubitabantque Macedones, deseruissent
28 urbem incolae, an fraude se occulerent: cum subito pate-
facta porta rex Indus cum duobus adultis filiis occurrit,
multum inter omnes barbaros eminens corporis specie.
29 vestis erat auro purpuraque distincta, quae etiam crura
velabat: aureis soleis inseruerat gemmas, lacerti quoque et

brachia margaritis ornata erant. pendebant ex auribus 30
insignes candore ac magnitudine lapilli. baculum aureum
berylli distinguebant: quo tradito precatus, ut sospes acci-
peret, et liberosque et gentem suam dedidit. nobiles ad 31
venandum canes in ea regione sunt: latratu abstinere dicun-
tur, cum viderunt feram, leonibus maxime infesti. horum 32
vim ut ostenderet Alexandro, in conseptum leonem eximiae
magnitudinis iussit emitti et IIII omnino admoveri canes, qui
celeriter feram occupaverunt. tum ex iis, qui adsueverant
talibus ministeriis, unus canis leoni cum aliis inhaerentis crus
avellere et, quia non sequebatur, ferro amputare coepit: ne 33
sic quidem pertinacia victa rursus aliam partem secare insti-
tit et inde non segnius inhaerentem ferro subinde caedebat.
ille in vulnere ferae dentes moribundus quoque infixerat:
tantam [in] illis animalibus ad venandum cupiditatem in-
generasse naturam memoriae proditum est. equidem plura 34
transcribo, quam credo: nam nec adfirmare sustineo, de qui-
bus dubito, nec subducere, quae accepi. relicto igitur Sopithe 35
in suo regno ad fluvium Hypasin processit, Hephaestione,
qui diversam regionem subegerat, coniuncto. Phegeus erat 36
gentis proximae rex: qui popularibus suis colere agros, ut
adsueverant, iussis Alexandro cum donis occurrit, nihil,
quod imperaret, detrectans.

Biduum apud eum substitit rex: tertio die amnem supe- **2**
rare decreverat, transitu difficilem non spatio solum aqua-
rum, sed etiam saxis inpeditum. percontatus igitur Phegea, 2
quae noscenda erant, XI dierum ultra flumen per vastas
solitudines iter esse cognoscit: excipere deinde Gangen,
maximum totius Indiae fluminum: ulteriorem ripam colere 3
gentes Gangaridas et Prasios eorumque regem esse Aggram-
men, XX milibus equitum ducentisque peditum obsidentem
vias. ad hoc quadrigarum II milia trahere et praecipuum 4
terrorem elephantos, quos III milium numerum explere

5 dicebat. incredibilia regi omnia videbantur. igitur Porum—
nam cum eo erat—percontatur, an vera essent, quae dice-
6 rentur. ille vires quidem gentis et regni haud falso iactari
adfirmat: ceterum, qui regnaret, non modo ignobilem esse,
sed etiam ultimae sortis: quippe patrem eius, tonsorem vix
diurno quaestu propulsantem famem, propter habitum haud
7 indecorum cordi fuisse reginae. ab ea in propiorem eius,
qui tum regnasset, amicitiae locum admotum interfecto eo
per insidias sub specie tutelae liberum eius invasisse regnum
necatisque pueris hunc, qui nunc regnat, generasse, invisum
vilemque popularibus, magis paternae fortunae quam suae
8 memorem. adfirmatio Pori multiplicem animo regis inie-
cerat curam. hostem beluasque spernebat, situm locorum
9 et vim fluminum extimescebat: relegatos in ultimum paene
rerum humanarum terminum persequi et eruere arduum
videbatur. rursus avaritia gloriae et insatiabilis cupido
10 famae nihil invium, nihil remotum videri sinebat. et inter-
dum dubitabat, an Macedones, tot emensi spatia terrarum,
in acie et in castris senes facti, per obiecta flumina, per tot
naturae obstantes difficultates secuturi essent: abundantes
onustosque praeda magis parta frui velle, quam adquirenda
11 fatigari. non idem sibi et militibus animi esse: *se* totius
orbis imperium mente conplexum adhuc in operum suorum
primordio stare: militem labore defetigatum proximum
12 quemque fructum finito tandem periculo expetere. vicit
ergo cupido rationem, et ad contionem vocatis militibus ad
hunc maxime modum disseruit: 'non ignoro, milites, multa,
quae terrere vos possent, ab incolis Indiae per hos dies de
13 industria esse iactata: sed non est inprovisa vobis mentien-
tium vanitas. sic Ciliciae fauces, sic Mesopotamiae campos,
Tigrim et Euphraten, quorum alterum vado transivimus,
14 alterum ponte, terribilem fecerant Persae. numquam ad
liquidum fama perducitur: omnia illa tradente maiora sunt

vero. nostra quoque gloria, cum sit ex solido, plus tamen
habet nominis, quam operis. modo quis beluas offerentes 15
moenium speciem, quis Hydaspen amnem, quis cetera
auditu maiora quam vero sustineri posse credebat? olim,
hercule, fugissemus ex Asia, si nos fabulae debellare potuis-
sent. creditisne elephantorum greges maiores esse, quam 16
usquam armentorum sunt, cum et rarum sit animal nec
facile capiatur multoque difficilius mitigetur? atqui eadem 17
vanitas copias peditum equitumque numeravit. nam flumen,
quo latius fusum est, hoc placidius stagnat: quippe angustis
ripis coercita et in angustiorem alveum elisa torrentes aquas
invehunt, contra spatio alvei segnior cursus est. praeterea 18
in ripa omne periculum est, ubi adplicantes navigia hostis
expectat. ita quantumcumque flumen intervenit, idem
futurum discrimen est evadentium in terram. sed omnia 19
ista vera esse fingamus. utrumne vos magnitudo beluarum
an multitudo hostium terret? quod pertinet ad elephantos,
praesens habemus exemplum: in suos vehementius quam in
nos incucurrerunt: tam vasta corpora securibus falcibusque
mutilata sunt. quid autem interest, totidem sint, quot Porus 20
habuit, an III milia, cum uno aut altero vulneratis ceteros in
fugam declinari *videamus?* dein paucos quoque incom-
mode regunt: congregata vero tot milia ipsa se elidunt, ubi 21
nec stare nec fugere potuerint inhabiles vastorum corporum
moles. equidem sic animalia ista contempsi, ut, cum habe-
rem ipse, non opposuerim, satis gnarus, plus suis quam
hostibus periculi inferre. at enim equitum peditumque 22
multitudo vos commovet! cum paucis enim pugnare soliti
estis et nunc primum inconditam sustinebitis turbam. testis 23
adversus multitudinem invicti Macedonum roboris Granicus
amnis et Cilicia inundata cruore Persarum et Arbela, cuius
campi devictorum a nobis ossibus strati sunt. sero hostium 24
legiones numerare coepistis, postquam solitudinem in Asia

vincendo fecistis. cum per Hellespontum navigaremus, de paucitate nostra cogitandum fuit: nunc nos Scythae sequuntur, Bactriana auxilia praesto sunt, Dahae Sogdianique inter
25 nos militant. nec tamen illi turbae confido. vestras manus intueor, vestram virtutem rerum, quas gesturus sum, vadem praedemque habeo. quamdiu vobiscum in acie stabo, nec mei nec hostium exercitus numero: vos modo animos mihi
26 plenos alacritatis ac fiduciae adhibete. non in limine operum laborumque nostrorum, sed in exitu stamus: pervenimus ad solis ortum et oceanum: nisi obstat ignavia, inde victores perdomito fine terrarum revertemur in patriam. nolite, quod pigri agricolae faciunt, maturos fructus per
27 inertiam amittere e manibus. maiora sunt periculis praemia: dives eadem et inbellis est regio. itaque non tam ad gloriam vos duco, quam ad praedam. digni estis, qui opes, quas illud mare litoribus invehit, referatis in patriam, digni,
28 qui nihil inexpertum, nihil metu omissum relinquatis. per vos gloriamque vestram, qua humanum fastigium exceditis, perque et mea in vos et in me vestra merita, quibus invicti contendimus, oro quaesoque, ne humanarum rerum terminos adeuntem alumnum commilitonemque vestrum, ne dicam
29 regem, deseratis. cetera vobis imperavi: hoc unum debiturus sum. et is vos rogo, qui nihil umquam vobis praecepi, quin primus me periculis obtulerim, qui saepe aciem clipeo meo texi, ne infregeritis in manibus meis palmam, qua Herculem Liberumque patrem, si invidia afuerit, aequabo.
30 date hoc precibus meis et tandem obstinatum silentium rumpite. ubi est ille clamor, alacritatis vestrae index? ubi ille meorum Macedonum vultus? non adgnosco vos, milites, nec adgnosci videor a vobis. surdas iamdudum aures pulso:
31 aversos animos et infractos excitare conor.' cumque illi in terram demissis capitibus tacere perseverarent, 'nescio quid', inquit, 'in vos inprudens deliqui, quod me ne intueri

quidem vultis. in solitudine mihi videor esse. nemo re-
spondet, nemo saltem negat. quos adloquor? quid autem 32
postulo? vestram gloriam et magnitudinem vindicamus.
ubi sunt illi, quorum certamen paulo ante vidi contenden-
tium, qui potissimum vulnerati regis corpus exciperent?
desertus, destitutus sum, hostibus deditus. sed solus quo- 33
que ire perseverabo. obicite me fluminibus et beluis et
illis gentibus, quarum nomina horretis. inveniam, qui de-
sertum a vobis sequantur: Scythae Bactrianique erunt
mecum, hostes paulo ante, nunc milites nostri. mori prae- 34
stat, quam precario imperatorem esse. ite reduces domos!
ite deserto rege ovantes! ego hic a vobis desperatae victo-
riae aut honestae morti locum inveniam.' ne sic quidem **3**
ulli militum vox exprimi potuit. expectabant, ut duces
principesque ad regem perferrent, vulneribus et continuo
labore militiae fatigatos non detrectare munia, sed sustinere
non posse. ceterum illi metu attoniti in terram ora defix-
erant. igitur primo fremitus sua sponte, deinde gemitus 2
quoque oritur, paulatimque liberius dolor erigi coepit manan-
tibus lacrimis, adeo ut rex ira in misericordiam versa ne
ipse quidem, quamquam cuperet, temperare oculis potuerit.
tandem universa contione effusius flente Coenus ausus est 3
cunctantibus ceteris propius tribunal accedere, significans
se loqui velle. quem ut videre milites detrahentem galeam 4
capiti—ita enim regem adloqui mos est—hortari coeperunt,
ut causam exercitus ageret. tum Coenus, 'dii prohibeant', 5
inquit, 'a nobis inpias mentes: et profecto prohibent. idem
animus est tuis, qui fuit semper, ire, quo iusseris, pugnare,
periclitari, sanguine nostro commendare posteritati tuum
nomen. proinde si perseveras, inermes quoque et nudi et
exangues, utcumque tibi cordi est, sequimur vel antecedimus.
sed si audire vis non fictas tuorum militum voces, verum 6
necessitate ultima expressas, praebe, quaeso, propitias aures

imperium atque auspicium tuum constantissime secutis et,
7 quocumque pergis, secuturis. vicisti, rex, magnitudine rerum
non hostes modo, sed etiam milites. quidquid mortalitas
capere poterat, inplevimus. emensis maria terrasque melius
8 nobis quam incolis omnia nota sunt. paene in ultimo mundi
fine consistimus. in alium orbem paras ire et Indiam quaeris
Indis quoque ignotam: inter feras serpentesque degentes
eruere ex latebris et cubilibus suis expetis, ut plura, quam
9 sol videt, victoria lustres. digna prorsus cogitatio animo
tuo, sed altior nostro. virtus enim tua semper *in* incremento
10 erit, nostra vis iam in fine est. intuere corpora exanguia, tot
perfossa vulneribus, tot cicatricibus putria. iam tela hebetia
sunt: iam arma deficiunt. vestem Persicam induimus, quia
domestica subvehi non potest. in externum degeneravimus
11 cultum. quoto cuique lorica est? quis equum habet? iube
quaeri, quam multos servi ipsorum persecuti sint, quid cuique
supersit ex praeda. omnium victores omnium inopes sumus.
nec luxuria laboramus, sed bello instrumenta belli consump-
12 simus. hunc tu pulcherrimum exercitum nudum obicies
beluis? quarum ut multitudinem augeant de industria bar-
bari, magnum tamen esse numerum etiam ex mendacio
13 intellego. quodsi adhuc penetrare in Indiam certum est,
regio a meridie minus vasta est: qua subacta licebit decur-
rere in illud mare, quod rebus humanis terminum voluit esse
14 natura. cur circuitu petis gloriam, quae ad manum posita
est? hic quoque occurrit oceanus. nisi mavis errare, per-
15 venimus, quo tua fortuna ducit. haec tecum, quam sine te
cum his, loqui malui, non uti inirem circumstantis exercitus
gratiam, sed ut vocem loquentium potius quam gemitum
16 murmurantium audires.' ut finem orationi Coenus inpo-
suit, clamor undique cum ploratu oritur, regem, patrem,
17 dominum confusis appellantium vocibus. iamque et alii
duces praecipueque seniores, quis ob aetatem et excusatio

honestior erat et auctoritas maior, eadem precabantur. ille 18
nec castigare obstinatos nec mitigare poterat iratos. itaque
inops consilii desiluit e tribunali claudique regiam iussit
omnibus praeter adsuetos adire prohibitis. biduum irae 19
datum est: tertio die processit erigique duodecim aras ex
quadrato saxo, monumentum expeditionis suae, munimenta
quoque castrorum iussit extendi cubiliaque amplioris formae,
quam pro corporum habitu, relinqui, ut speciem omnium
augeret, posteritati fallax miraculum praeparans.

Hinc repetens, quae emensus erat, ad flumen Acesinem 20
locat castra. ibi forte Coenus morbo extinctus est: cuius
morte ingemuit quidem rex, adiecit tamen, propter paucos
dies longam orationem eum exorsum, tamquam solus Mace-
doniam visurus esset. iam in aqua classis, quam aedificari 21
iusserat, stabat. inter haec Memnon ex Thracia in supple-
mentum equitum V milia, praeter eos ab Harpalo peditum
VII milia adduxerat armaque XXV milibus auro et argento
caelata pertulerat, quis distributis vetera cremari iussit.
mille navigiis aditurus oceanum discordesque et vetera odia 22
retractantes Porum et Taxilen, Indiae reges, firmatae per
adfinitatem gratiae relinquit in suis regnis, summo in aedifi-
canda classe amborum studio usus. oppida quoque duo 23
condidit, quorum alterum Nicaeam appellavit, alterum Buce-
phala, equi, quem amiserat, memoriae ac nomini dedicans
urbem. elephantis deinde et inpedimentis terra sequi iussis 24
secundo amne defluxit, quadraginta ferme stadia singulis
diebus procedens, ut opportunis locis exponi subinde copiae
possent.

Perventum erat in regionem, in qua Hydaspes amnis **4**
Acesini committitur. hinc decurrit in fines Siborum. hi 2
de exercitu Herculis maiores suos esse memorant: aegros
relictos esse, cepisse sedem, quam ipsi obtinebant. pelles 3
ferarum pro veste, clavae tela erant: multaque, etiam cum

4 Graeci mores exolevissent, stirpis ostendebant vestigia. hinc
excensione facta CC et L stadia excessit depopulatusque
5 regionem oppidum, caput eius, corona cepit. XL peditum
milia gens in ripa fluminum opposuerat: quae amne superato
in fugam conpulit inclusosque moenibus expugnat. puberes
6 interfecti sunt, ceteri venierunt. alteram deinde urbem
expugnare adortus magnaque vi defendentium pulsus multos
Macedonum amisit. sed cum in obsidione perseverasset,
oppidani desperata salute ignem subiecere tectis seque ac
7 liberos coniugesque incendio cremant. quod cum ipsi
augerent, hostes extinguerent, nova forma pugnae erat. de-
lebant incolae urbem, hostes defendebant: adeo etiam na-
8 turae iura bellum in contrarium mutat. arx erat oppidi in-
tacta, in qua praesidium dereliquit: ipse navigiis circum-
vectus est arcem. quippe III flumina tota India praeter
Gangen maxima munimento arcis adplicant undas. a sep-
tentrione Indus adluit, a meridie Acesines Hydaspi con-
9 funditur. ceterum amnium coetus maritimis similes fluctus
movet, multoque ac turbido limo, quod aquarum concursu
subinde turbatur, iter, qua meant navigia, in tenuem alveum
10 cogitur. itaque cum crebri fluctus se inveherent et navium
hinc proras, hinc latera pulsarent, subducere nautae vela
coeperunt. sed ministeria eorum hinc metu, hinc praerapida
11 celeritate fluminum occupantur. in oculis omnium duo
maiora navigia submersa sunt: leviora, cum et ipsa nequi-
rent regi, in ripam tamen innoxia expulsa sunt. ipse rex in
rapidissimos vertices incidit, quibus intorta navis obliqua et
12 gubernaculi inpatiens agebatur. iam vestem detraxerat cor-
pori proiecturus semet in flumen, amicique, ut exciperent
eum, haud procul nabant, adparebatque anceps periculum
13 tam nataturi, quam navigare perseverantis. ergo ingenti
certamine concitant remos, quantaque vis humana esse pote-
rat, admota est, ut fluctus, qui se invehebant, everberarentur.

findi crederes undas et retro gurgites cedere. quibus tan- 14
dem navis erepta, non tamen ripae adplicatur, sed in proxi-
mum vadum inliditur. cum amni bellum fuisse crederes.
ergo aris pro numero fluminum positis sacrificioque facto
xxx stadia processit.

Inde ventum est in regionem Sudracarum Mallorumque, 15
quos alias bellare inter se solitos tunc periculi societas
iunxerat. nonaginta milia iuniorum peditum in armis erant,
praeter hos equitum x milia nongentaeque quadrigae. at 16
Macedones, qui omni discrimine iam defunctos se esse
crediderant, postquam integrum bellum cum ferocissimis
Indiae gentibus superesse cognoverunt, inproviso metu
territi rursus seditiosis vocibus regem increpare coeperunt:
Gangen amnem et, quae ultra essent, coactum transmittere, 17
non tamen finisse, sed mutasse bellum. indomitis gentibus
se obiectos, ut sanguine suo aperirent ei oceanum. trahi 18
extra sidera et solem cogique adire, quae mortalium oculis
natura subduxerit. novis identidem armis novos hostes
existere. quos ut omnes fundant fugentque, quod praemium
ipsos manere? caliginem ac tenebras et perpetuam noctem
profundo incubantem mari, repletum inmanium beluarum
gregibus fretum, inmobiles undas, in quibus emoriens natura
defecerit. rex non sua, sed militum sollicitudine anxius 19
contione advocata docet, inbelles esse, quos metuant. nihil
deinde praeter has gentes obstare, quominus terrarum spatia
emensi ad finem simul mundi laborumque perveniant. ces- 20
sisse illis metuentibus Gangen et multitudinem nationum,
quae ultra amnem essent: declinasse iter eo, ubi par gloria,
minus periculum esset. iam prospicere se oceanum, iam 21
perflare ad ipsos auram maris: ne inviderent sibi laudem,
quam peteret. Herculis et Liberi patris terminos transituros
illos, regi suo parvo inpendio inmortalitatem famae daturos.
paterentur se ex India redire, non fugere. omnis multitudo 22

et maxime militaris mobili impetu effertur. ita seditionis
23 non remedia quam principia maiora sunt. non alias tam
alacer clamor ab exercitu est redditus, iubentium duceret dis
secundis aequaretque gloria, quos aemularetur. laetus his
24 adclamationibus ad hostes protinus castra movit. validissi-
mae Indorum gentes erant et bellum inpigre parabant ducem-
que ex natione Sudracarum spectatae virtutis elegerant, qui
sub radicibus montis castra posuit lateque ignes, ut speciem
multitudinis augeret, ostendit, clamore quoque ac sui moris
ululatu identidem adquiescentes Macedonas frustra terrere
25 conatus. iam lux adpetebat, cum rex fiduciae ac spei plenus
alacres milites arma capere et exire in aciem iubet. sed
haud traditur, metune an oborta seditione inter ipsos subito
profugerint barbari: certe avios montes et inpeditos occupa-
verunt, quorum agmen rex frustra persecutus inpedimenta
cepit.

26 Perventum deinde est ad oppidum Sudracarum, in quod
plerique confugerant, haud maiore fiducia moenium, quam
27 armorum. iam admovebat rex, cum vates monere eum coepit,
ne committeret aut certe differret obsidionem: vitae eius
28 periculum ostendi. rex Demophontem—is namque vates
erat—intuens, 'si quis', inquit, 'te arti tuae intentum et
exta spectantem sic interpellet, non dubitem, quin incom-
29 modus ac molestus videri tibi possit.' et cum ille ita prorsus
futurum respondisset, 'censesne', inquit, 'tantas res, non
pecudum fibras ante oculos habenti ullum esse maius inpe-
30 dimentum, quam vatem superstitione captum?' nec diutius,
quam respondit, moratus admoveri iubet scalas cunctanti-
busque ceteris evadit in murum. angusta muri corona erat:
non pinnae sicut alibi fastigium eius distinxerant, sed per-
31 petua lorica obducta transitum saepserat. itaque rex haere-
bat magis quam stabat in margine, clipeo undique incidentia
tela propulsans: nam ubique eminus ex turribus petebatur.

nec subire milites poterant, quia superne vi telorum obrue- 32
bantur. tandem magnitudinem periculi pudor vicit: quippe
cernebant cunctatione sua dedi hostibus regem. sed fes- 33
tinando morabantur auxilia. nam dum pro se quisque
certat evadere, oneravere scalas: quis non sufficientibus
devoluti unicam spem regis fefellerunt. stabat enim in
conspectu tanti exercitus velut in solitudine destitutus. iam- **5**
que laevam, qua clipeum ad ictus circumferebat, lassaverat
clamantibus amicis, ut ad ipsos desiliret, stabantque excep-
turi: cum ille rem ausus est incredibilem atque inauditam
multoque magis ad famam temeritatis quam gloriae insignem.
namque in urbem hostium plenam praecipiti saltu semetipse 2
inmisit, cum vix sperare posset, dimicantem certe et non
inultum esse moriturum: quippe antequam adsurgeret, op-
primi poterat et capi vivus. sed forte ita libraverat corpus, 3
ut se pedibus exciperet. itaque stans init pugnam: et, ne
circumiri posset, fortuna providerat. vetusta arbor haud 4
procul muro ramos multa fronde vestitos, velut de industria
regem protegentes, obiecerat: huius spatioso stipiti corpus,
ne circumiri posset, adplicuit, clipeo tela, quae ex adverso
ingerebantur, excipiens. nam cum unum procul tot manus 5
peterent, nemo tamen audebat propius accedere: missilia
ramis plura quam clipeo incidebant. pugnabat pro rege 6
primum celebrati nominis fama, deinde desperatio, mag-
num ad honeste moriendum incitamentum. sed cum 7
subinde hostis adflueret, iam ingentem vim telorum ex-
ceperat clipeo, iam galeam saxa perfregerant, iam continuo
labore gravia genua succiderant. itaque contemptim et 8
incaute, qui proximi steterant, incurrerunt: e quibus duos
gladio ita excepit, ut ante ipsum exanimes procumberent.
nec cuiquam deinde propius incessendi eum animus fuit:
procul iacula sagittasque mittebant. ille ad omnes ictus 9
expositus non aegre tamen exceptum poplitibus corpus tue-

batur, donec Indus duorum cubitorum sagittam — namque
Indis, ut antea diximus, huius magnitudinis sagittae erant —
ita excussit, ut per thoracem paulum super latus dextrum
10 infigeret. quo vulnere adflictus magna vi sanguinis emi-
cante remisit arma moribundo similis adeoque resolutus, ut
ne ad vellendum quidem telum sufficeret dextera. itaque
ad spoliandum corpus, qui vulneraverat, alacer gaudio ac-
11 currit. quem ut inicere corpori suo manus sensit, credo,
ultimi dedecoris indignitate commotus linquentem revocavit
animum et nudum hostis latus subiecto mucrone hausit.
12 iacebant circa regem tria corpora procul stupentibus ceteris:
ille ut, antequam ultimus spiritus deficeret, dimicans iam
13 extingueretur, clipeo se adlevare conatus est et, postquam
ad conitendum nihil supererat virium, dextera inpendentes
ramos conplexus temptabat adsurgere. sed ne sic quidem
potens corporis rursus in genua procumbit, manu provocans
14 hostes, si quis congredi auderet. tandem Peucestes per
aliam oppidi partem deturbatis propugnatoribus muri ves-
15 tigia persequens regi supervenit. quo conspecto Alexander,
iam non vitae suae, sed mortis solacium supervenisse ratus,
clipeo fatigatum corpus excepit. subit inde Timaeus et
16 paulo post Leonnatus, huic Aristonus supervenit. Indi
quoque, cum intra moenia regem esse conperissent, omissis
ceteris illuc concurrerunt urgebantque protegentes. ex qui-
bus Timaeus multis adverso corpore vulneribus acceptis
17 egregiaque edita pugna cecidit: Peucestes quoque tribus
iaculis confossus non se tamen scuto, sed regem tuebatur:
Leonnatus, dum avide ruentes barbaros submovet, cervice
18 graviter icta semianimis procubuit ante regis pedes. iam et
Peucestes vulneribus fatigatus submiserat clipeum: in Arist-
ono spes ultima haerebat. hic quoque graviter saucius
19 tantam vim hostium ultra sustinere non poterat. inter haec
ad Macedonas regem cecidisse fama perlata est. terruisset

alios, quod illos incitavit. namque periculi omnis inmemo-
res dolabris perfregere murum et, qua moliti erant aditum,
inrupere in urbem Indosque plures fugientes, quam congredi
ausos ceciderunt. non senibus, non feminis, non infantibus 20
parcitur: quisquis occurrerat, ab illo vulneratum regem esse
credebant. tandemque internecione hostium iustae irae
parentatum est. Ptolomaeum, qui postea regnavit, huic 21
pugnae adfuisse auctor est Clitarchus et Timagenes. sed
ipse, scilicet gloriae suae non refragatus, afuisse se, missum
in expeditionem, memoriae tradidit. tanta conponentium
vetusta rerum monumenta vel securitas vel, par huic vitium,
credulitas fuit! rege in tabernaculum relato medici lignum 22
sagittae corpori infixum ita, ne spiculum moveretur, absci-
dunt. corpore deinde nudato animadvertunt hamos inesse 23
telo, nec aliter id sine pernicie corporis extrahi posse, quam
ut secando vulnus augerent. ceterum, ne secantes proflu- 24
vium sanguinis occuparet, verebantur: quippe ingens telum
adactum erat et penetrasse in viscera videbatur. Critobulus, 25
inter medicos artis eximiae, sed in tanto periculo territus,
manus admovere metuebat, ne in ipsius caput parum pros-
perae curationis recideret eventus. lacrimantem eum ac 26
metuentem et sollicitudine propemodum exanguem rex con-
spexerat. 'quid', inquit, 'quodve tempus expectas et non
quamprimum hoc dolore me saltem moriturum liberas? an
times, ne reus sis, cum insanabile vulnus acceperim?' at 27
Critobulus tandem vel finito vel dissimulato metu hortari
eum coepit, ut se continendum praeberet, dum spiculum
evelleret: etiam levem corporis motum noxium fore. rex 28
cum adfirmasset nihil opus esse iis, qui semet continerent,
sicut praeceptum erat, sine motu praebuit corpus. igitur
patefacto latius vulnere et spiculo evolso ingens vis sangui-
nis manare coepit linquique animo rex et caligine oculis
offusa velut moribundus extendi. cumque profluvium medi- 29

camentis frustra inhiberent, clamor simul atque ploratus amicorum oritur, regem expirasse credentium. tandem constitit sanguis, paulatimque animum recepit et circumstantes
30 coepit adgnoscere. toto eo die ac nocte, quae secuta est, armatus exercitus regiam obsedit, confessus omnes unius spiritu vivere. nec prius recesserunt, quam conpertum est somno paulisper adquiescere. hinc certiorem spem salutis eius in castra rettulerunt.

6 Rex VII diebus curato vulnere necdum obducta cicatrice, cum audisset convaluisse apud barbaros famam mortis suae, duobus navigiis iunctis statui in medium undique conspicuum tabernaculum iussit, ex quo se ostenderet perisse credentibus: conspectusque ab incolis spem hostium falso nuntio
2 conceptam inhibuit. secundo deinde amne defluxit, aliquantum intervalli a cetera classe praecipiens, ne quies corpori invalido adhuc necessaria pulsu remorum inpediretur.

3 Quarto, postquam navigare coeperat, die pervenit in regionem desertam quidem ab incolis, sed frumento et pecoribus abundantem. placuit is locus et ad suam et ad
4 militum requiem. mos erat principibus amicorum et custodibus corporis excubare ante praetorium, quotiens adversa regi valitudo incidisset. hoc tum quoque more servato uni-
5 versi cubiculum eius intrant. ille sollicitus, ne quid novi adferrent, quia simul venerant, percontatur, num hostium
6 recens nuntiaretur adventus. at Craterus, cui mandatum erat, ut amicorum preces perferret ad eum, 'Credisne', inquit, 'adventu magis hostium—ut iam in vallo consisterent—
7 sollicitos esse, quam cura salutis tuae, ut nunc est, tibi vilis? quantalibet vis omnium gentium conspiret in nos, inpleat armis virisque totum orbem, classibus maria consternat,
8 inuisitatas beluas inducat: tu nos praestabis invictos. sed quis deorum hoc Macedoniae columen ac sidus diuturnum *fore* polliceri potest, cum tam avide manifestis periculis

offeras corpus, oblitus tot civium animas trahere te in casum?
quis enim tibi superstes aut optat esse aut potest? eo per- 9
venimus auspicium atque imperium secuti tuum, unde nisi
te reduce nulli ad penates suos iter est. quodsi adhuc de 10
Persidis regno cum Dareo dimicares, etsi nemo vellet, tamen
ne admirari quidem posset, tam promptae esse te ad omne
discrimen audaciae: nam ubi paria sunt periculum ac
praemium, et secundis rebus amplior fructus est et adversis
solacium maius: tuo vero capite ignobilem vicum emi, quis 11
ferat non tuorum modo militum, sed ullius gentis barbarae
civis, qui tuam magnitudinem novit? horret animus cogita- 12
tionem rei, quam paulo ante vidimus. eloqui timeo, invicti
corporis spolia inertissimas manus fuisse infecturas, nisi te
interceptum misericors in nos fortuna servasset. totidem pro-
ditores, totidem desertores sumus, quot te non potuimus per-
sequi. universos licet milites ignominia notes, nemo recusabit 13
luere id, quod ne admitteret, praestare non potuit. patere nos, 14
quaeso, alio modo esse viles tibi. quocumque iusseris, ibimus.
obscura pericula et ignobiles pugnas nobis deposcimus: temet-
ipsum ad ea serva, quae magnitudinem tuam capiunt. cito
gloria obsolescit in sordidis hostibus, nec quicquam indignius
est, quam consumi eam, ubi non possit ostendi.' eadem fere 15
Ptolomaeus et similia his ceteri. iamque confusis vocibus
flentes eum orabant, ut tandem exsatiatus laudi modum
faceret ac saluti suae, id est publicae, parceret. grata erat 16
regi pietas amicorum. itaque singulos familiarius amplexus
considere iubet. altiusque sermone repetito, 'vobis quidem', 17
inquit, 'o fidissimi piissimique civium atque amicorum,
grates ago habeoque non solum eo nomine, quod hodie
salutem meam vestrae praeponitis, sed quod a primordiis
belli nullum erga me benivolentiae pignus atque indicium
omisistis, adeo ut confitendum sit numquam mihi vitam
meam fuisse tam caram, quam esse coepit, ut vobis diu frui

18 possim. ceterum non eadem est cogitatio eorum, qui pro me
mori optant, et mea, *qui* quidem hanc benivolentiam vestram
virtute meruisse me iudico. vos enim diuturnum fructum
ex me, forsitan etiam perpetuum percipere cupiatis: ego me
19 metior non aetatis spatio, sed gloriae. licuit paternis opibus
contento intra Macedoniae terminos per otium corporis ex-
pectare obscuram et ignobilem senectutem: quamquam ne
pigri quidem sibi fata disponunt, sed unicum bonum diutur-
nam vitam existimantes saepe acerba mors occupat: verum
ego, qui non annos meos, sed victorias numero, si munera
20 fortunae bene conputo, diu vixi. orsus a Macedonia im-
perium Graeciae teneo, Thraciam et Illyrios subegi, Triballis
Maedisque imperito, Asiam, qua Hellesponto, qua rubro
mari subluitur, possideo. iamque haud procul absum fine
mundi, quem egressus aliam naturam, alium orbem aperire
21 mihi statui. ex Asia in Europae terminos momento unius
horae transivi. victor utriusque regionis post nonum regni
mei, post vicesimum atque octavum *aetatis* annum, videorne
vobis in excolenda gloria, cui me uni devovi, posse cessare?
ego vero non deero et, ubicumque pugnabo, in theatro
22 terrarum orbis esse me credam. dabo nobilitatem ignobili-
bus locis, aperiam cunctis gentibus terras, quas natura longe
submoverat. in his operibus extingui mihi, si fors ita feret,
pulchrum est: ea stirpe sum genitus, ut multam prius quam
23 longam vitam debeam optare. obsecro vos, cogitate nos
pervenisse in terras, quibus feminae ob virtutem celeberri-
mum nomen est. quas urbes Samiramis condidit! quas
gentis redegit in potestatem! quanta opera molita est! non-
dum feminam aequavimus gloria, et iam nos laudis satietas
24 cepit? di faveant, maiora adhuc restant. sed ita nostra
erunt, quae nondum attigimus, si nihil parvum duxerimus,
in quo magnae gloriae locus est. vos modo me ab intestina
fraude et domesticorum insidiis praestate securum: belli

Martisque discrimen inpavidus subibo. Philippus in acie 25
tutior, quam in theatro fuit: hostium manus saepe vitavit,
suorum effugere non valuit. aliorum quoque regum exitus
si reputaveritis, plures a suis quam ab hoste interemptos
numerabitis. ceterum, quoniam olim rei agitatae in animo 26
meo nunc promendae occasio oblata est, mihi maximus laborum atque operum meorum erit fructus, si Olympias mater
inmortalitati consecretur, quandoque excesserit vita. si
licuerit, ipse praestabo hoc: si me praeceperit fatum, vos
mandasse mementote.' ac tum quidem amicos dimisit:
ceterum per conplures dies ibi stativa habuit.

Haec dum in India geruntur, Graeci milites nuper in co- 7
lonias a rege deducti circa Bactra orta inter ipsos seditione
defecerant, non tam Alexandro infensi, quam metu supplicii.
quippe occisis quibusdam popularium, qui validiores erant, 2
arma spectare coeperunt et Bactriana arce, quae casu neglegentius adservata erat, occupata barbaros quoque in societatem inpulerant. Athenodorus erat princeps eorum, qui regis 3
quoque nomen adsumpserat, non tam imperii cupidine, quam
in patriam revertendi cum iis, qui auctoritatem ipsius sequebantur. huic Biton quidam nationis eiusdem, sed ob aemu- 4
lationem infestus conparavit insidias invitatumque ad epulas
per Boxum quendam Margianum in convivio occidit. postero 5
die contione advocata Bito ultro insidiatum sibi Athenodorum
plerisque persuaserat: sed aliis suspecta erat fraus Bitonis,
et paulatim in plures coepit manare suspitio. itaque Graeci 6
milites arma capiunt occisuri Bitonem, si daretur occasio:
ceterum principes eorum iram multitudinis mitigaverunt.
praeter spem suam Biton praesenti periculo ereptus paulo 7
post *est* insidiatus auctoribus salutis suae: cuius dolo cognito
et ipsum conprehenderunt et Boxum. ceterum Boxum 8
protinus placuit interfici, Bitonem etiam per cruciatum
necari. iamque corpori tormenta admovebantur, cum

milites—incertum ob quam causam—lymphatis similes ad
9 arma discurrunt. quorum fremitu exaudito, qui torquere
Bitonem iussi erant, omisere, veriti, ne id facere tumultu-
10 antium vociferatione prohiberentur. ille, sicut nudatus erat,
pervenit ad Graecos, et miserabilis facies supplicio destinati
in diversum animos repente mutavit, dimittique eum iusse-
11 runt. hoc modo poena bis liberatus cum ceteris, qui colonias
a rege attributas reliquerunt, revertit in patriam. haec circa
Bactra et Scytharum terminos gesta.

12 Interim regem duarum gentium, de quibus ante dictum
est, C legati adeunt. omnes curru vehebantur, eximia mag-
nitudine corporum, decoro habitu: lineae vestes intexto
13 auro purpuraque distinctae. ei se dedere ipsos, urbes agros-
que referebant, per tot aetates inviolatam libertatem illius
primum fidei dicionique permissuros: deos sibi deditionis
auctores, non metum: quippe intactis viribus iugum excipere.
14 rex consilio habito deditos in fidem accepit, stipendio, quod
Arachosiis utraque natio pensitabat, inposito. praeterea II
milia et D equites imperat: et omnia oboedienter a barbaris
15 facta. invitatis deinde ad epulas legatis gentium regulisque
exornari convivium iussit. C aurei lecti modicis intervallis
positi erant, lectis circumdederat aulaea purpura auroque
fulgentia; quidquid aut apud Persas vetere luxu aut apud
Macedonas nova inmutatione corruptum erat, confusis utri-
16 usque gentis vitiis, in illo convivio ostendens. intererat epulis
Dioxippus Atheniensis, pugil nobilis et ob eximiam virtutem
virium iam regi pernotus et gratus. invidi malignique in-
crepabant per seria et ludum saginati corporis sequi inutilem
beluam: cum ipsi proelium inirent, oleo madentem prae-
17 parare ventrem epulis. eadem igitur in convivio Horratas
Macedo iam temulentus exprobrare ei coepit et postulare, ut,
si vir esset, postero die secum ferro decerneret: regem tan-
dem vel de sua temeritate vel de illius ignavia iudicaturum.

et a Dioxippo contemptim militarem eludente ferociam ac- 18
cepta condicio est. ac postero die rex, cum etiam acrius
certamen exposcerent, quia deterrere non poterat, destinata
exequi passus est. ingens hic militum conventus erat, inter 19
quos qui erant Graeci Dioxippo studebant. Macedo iusta ar-
ma sumpserat, aereum clipeum, hastam, quam sarisam vocant,
laeva tenens, dextera lanceam gladioque cinctus, velut cum
pluribus simul dimicaturus. Dioxippus oleo nitens et coro- 20
natus laeva puniceum amiculum, dextra validum nodosum-
que stipitem praeferebat. ea ipsa res omnium animos ex-
pectatione suspenderat: quippe armato congredi nudum
dementia, non temeritas videbatur. igitur Macedo, haud 21
dubius eminus interfici posse, lanceam emisit: quam Dioxip-
pus cum exigua corporis declinatione vitasset, antequam ille
hastam transferret in dextram, adsiluit et stipite mediam
eam fregit. amisso utroque telo Macedo gladium coeperat 22
stringere: quem occupatum conplexu pedibus repente sub-
ductis Dioxippus arietavit in terram ereptoque gladio pedem
super cervicem iacenti inposuit, stipitem intentans elisurus-
que eo victum, ni prohibitus esset a rege. tristis spectaculi 23
eventus non Macedonibus modo, sed etiam Alexandro fuit,
maxime quia barbari adfuerant: quippe celebratam Mace-
donum fortitudinem ad ludibrium recidisse verebatur. hinc 24
ad criminationem invidorum adapertae sunt aures regis. et
post paucos dies inter epulas aureum poculum ex conposito
subducitur, ministrique, quasi amisissent, quod amoverant,
regem adeunt. saepe minus est constantiae in rubore, quam 25
in culpa. coniectum oculorum, quibus ut fur destinabatur,
Dioxippus ferre non potuit et, cum excessisset convivio,
litteris conscriptis, quae regi redderentur, ferro se interemit.
graviter mortem eius tulit rex, existimans indignationis esse, 26
non paenitentiae testem, utique postquam falso insimulatum
eum nimium invidorum gaudium ostendit.

8 Indorum legati dimissi domos paucis post diebus cum
donis revertuntur. CCC erant equites, MXXX currus, quos
quadriiugi equi ducebant, lineae vestis aliquantum; mille
2 scuta Indica et ferri candidi talenta C leonesque rarae mag-
nitudinis et tigres, utrumque animal ad mansuetudinem
domitum, lacertarum quoque ingentium pelles et dorsa testu-
3 dinum. Cratero deindc imperat rex, haud procul amne, per
quem erat ipse navigaturus, copias duceret: eos autem, qui
comitari eum solebant, inponit in naves et in fines Mallorum
secundo amne devehitur.

4 Inde Sabarcas adiit, validam Indiae gentem, quae populi,
non regum imperio regebatur. LX milia peditum habebant,
5 equitum sex milia: has copias currus D sequebantur. III
duces spectatos virtute bellica elegerant. at qui in agris
erant proximi flumini—frequentes autem vicos maxime in
ripa habebant—ut videre totum amnem, qua prospici poterat,
navigiis constratum et tot militum arma fulgentia, territi nova
facie, deorum exercitum et alium Liberum patrem, celebre
6 in illis gentibus nomen, adventare credebant. hinc militum
clamor, hinc remorum pulsus variaeque nautarum voces hor-
7 tantium pavidas aures inpleverant. ergo universi ad eos,
qui in armis erant, currunt, furere clamitantes et cum dis
proelium inituros: navigia non posse numerari, quae invictos
viros veherent. tantumque in exercitum suorum intulere
terroris, ut legatos mitterent gentem dedituros.

8 His in fidem acceptis ad alias deinde gentes quarto die
pervenit. nihilo plus animi his fuit, quam ceteris fuerat.
itaque oppido ibi condito, quod Alexandream appellari
9 iusserat, fines eorum, qui Musicani appellantur, intravit. hic
de Teriolte satrape, quem Parapamisadis praefecerat, isdem
arguentibus cognovit multaque avare ac superbe fecisse con-
10 victum interfici iussit. Oxyartes, praetor Bactrianorum, non
absolutus modo, sed etiam iure amoris amplioris imperii

donatus est finibus. Musicanis deinde in dicionem redactis
urbi eorum praesidium inposuit.

Inde Praestos, et ipsam Indiae gentem, perventum est. 11
Porticanus rex erat, qui se munitae urbi cum magna manu
popularium incluserat. hanc Alexander tertio die, quam coe-
perat obsidere, expugnavit. et Porticanus, cum in arcem 12
confugisset, legatos de condicione deditionis misit ad regem:
sed antequam adirent eum, duae turres cum ingenti fragore
prociderant, per quarum ruinas Macedones evasere in arcem,
qua capta Porticanus cum paucis repugnans occiditur.

Diruta igitur arce et omnibus captivis venundatis Sambi 13
regis fines ingressus est multisque oppidis in fidem acceptis
validissimam gentis urbem cuniculo cepit. barbaris simile 14
monstri visum est, rudibus militarium operum; quippe in
media ferme urbe armati terra existebant, nullo suffossi
specus ante vestigio facto. LXXX milia Indorum in ea re- 15
gione caesa Clitarchus est auctor multosque captivos sub
corona venisse. rursus Musicani defecerunt, ad quos op- 16
primendos missus est Pithon, qui captum principem gentis
eundemque defectionis auctorem adduxit ad regem. quo
Alexander in crucem sublato rursus amnem, in quo classem
expectare se iusserat, repetit.

Quarto deinde die secundo amne pervenit ad oppidum, 17
quod in regno imo erat Sambi. nuper se ille dediderat, sed
oppidani detrectabant imperium et clauserant portas. quo- 18
rum paucitate contempta rex D Agrianos moenia subire iussit
et sensim recedentes elicere extra muros hostem, secuturum
profecto, si fugere eos crederet. Agriani, sicut imperatum 19
erat, lacessito hoste subito terga verterunt: quos barbari
effuse sequentes in alios, inter quos ipse rex erat, incidunt.
renovato ergo proelio ex III milibus barbarorum DC caesi
sunt, mille capti, ceteri moenibus urbis inclusi. sed non ut 20
prima specie laeta victoria, ita eventu quoque fuit: quippe

barbari veneno tinxerant gladios. itaque saucii subinde ex-
pirabant, nec causa tam strenuae mortis excogitari poterat a
21 medicis, cum etiam leves plagae insanabiles essent. barbari
autem speraverant incautum et temerarium regem excipi
posse. et forte inter promptissimos dimicans intactus evas-
22 erat. praecipue Ptolomaeus, laevo humero leviter quidem
saucius, sed maiore periculo quam vulnere adfectus, regis
sollicitudinem in se converterat. sanguine coniunctus erat,
et quidam Philippo genitum esse credebant, certe pelice
23 eius ortum constabat. idem corporis custos promptissimus-
que bellator et pacis artibus quam militiae maior et clarior
modico civilique cultu liberalis in primis adituque facili nihil
24 ex fastu regiae adsumpserat. ob haec regi an popularibus
carior esset, dubitari poterat, tum certe primum expertus
suorum animos, adeo ut fortunam, in quam postea ascendit,
25 in illo periculo Macedones ominati esse videantur. quippe
non levior illis Ptolomaei fuit cura, quam regis: qui et proe-
lio et sollicitudine fatigatus cum Ptolomaeo adsideret, lec-
26 tum, in quo ipse adquiesceret, iussit inferri. in quem ut se
recepit, protinus altior insecutus est somnus. ex quo exci-
tatus per quietem vidisse se exponit speciem draconis obla-
tam herbam ferentis ore, quam veneni remedium esse mon-
27 strasset: colorem quoque herbae referebat, adgniturum, si quis
repperisset, adfirmans. inventam deinde — quippe a multis
simul erat requisita — vulneri inposuit, protinusque dolore
28 finito intra breve spatium cicatrix quoque obducta est. barba-
ros ut prima spes fefellerat, se ipsos urbemque dediderunt.

Hinc in proximam gentem Pataliam perventum est. rex
29 erat Moeris, qui urbe deserta in montes profugerat. itaque
Alexander oppido potitur agrosque populatur. magnae inde
praedae actae sunt pecorum armentorumque, magna vis
30 reperta frumenti. ducibus deinde sumptis amnis peritis
defluxit ad insulam medio ferme alveo enatam.

Ibi diutius subsistere coactus, quia duces socordius 9
adservati profugerant, misit, qui conquirerent alios, nec repertis pervicax cupido visendi oceanum adeundique terminos mundi sine regionis peritis flumini ignoto caput suum totque fortissimorum virorum salutem permittere *coegit*. naviga- 2
bant ergo omnium, per quae ferebantur, ignari. quantum inde abesset mare, quae gentes colerent, quam placidum amnis os, quam patiens longarum navium esset, anceps et caeca aestimatio augurabatur: unum erat temeritatis sola- 3
cium perpetua felicitas. iam CCCC stadia processerant, cum gubernatores adgnoscere ipsos auram maris et haud procul videri sibi oceanum abesse indicant regi. laetus ille hortari 4
nauticos coepit, incumberent remis: adesse finem laboris omnibus votis expetitum: iam nihil gloriae deesse, nihil obstare virtuti, sine ullo Martis discrimine, sine sanguine orbem terrae ab illis capi: ne naturam quidem longius posse procedere: brevi incognita nisi inmortalibus esse visuros. paucos tamen navigio emisit in ripam, qui agrestes vagos 5
exciperent, e quibus certiora nosci posse sperabat. illi scrutati omnia tuguria tandem latentes repperere. qui interrogati, 6
quam procul abesset mare, responderunt nullum ipsos mare ne fama quidem accepisse: ceterum tertio die perveniri posse ad aquam amaram, quae corrumperet dulcem. intellectum est mare destinari ab ignaris naturae eius. itaque 7
ingenti alacritate nautici remigant, et proximo quoque die, quo propius spes admovebatur, crescebat ardor animorum. tertio iam die mixtum flumini subibat mare, leni adhuc aestu confundente dispares undas. tum aliam insulam me- 8
dio amni sitam evecti paulo lentius, quia cursus aestu reverberabatur, adplicant classem et ad commeatus petendos discurrunt, securi casus eius, qui supervenit ignaris. tertia 9
ferme hora erat, cum stata vice oceanus exaestuans invehi

coepit et retro flumen urgere: quod primo coercitum, deinde
vehementius pulsum maiore impetu adversum agebatur,
10 quam torrentia praecipiti alveo incurrunt. ignota vulgo freti
natura erat, monstraque et irae deum indicia cernere vide-
bantur. identidem intumescens mare et in campos paulo
11 ante siccos descendere superfusum. iamque levatis navigiis
et tota classe dispersa, qui expositi erant, undique ad naves
12 trepidi et inproviso malo attoniti recurrunt. sed in tumultu
festinatio quoque tarda est. hi contis navigia pellebant, hi,
13 dum remos aptari prohibebant, consederant: quidam enavi-
gare properantes, sed non expectatis, qui simul esse debe-
bant, clauda et inhabilia navigia languide moliebantur, aliae
navium inconsulte ruentes non receperant: pariterque et
14 multitudo et paucitas festinantes morabatur. clamor hinc
expectare, hinc ire iubentium dissonaeque voces numquam
idem atque unum tendentium non oculorum modo usum,
15 sed etiam aurium abstulerant. ne in gubernatoribus quidem
quicquam opis erat, quorum nec exaudiri vox a tumultuanti-
bus poterat nec imperium a territis inconpositisque servari.
16 ergo conlidi inter se naves abstergerique invicem remi et alii
aliorum navigia urgere coeperunt. crederes non unius exer-
17 citus classem vehi, sed duorum navale inisse certamen. in-
cutiebantur puppibus prorae: premebantur a sequentibus,
qui antecedentes turbaverant: iurgantium ira perveniebat
18 etiam ad manus. iamque aestus totos circa flumen campos
inundaverat tumulis dumtaxat eminentibus velut insulis
parvis, in quos plerique trepidi omissis navigiis enare prope-
19 rant. dispersa classis partim in praealta aqua stabat, qua
subsederant valles, partim in vado haerebat, utcumque inae-
quale terrae fastigium occupaverant undae: cum subito
20 novus et pristino maior terror incutitur. reciprocari coepit
mare magno tractu aquis in suum fretum recurrentibus red-

debatque terras paulo ante profundo salo mersas. igitur
destituta navigia alia praecipitantur in proras, alia in latera
procumbunt. strati erant campi sarcinis, armis, avulsarum
tabularum remorumque fragmentis. miles nec egredi in 21
terram nec in nave subsistere audebat, identidem praesenti-
bus graviora, quae sequerentur, expectans. vix, quae per-
petiebantur, videre ipsos credebant, in sicco naufragia, in
amni mare. nec finis malorum: quippe aestum paulo post 22
mare relaturum, quo navigia adlevarentur, ignari, famem et
ultima sibimet ominabantur. beluae quoque fluctibus desti-
tutae terribiles vagabantur. iamque nox adpetebat, et regem 23
quoque desperatio salutis aegritudine adfecerat. non tamen
invictum animum curae obruunt, quin tota nocte persideret
in speculis equitesque praemitteret ad os amnis, ut, cum
mare rursus exaestuare sensissent, praecederent. navigia 24
quoque et lacerata refici et eversa fluctibus erigi iubet para-
tosque esse et intentos, cum rursus mare terras inundasset.
tota ea nocte inter vigilias adhortationesque consumpta cele- 25
riter et equites ingenti cursu refugere et secutus est aestus.
qui primo aquis leni tractu subeuntibus coepit levare navi-
gia, mox totis campis inundatis etiam inpulit classem. plau- 26
susque militum nauticorumque insperatam salutem inmodico
celebrantium gaudio litoribus ripisque resonabat. unde tan-
tum redisset subito mare, quo pridie refugisset, quaenam
esset eiusdem elementi natura, modo discors, modo imperio
temporum obnoxia, mirabundi requirebant. rex cum ex eo, 27
quod acciderat, coniectaret post solis ortum statum tempus
esse, media nocte, ut aestum occuparet, cum paucis navigiis
secundo amne defluxit. evectusque os eius CCCC stadia
processit in mare, tandem voti sui compos: praesidibus-
que et maris et locorum dis sacrificio facto ad classem
rediit.

10 Hinc adversum flumen subit classis et altero die adpulsa
est haud procul lacu salso, cuius incognita natura plerosque
decepit temere ingressos aquam. quippe scabies corpora
invasit, et contagium morbi etiam in alios vulgatum est.
2 oleum remedio fuit. Leonnato deinde praemisso, ut puteos
foderet, qua terrestri itinere ducturus exercitum videbatur —
quippe sicca erat regio — ipse cum copiis substitit, vernum
3 tempus expectans. interim et urbes plerasque condidit. Ne-
archo atque Onesicrito nauticae rei peritis imperavit, ut vali-
dissimas navium deducerent in oceanum progressique,
quoad tuto possent, naturam maris noscerent: vel eodem
amne vel Euphrate subire eos posse, cum reverti ad se
vellent.

4 Iamque mitigata hieme et navibus, quae inutiles vide-
5 bantur, crematis terra ducebat exercitum. nonis castris in
regionem Arabiton, inde totidem diebus in Cedrosiorum
perventum est. liber hic populus concilio habito dedidit se,
nec quicquam deditis praeter commeatus imperatum est.
6 quinto hinc die venit ad flumen: Arabum incolae appellant.
regio deserta et aquarum inops excipit. quam emensus in
Oritas transit: ibi maiorem exercitus partem Hephaestioni
tradidit, levem armaturam cum Ptolomaeo Leonnatoque
7 partitus est. tria simul agmina populabantur Indos, mag-
naeque praedae actae sunt: maritimos Ptolomaeus, ceteros
ipse rex et ab alia parte Leonnatus urebant. in hac quoque
regione urbem condidit, deductique sunt in eam Arachosii.

8 Hinc pervenit ad maritimos Indos. desertam vastamque
regionem late tenent ac ne cum finitimis quidem ullo com-
9 mercii iure miscentur. ipsa solitudo natura quoque inmitia
efferavit ingenia: prominent ungues numquam recisi, comae
10 hirsutae et intonsae sunt. tuguria conchis et ceteris purga-
mentis maris instruunt. ferarum pellibus tecti piscibus sole

duratis et maiorum quoque beluarum, quas fluctus eiecit,
carne vescuntur. consumptis igitur alimentis Macedones 11
primo inopiam, deinde ad ultimum famem sentire coeperunt,
radices palmarum, namque sola ea arbor gignitur, ubique
rimantes. sed cum haec quoque alimenta defecerant, iu- 12
menta caedere adgressi ne equis quidem abstinebant: et
cum deessent, quae sarcinas veherent, spolia de hostibus,
propter quae ultima Orientis peragraverant, cremabant in-
cendio. famem deinde pestilentia secuta est, quippe insalu- 13
brium ciborum novi suci, ad hoc itineris labor et aegritudo
animi vulgaverant morbos, et nec manere sine clade nec
progredi poterant: manentes fames, progressos acrior pes-
tilentia urgebat. ergo strati erant campi paene pluribus 14
semivivis quam cadaveribus. ac ne levius quidem aegri
sequi poterant: quippe agmen raptim agebatur tantum sin-
gulis ad spem salutis ipsos proficere credentibus, quantum
itineris festinando praeciperent. igitur qui defecerant, notos 15
ignotosque, ut adlevarenter, orabant: sed nec iumenta erant,
quibus excipi possent, et miles vix arma portabat, imminen-
tisque et ipsis facies mali ante oculos erat. ergo saepius
revocati ne respicere quidem suos sustinebant misericordia
in formidinem versa. illi relicti deos testes et sacra com- 16
munia regisque inplorabant opem: cumque frustra surdas
aures fatigarent, in rabiem desperatione versa parem suo
exitum similesque ipsis amicos et contubernales precabantur.
rex dolore simul ac pudore anxius, quia causa tantae cladis 17
ipse esset, ad Phrataphernen, Parthyaeorum satrapen, misit,
qui iuberet camelis cocta cibaria adferri, aliosque finitima-
rum regionum praefectos certiores necessitatis suae fecit.
nec cessatum est ab his. itaque fame dumtaxat vindicatus 18
exercitus tandem in Cedrosiae fines perducitur. omnium
rerum sola fertilis regio est, in qua stativa habuit, ut vexatos

19 milites quiete firmaret. hic Leonnati litteras accepit conflixisse ipsum cum VIII milibus peditum et CCC equitibus Oritarum prospero eventu. a Cratero quoque nuntius venit Ozinen et Zariaspen, nobilis Persas, defectionem molientes
20 oppressos a se in vinculis esse. praeposito igitur regioni Sibyrtio—namque Menon, praefectus eius, nuper interierat
21 morbo—in Carmaniam ipse processit. Aspastes erat satrapes gentis, suspectus res novare voluisse, dum in India rex
22 est. quem occurrentem dissimulata ira comiter adlocutus, dum exploraret, quae delata erant, in eodem honore habuit. cum inde praefecti, sicut imperatum erat, equorum iumentorumque iugalium vim ingentem ex omni, quae sub imperio erat, regione misissent, quibus deerant inpedimenta, resti-
23 tuit. arma quoque ad pristinum refecta sunt cultum: quippe haud procul a Perside aberant, non pacata modo, sed etiam
24 opulenta. igitur, ut supra dictum est, aemulatus patris Liberi non gloriam solum, quam ex illis gentibus deportaverat, sed etiam famam, sive illud triumphus fuit ab eo primum institutus, sive bacchantium lusus, statuit imitari, animo super
25 humanum fastigium elato. vicos, per quos iter erat, floribus coronisque sterni iubet, liminibus aedium crateras vino repletas et alia eximiae magnitudinis vasa disponi: vehicula deinde constrata, ut plures capere milites possent, in tabernaculorum modum ornari, alia candidis velis, alia veste pre-
26 tiosa. primi ibant amici et cohors regia, variis redimita floribus coronisque: alibi tibicinum cantus, alibi lyrae sonus audiebatur: item *in* vehiculis pro copia cuiusque adornatis comissabundus exercitus, armis, quae maxime decora erant, circumpendentibus. ipsum convivasque currus vehebat crateris aureis eiusdemque materiae ingentibus poculis
27 praegravis. hoc modo per dies VII bacchabundum agmen incessit, parata praeda, si quid victis saltem adversus comis-

santes animi fuisset: mille, hercule, viri modo et sobrii VII dierum crapula graves in suo triumpho capere potuerunt. sed fortuna, quae rebus famam pretiumque constituit, hoc 28
quoque militiae probrum vertit in gloriam. et praesens aetas et posteritas deinde mirata est per gentes nondum satis domitas incessisse temulentos, barbaris, quod temeritas erat, fiduciam esse credentibus. hunc apparatum carnifex seque- 29
batur: quippe satrapes Aspastes, de quo ante dictum est, interfici iussus est: adeo nec luxuriae quicquam crudelitas 30
nec crudelitati luxuria obstat.

VARIATIONS FROM THE TEXT OF HEDICKE

(BERLIN, 1867).

	Hedicke.	
VIII 9 § 10	Ethymandrus	Ethimantus Z F
§ 12	mitis Z	mitia F V
10 § 14	germinum	seminum Z M F V
	baccarisque [et]	baccarisque Z M F
§ 24	obmolita V	admolita Z M F
§§ 27, 28	percussit eum. forte V	percussit. tum forte Z M F
§ 30	demoliebantur V	moliebantur Z M F
§ 32	admotas F	adiutas V
11 § 8	exercitus [se] index V	exercitus index Z M F
§ 25	quos subire M	quo subire Z F V [so Madvig in Advers vol 2]
14 § 13	magnitudini Pori Z M F	magnitudinem corpori V
IX 2 § 9	persequi terminum Z M F	terminum persequi V
§ 21	quoque [et]	quoque Z M F V
§ 25	adhibite (? misprint)	adhibete Z M F V
§ 28	invicem	invicti Z M F V
3 § 21	xxv milia Z M F V	xxv milibus [so Madvig in Advers vol 2]
4 § 6	subicere V	subiecere Z M F
§ 9	qua meatur navigiis V	qua meant navigia Z M F
§ 10	aestu F	metu M
§ 15	Oxydracarum Z M F	Sudracarum V
§ 23	ducere	duceret Z M F V
	aequareque	aequaretque Z M F V
§ 24	Oxydracarum Z M F	Sudracarum V
§ 26	Oxydracarum Z M F	Sudracarum V
§ 27	ni omitteret, at	ne committeret aut Z M F V

	§ 32 magnitudinem terrorum	magnitudinem Z M F V
5	§ 5 cum comminus unum	cum unum Z M F V
6	§ 2 perinvalido V	corpori invalido Z M F
	§ 23 Sameramis	Samiramis V
7	§ 5 suspicio Z M F V	suspitio
	§ 16 virium etiam regi	virium iam regi [so the MSS]
	§ 19 ingens vis militum, inter quos erant Graeci, Dioxippo studebant	ingens hic militum conventus erat, inter quos qui erant Graeci Dioxippo studebant
8	§ 7 vivos (misprint)	viros Z M F V
	§ 11 in Depraestos	inde Praestos Z M F
9	§ 1 *instigabat*	*coegit* [conjecture of Freinsheim and Z]
	§ 13 [non] receperant	non receperant Z M V
10	§ 18 copia fertilis V	sola fertilis Z M F

The letters subjoined to readings in this table are initials denoting the texts of the editions of Zumpt (Brunswick 1849), Mützell (Berlin 1841), Foss (Leipsic 1857), and Vogel (Leipsic 1872). The critical edition of Hedicke is the basis of the present text, and has never been departed from without grave reasons and careful deliberation, and only once or twice without the support of a preponderance of manuscript or other authority. Where difficult questions arise they are briefly discussed in the notes.

NOTES.

BOOK VIII, CHAPTER IX.

§ 1. *ne...aleret*] Curtius, like Livy and other rhetorical historians, gives the motives of actions with the utmost confidence.

natum] for the construction compare Terence adelph 545 *nisi me credo huic esse natum rei, ferundis miseriis*, Horace de art poet 82 *natum rebus agendis*. For the matter see Curtius VI 2 § 15 *rumor, otiosi militis vitium*.

in Indiam movit] Arrian IV 22 § 3 says in much the same sense προὐχώρει ὡς ἐπὶ Ἰνδούς. For *movit* intransitive or = *movit castra* compare V 13 § 1 *audito Dareum movisse ab Ecbatanis*, IX 4 § 27, Livy XXI 39 § 6, XXII 1 § 1.

semper...clarior] this dry remark is particularly suggested by the matter of the four chapters just preceding, namely the unjust accusation and death of the sophist Kallisthenes. Curtius means that Alexander did himself no credit by his acts during an interval of rest. For *clarior* compare IX 8 § 23.

§ 2. *spectat orientem*] 'lies towards the East'. Curtius speaks from the point of view of one coming from central Asia as Alexander did. That the above rendering is correct seems to be shewn by VII 10 § 15 *circa eam* VI *oppidis condendis electa sedes est, duo ad meridiem versa, quattuor spectantia orientem*, VIII 10 § 23, VI 6 § 23 *praerupta rupes est qua spectat occidentem*, and other such passages. Pratt renders 'slopes eastward', but his reasons seem weak. We must remember that the ancients knew very little of India [see Strabo XV 1 §§ 1—12], and that Eratosthenes [in Strabo XV 1 § 11] evidently makes the Indus flow north and south, and places the southern angle of the rhomboid to which he likens India a good way to the east of the northern one. See also Arrian Indica 3.

in latitudinem...recta regione] 'broadways'...'straightways', that is 'in breadth' and 'straight ahead' = 'in length'. That writers differed, some reckoning the length from north to south and the breadth from east to west, while others adopted the contrary arrangement, is clear from Arrian Indica 3. Curtius seems to reckon the length from east to west. See on § 6 *rubro mari*. For *in latitudinem* compare VII 10 § 1 *octingenta fere stadia in latitudinem vastae solitudines tenent*. For *recta regione* compare VII 7 § 4 *recta deinde regione saltum ultra*

Istrum iacentem colit (Scytharum gens), 10 § 2 *ingens spatium rectae regionis est*, Livy XXI 31 § 9.

§ 3. *fastigium*] peak, ridge, slope. The word is often used of the gable slope of a roof. The metaphorical sense is common, as in IX 2 § 28, 10 § 24. Compare our use of 'pitch' in both senses. See on 10 § 31 below, and compare 11 § 6, IX 9 § 19.

excedunt] rise, stand out. Compare VII 3 § 22 *rupes quattuor (stadia) in altitudinem excedit*. Mützell remarks that the parts spoken of are the Vindhya mountains and the Deckan.

plana] this bold statement is rather sweeping, but more nearly accurate than that of Pliny N H VI § 60 where speaking of the northern mountains he says *iunguntur inter se Imaus Emodus Paropamisus Caucasus, a quibus tota (India) decurrit in planitiem immensam et Aegypto similem*. Strabo and Arrian more cautiously speak of τὰ πεδία.

Caucaso] this name was given generally to the mountains north of India by the Greeks, especially to the range of the Hindu Kush. Arrian Indica 2 §§ 3, 4 ἄλλῃ δὲ ἄλλο καλέεται τὸ οὖρος, τῇ μὲν Παραπαμισός, τῇ δὲ Ἠμωδός· ἄλλῃ δὲ Ἴμαον κληΐζεται, καὶ τυχὸν ἄλλα καὶ ἄλλα ἔχει οὐνόματα. Μακεδόνες δὲ οἱ σὺν Ἀλεξάνδρῳ στρατεύσαντες Καύκασον αὐτὸ ἐκάλεον, ἄλλον τοῦτον Καύκασον, οὐ τὸν Σκυθικόν. So before him Strabo XV 1 § 11, following Eratosthenes; in § 13 he says of the rivers ἅπαντες δ' ἀπὸ τοῦ Καυκάσου τὴν ἀρχὴν ἔχουσι. See also Curtius VII 3 §§ 19—22, Pliny N H VI §§ 60, 71, Horace carm I 22 7.

§ 4. *Indus*] the name is interesting. Prof M Williams (*Hinduism* chap 1) says, speaking of the districts near the river Sindhu [now called the Indus] "the Persians pronounced this word Hindhū, and named their Aryan brethren Hindūs. The Greeks, who probably gained their first idea of India from the Persians, dropped the hard aspirate and called the Hindus Ἰνδοί." Compare the words of Pliny N H VI § 71 *Indus incolis Sindus appellatus*. This river was generally recognized as the western boundary of India, though that name was occasionally extended. See IX 10 § 7 and Elphinstone appendix III *on the Greek accounts of India*. The river and its affluents are described by Strabo XV 1 § 13, Arrian Indica 4 §§ 8—13, Pomponius Mela III 7, Pliny N H VI §§ 71, 72, and are often referred to by other authors. It was regarded as the greatest of all rivers but the Ganges. Herod IV 44 Ἰνδὸν ποταμόν, ὃς κροκοδείλους δεύτερος οὗτος ποταμῶν πάντων παρέχεται, Lucan III 236 *vastis Indus aquis mixtum non sentit Hydaspen*.

gelidior] this statement and that concerning the colour of the water are supported by Burnes [Travels into Bokhara vol I pp 74, 77, 79], quoted by Mützell with the remark that the coldness of the Indus is in interesting contrast to the warmth of the Ganges.

§ 5. *Ganges*] the Ganga or Ganges, thought by the ancients to be the greatest river in the world, is described by Strabo XV 1 § 13, Arrian Indica 4 §§ 2—7, Pomponius Mela III 7, Pliny N H VI § 65. It is often referred to by other authors as representing the far east. Lucan III 229—234, Juvenal X 1, 2 *omnibus in terris quae sunt a Gadibus usque Auroram et Gangen*.

omnium] genitive after *eximius*, which is equivalent to a superlative. Compare Statius Theb VI 15 *eximii regum*.

ab oriente] on the eastern side of the world, in the east. Compare the similar usage of *a meridie* in 10 § 24, and other expressions. This reading, being adopted by Zumpt Mützell Foss and Hedicke and having the MSS authority on its side, has been retained. But the sense thus given is feeble in the extreme. Aldus read *ab ortu* which he probably meant to mean 'from its source', and he may have had authority for the reading. Anyhow Arrian says of the Ganges on the authority of Megasthenes *αὐτόν τε γὰρ μέγαν ἀνίσχειν ἐκ τῶν πηγέων*, and Pliny *alii (dixerunt) cum magno fragore ipsius statim fontis erumpere*, statements such as Curtius loves to make.

recto alveo] with straight bed = running straight ahead. Compare *recta regione* above.

stringit] grazes, washes. Compare Virgil Aen VIII 62, 63 where father Tiber says *ego sum pleno quem flumine cernis stringentem ripas et pinguia culta secantem*. Also Seneca nat quaest III 27 § 9.

inclinant] see Strabo XV 1 § 13, speaking of the Indian rivers, *ἅπαντες δ' ἀπὸ τοῦ Καυκάσου τὴν ἀρχὴν ἔχουσι καὶ φέρονται μὲν ἐπὶ τὴν μεσημβρίαν τὸ πρῶτον, εἶθ' οἱ μὲν μένουσιν ἐπὶ τῆς αὐτῆς φορᾶς καὶ μάλιστα οἱ εἰς τὸν Ἰνδὸν συμβάλλοντες, οἱ δ' ἐπιστρέφονται πρὸς ἕω καθάπερ καὶ ὁ Γάγγης ποταμός. οὗτος μὲν οὖν καταβὰς ἐκ τῆς ὀρεινῆς ἐπειδὰν ἅψηται τῶν πεδίων ἐπιστρέψας πρὸς ἕω καὶ ῥυεὶς παρὰ τὰ Παλίβοθρα μεγίστην πόλιν πρόεισιν ἐπὶ τὴν ταύτῃ θάλατταν*, also § 72. Mützell points out that modern researches confirm the statement of Curtius assigning *obiectae rupes* as the cause of the river's change of course.

§ 6. *rubro mari*] this of course stands for the Indian ocean generally. So often in Curtius and in rhetorical or poetical writers. See III 2 § 9 *Indos ceterosque rubri maris accolas*, IV 12 § 9, VI 2 § 12, IX 6 § 20, X 10 § 4, Virgil Aen VIII 686 (compare 605), Horace carm I 35 32, pseudo-Tibullus IV 2 19 *et quascunque niger rubro de litore conchas proximus eois colligit Indus aquis*. If the text be sound here, the making both rivers (Indus and Ganges) run into the same sea is in favour of the view put forth in a note on § 2, that Curtius thought India longer from east to west than from north to south; he being in fact ignorant that there was a great tongue of land projecting southwards. Ptolemy afterwards had the same imperfect conception.

§ 7. *reverberatur*] compare IX 9 § 8.

stagnat] forms pools or meres. Arrian VI 14 § 5 says that the river may perhaps be more than 100 stadia broad *ἵναπερ λιμνάζει μᾶλλον*. In his Indica 6 § 5 he speaks of the summer floods in the Indian rivers generally, so too Strabo XV 1 § 13 *βρέχεται τοῖς θερινοῖς ὄμβροις ἡ Ἰνδικὴ καὶ λιμνάζει τὰ πεδία*, also §§ 17—20.

insulas] alluvial banks. For these vast silt deposits see IX 8 § 30, Strabo XV 1 § 16, and for the Indus in particular Pliny N H VI § 71.

molitur] builds up, forms. Compare Virgil Aen III 132 *ergo avidus muros optatae molior urbis* and other passages.

§ 8. *Acesines*] now the Chenab. For this river and its affluents Hydaspes (Jhelam) Hydraotes (Ravi) and Hyphasis (Satlej), the waters of which it carries to the Indus, see Arrian VI 14 § 5. The Hyphasis (or Hypasis, Vipasa) seems properly to mean the Bias river, but to have been applied to the stream formed by the junction of that river with the Satlej. See however note 1 on § 7 of introduction B.

Iomanen] a clever conjectural insertion, due to Hedicke. Foss had suspected some such omission, as the old attempt to make the Acesines run into the Ganges by finding some other modern name for it was preposterous. For the junction of the Jamna and Ganges see Pliny N H VI § 63 *ad confluentem Iomanis amnis et Gangis*, § 69 *amnis Iomanes in Gangen per Palibothros decurrit*.

quippe] this word is especially frequent in Curtius in the sense of 'the fact is', 'in truth'. Compare § 19, 10 § 35, 11 § 19, 13 § 3, IX 7 §§ 2, 23 and elsewhere. See introduction A § 3.

os] used generally of the mouth of a river, here of the mouth or face that one river presents to another at their junction. Render 'in truth the Ganges presents a rough face to its entrance, and its waters though beaten back (in eddies) do not give way'.

repercussae] see on 13 § 9.

§ 9. *Dyardenes*] cannot be identified. It is however worth comparing the report given in Strabo XV 1 § 72 of Artemidorus' account of the Ganges, where an obscure river-name occurs, with a description very like that of the Dyardenes; τῶν δὲ συρρεόντων εἰς αὐτὸν Οἰδάνην τινὰ καλεῖ· τρέφειν δὲ καὶ κροκοδείλους καὶ δελφῖνας· λέγει δὲ καὶ ἄλλα τινά, συγκεχυμένως δὲ καὶ ἀργῶς, ὧν οὐ φροντιστέον. This passage has been noticed by Mützell.

uti Nilus] Alexander on seeing crocodiles in the Indus jumped to the conclusion that he had found the source of the Nile. See Arrian VI 1 §§ 2, 3, Herod IV 44 (quoted on § 4), Strabo XV 1 § 25 (of the Hydaspes), Arrian Indica 6 § 8 (of Indian rivers in general).

delphinos] this, as Zumpt remarks, is the proper Latin form of the accusative plural, and should be kept in prose.

§ 10. *Ethimantus*] this spelling has been kept, as nearer to the MSS. Mützell has shewn that Ritter was wrong in identifying this with the Etymandrus of Arrian IV 6 § 6.

subinde] 'now and then', 'often'. The regular silver-age use of the word. Compare 13 § 18, IX 3 § 24, 4 § 9, 5 § 7.

rigantibus] Strabo XV 1 § 50 speaks of a board charged with the supervision of irrigation works, but this is from Megasthenes, and refers to the Ganges.

carpitur] is spent, used up. Compare Virgil georg III 215 *carpit enim vires paulatim*, Aen IV 2 *caeco carpitur igni*, 32 *solane perpetua maerens carpere iuventa*. The word is used in military history of cutting off stragglers and detachments (*carpere agmen*), or of dividing an army into portions. See Livy VI 32, XXII 32, XXVII 46, XXVI 38.

ea causa] 'that is the reason'. The pronoun as usual is attracted to the gender of the substantive instead of being made neuter. Compare Virgil Aen IV 379 *scilicet is superis labor est*, Tacitus ann III 38 *quae causa fuit*.

iam sine nomine] which by that time have ceased to have a name, ἤδη ἀνώνυμα.

§ 11. *non adeo*] the theory of the construction will be best explained by Virgil Aen XI 436, 437 *non adeo has exosa manus Victoria fugit ut tanta quicquam pro spe temptare recusem*. Here if completed it would run *non adeo interfluunt ut nobiles fiant*.

interfluunt] run through. Compare III 1 § 12 *Gordium nomen est urbi, quam Sangarius amnis interfluit*.

§ 12. *ceterum*] like the Greek δ' οὖν, resuming the thread of narrative after a parenthesis or digression. Here we turn back to § 3, since which we have been dealing with rivers.

aquilone] how this mention of a hot north wind can possibly refer to the storms and rains of the SW Monsoon [see Elphinstone introd p 5, Meadows Taylor bk I c I] is just what Zumpt and Mützell do not explain, though they refer it to that season. Nor will the NE Monsoon, blowing in October and November on the Coromandel coast, answer the description. Pratt does really try to meet the difficulty, remarking 'As to the heat attributed to the north wind, it may be acquired by passing over torrefied deserts in the last stages of its course', and quoting from Elphinstone's *Caubul* p 133 "We experienced a whole night of strong hot wind from the North-West" [at Peshawer].

deuruntur] may either refer to the effect of heat or (as in Livy XL 45) to that of cold. How to explain the statement of Curtius on either supposition is very far from clear. The MSS read *aquiloni* and *decurrunt* which if retained would need some other explanation than that of Zumpt.

ita...mitia] 'which thus (=for this reason) are mild and nourish the crops'. As οὕτω so *ita* often means 'under such conditions'. See IX 4 § 22. In this place however there is no verb and the clause is so to speak participial. Compare use of *ideo* in Plin N H III § 78. If we had *ea* after *ita* we might put a colon at *penetrat* and understand *sunt*.

§ 13. *adeo*] to such an extent.

mundus] the world, or universal order of things, ὁ κόσμος. See IV 11 § 22 *nec mundus duobus solibus potest regi*. The exaggeration of the differences between the climate of India and that of Europe is quite in Curtius' rhetorical manner. Pliny N H VI § 58 is more sober and accurate. Pratt well remarks 'Possibly the Macedonian-Greeks might have encountered extreme cold in the elevated mountain tracts of India, in the season corresponding to summer in a European climate; and again, in descending the valleys of the south, have experienced oppressive heat when the rigours of winter prevail in their own country; and on these unexpected vicissitudes have founded the erroneous conclusion that the *times* of both seasons were inverted in respect to Europe'. See Strabo XV 1 §§ 17, 18, and introduction A § 5.

statas temporum vices] 'the regular changes of seasons'. Compare IX 9 §§ 9, 27.

inverterit se] has turned itself round, as we say 'wrong way about'. The text is very uncertain here. For the present compare the *inversi mores* of Horace carm III 5 7.

causa] that is, *satis constat* or *apparet*. The MSS are corrupt here, and Hedicke's emended reading is only accepted provisionally. It must be granted that the omission of the verb is very harsh.

§ 14. *Erythro*] so in the report of Nearchus after his voyage to the Persian gulf, X 1 §§ 13, 14, and Arrian Indica 37 § 3 ἐν ταύτῃ τῇ νήσῳ ἔλεγον καὶ τοῦ πρώτου δυναστεύσαντος τῆς χώρης ταύτης δείκνυσθαι τὸν τάφον· οὔνομα δὲ αὐτῷ Ἐρύθρην εἶναι, ἀπ' ὅτου καὶ τὴν ἐπωνυμίην τῇ θαλάσσῃ ταύτῃ εἶναι, ἐρυθρὴν καλέεσθαι.

§ 15. *lini*] this usually stands for flax, though here perhaps cotton is meant. Compare Strabo XV 1 § 13 βρέχεται τοῖς θερινοῖς ὄμβροις ἡ Ἰνδική, καὶ λιμνάζει τὰ πεδία· ἐν μὲν οὖν τούτοις τοῖς ὄμβροις λίνον σπείρεται καὶ κέγχρος, πρὸς τούτοις σήσαμον ὄρυζα βόσμορον.

vestes] see IX 7 § 12, 8 § 1, Strabo XV 1 § 71, Arriana Indic 16 §§ 1, 2 ἐσθῆτι δὲ Ἰνδοὶ λινέῃ χρέονται, κατάπερ λέγει Νέαρχος, λίνου τοῦ ἀπὸ τῶν δένδρεων ὑπὲρ ὅτων μοι ἤδη λέλεκται. τὸ δὲ λίνον τοῦτο ἢ λαμπρότερον τὴν χροιήν ἐστιν ἄλλου λίνου παντός, ἢ μέλανες αὐτοὶ ἐόντες λαμπρότερον τὸ λίνον φαίνεσθαι ποιέουσιν. ἔστι δὲ κιθὼν λίνεος αὐτοῖσιν ἔστε ἐπὶ μέσην τὴν κνήμην, εἷμα δὲ τὸ μὲν περὶ τοῖσιν ὤμοισι περιβεβλημένον, τὸ δὲ περὶ τῇσι κεφαλῇσιν εἱλιγμένον. Pomponius Mela III 7 calls the cotton *lana* (*tam feracis soli ut...lanas silvae ferant*) and says of the people *lino alii vestiuntur aut lanis quas diximus, alii avium ferarumque pellibus; pars nudi agunt.* Herodotus (III 106) had heard of the 'tree-wool'. Compare Virgil georg II 120, 121. Meadows Taylor bk I c 3 'The costume of the male Hindoos, as depicted in ancient sculptures, is still used. It consists of two pieces of broad cotton cloth, one of which is folded round the waist, reaching to the calf of the leg, the other cast gracefully over the shoulders'. The latter, says Elphinstone bk III c 11 p 201 'is occasionally stretched over the head, which has no other covering'. See below § 21.

libri] *liber* originally means 'bark' (see Virgil georg II 77), then 'book'. *charta* is the papyrus-paper, so extensively used in ancient times. Pliny NH XIII §§ 68—89 describes the growth and preparation of it: in § 69 he remarks *in palmarum foliis primo scriptitatum, dein quarundam arborum libris*. Strabo XV 1 §§ 67, 73 mentions Indian writing on fine pressed linen and on skins, but says nothing of the bark-paper. Pratt quotes Hamilton's *Description of India* to the effect that bark is used for writing upon in Kashmir.

§ 16. *aves*] Pliny NH X §§ 117—120 treats of birds taught to talk. In § 117 he says *super omnia humanas voces reddunt, psittaci quidem etiam sermocinantes. India hanc avem mittit, septagen vocat, viridem toto corpore, torque tantum miniato in cervice distinctam. imperatores salutat et quae accipit verba pronuntiat, in vino praecipue lasciva*, Arrian Indica 15 §§ 8, 9, Strabo XV 1 § 69, Ovid amores II 6 *psittacus eois imitatrix ales ab Indis.* Elphinstone introd p 10 speaks of 'parrots, or rather peroquets' in India.

invisitata] some editors prefer the form *inusitata* here and in IX 1 § 4 and other places. Both words are recognized and there is hardly any perceptible difference in sense. Mützell on V 5 § 7 discusses the question with much learning. We may render either 'uncommon' or 'unknown'. The frequentative form has here as in many other cases lost its proper meaning. See for instance Virgil Aen VI 258 *adventante dea.* The strange animals referred to are probably the gold-digging ants, flying snakes and scorpions, griffins and other marvellous creatures of fabulous or exaggerated powers. See Arrian V 4 § 3, Indica 15 §§ 1—10, Strabo XV 1 §§ 35, 37, 44, 69, Pomponius Mela III 7, Pliny NH XI § 111, XXXIII § 66, VII §§ 21—30.

nisi] so IX 9 § 4 *incognita nisi inmortalibus.*

alit non generat] for the words compare Horace carm I 22 13—16. As to the matter Mützell well observes that the statement is found only in Curtius, who seems to contradict himself in IX 1 § 5. Elphinstone intr p 9 says that the rhinoceros is found in India but is confined to the forests. It would seem therefore to be indigenous. See Aelian hist anim XVI 20 translated by M'Crindle p 59.

§ 17. *elephantorum*] for the use of elephants in India in ancient times, and the method of catching and taming them etc see Strabo XV 1 §§ 41—43, Arrian Indica 13, 14, 17, Diodorus II 35, 42, Elphinstone bk III c 11 p 201.

magnitudo] the superiority of the Indian to the African elephants in size and strength is set forth in Strabo (only on the authority of Onesikritus) and Diodorus.

§ 18. *aurum*] see Herod III 106, Strabo XV 1 §§ 57, 69.

§ 19. *gemmas*] for the precious stones of India and their use by the natives see Pliny NH XXXVII §§ 76—80, 84—96, 100, 101, 105, 110, 114, 115, 121, 122, 128—132, 177, 185, 200. Mützell well compares Strabo II 3 § 4 of the voyage of Eudoxus to India πλεύσαντα δὴ μετὰ δώρων ἐπανελθεῖν ἀντιφορτισάμενον ἀρώματα καὶ λίθους πολυτελεῖς ὧν τοὺς μὲν καταφέρουσιν οἱ ποταμοὶ μετὰ τῶν ψήφων τοὺς δ' ὀρυκτοὺς εὑρίσκουσι πεπηγότας ἐξ ὑγροῦ καθάπερ τὰ κρυστάλλινα παρ' ἡμῖν. See Elphinstone intr p 10, Strabo XV 1 § 67.

margaritas] 'most of the pearls in the world, and all the best, are taken up from beds near Ceylon'. Elphinstone. Athenaeus III 93a refers to Theophrastus de lapidibus § 36 which runs τῶν σπουδαζομένων δὲ λίθων ἐστὶ καὶ ὁ μαργαρίτης καλούμενος, διαφανὴς μὲν τῇ φύσει, ποιοῦσι δ' ἐξ αὐτοῦ τοὺς πολυτελεῖς ὅρμους. γίνεται δὲ ἐν ὀστρείῳ τινὶ παραπλησίῳ ταῖς πίνναις, φέρει δὲ ἥ τε Ἰνδικὴ χώρα καὶ νῆσοί τινες τῶν ἐν τῇ ἐρυθρᾷ. See Pliny NH IX §§ 106—123, Arrian Indica 8 §§ 9—13, 38 § 3.

litoribus] compare IX 2 § 27.

opulentiae] the word here stands for 'wealth'. In Pliny NH VI § 89 it means 'splendour', 'show of wealth', *sed ne Taprobane quidem, quamvis extra orbem a natura relegata, nostris vitiis caret. aurum argentumque et ibi in pretio. marmor testudinis simile, margaritae gemmaeque in honore multo, praestantiorum et totius luxuriae nostrae cumulus. ipsorum opes maiores esse dicebant, sed apud nos opulentiae maiorem usum.* See also XXXIV § 163 *India neque aes neque plumbum habet gemmisque ac margaritis suis haec permutat.*

utique postquam] compare IX 7 § 26. Render 'especially since they spread the community of evil to foreign nations'. *vitia* here as in §§ 23, 31 are the moral defects that make men love luxury and vain display. Compare IX 7 § 15, Juvenal I 87 *et quando uberior vitiorum copia*, 149 *omne in praecipiti vitium stetit.* These are the constant theme of the rhetoricians and satirists of imperial Rome. In the matter of pearls Tacitus Agr 12, Pliny NH IX §§ 112—123 may be referred to.

commercium] the sharing or having in common, hence 'intercourse'. Compare VI 3 § 8 *tot gentes alterius imperio ac nomine adsuetas, non sacris non moribus non commercio linguae nobiscum cohaerentes*, and IX 10 § 8 below.

purgamenta] excretions, things cast out by the sea. Compare IX 10 § 10. The word is an ignoble one, and is used metaphorically as we say 'offscourings'. Compare VIII 5 § 8 where the fawning flatterers of Alexander are described as *urbium suarum purgamenta.*

libido] 'fashion' is our nearest word. Compare with Mützell Pliny NH XXXVII § 85 *singulorum enim libido pretia singulis facit.*

constituit] see II § 4, IX 10 § 28.

§ 20. *ingenia*] their 'natures' or 'characters'. So IX 10 § 9. For the matter of the effect of various countries on their inhabitants see Herod I 142, III 106, IX 2, 122, Aristotle Pol VII 7 §§ 1—4, Cic de deor nat II § 42, Livy XXIX 25, Draper's History of the American civil war sect I cc 4—6, Vegetius I 2 *passim* especially *plaga caeli ad robur non tantum corporum sed etiam animorum plurimum valet.* For India in particular see Strabo XV I § 13, Arrian V 4 § 4, Indica 6 § 9, 17 § 1, Diodorus II 36, Pomponius Mela III 7, Elphinstone bk III c II pp 214, 215.

locorum situs] this expression seems generally to mean the 'lie of the ground' viewed with the eye of a general or engineer. See 10 §§ 13, 23, IX 2 § 8. Here it seems to mean rather what we call 'the surroundings' of the people, that is, the position of their country and its climate. See Tacitus Agr 10.

quoque] goes in sense with *illos.* This licentious misplacement of *quoque* is common in Livy and Curtius.

§ 21. *usque pedes*] for the use of *usque* as a preposition compare Juvenal X 1, 2 *omnibus in terris quae sunt a Gadibus usque Auroram et Gangen.* Curtius seems not to use it thus elsewhere. For the matter see IX 1 § 29.

carbaso] Strabo XV I § 71 ὡς δ' εἰπεῖν, Ἰνδοὺς ἐσθῆτι λευκῇ χρῆσθαι καὶ σινδόσι λευκαῖς καὶ καρπάσοις, ὑπεναντίως τοῖς εἰποῦσιν εὐανθέστατα *αὐτοὺς ἀμπέχεσθαι φορήματα*, reporting the account of Klitarchus. See also Elphinstone bk III c 11 pp 201, 202 'The full dress is a long white gown of almost transparent muslin, close over the body, but in innumerable loose folds below the waist'. The writer thinks however that some of the dress is borrowed from the Mahometans: whether this part or not he does not say. Pratt remarks that the Sanskrit term for muslins or fine calicoes is *karpasi*.

soleis] slippers, covering little more than the sole of the foot. Mützell observes that Philostratus in Photius says that the Indians wear *ὑποδήματα βύβλου*. But Arrian Indica 16 § 5 says on the authority of Nearchus that *ὑποδήματα δὲ λευκοῦ δέρματος φορέουσι, περισσῶς καὶ ταῦτα ἠσκημένα, καὶ τὰ ἴχνεα τῶν ὑποδημάτων αὐτοῖσι ποικίλα καὶ ὑψηλὰ τοῦ μέζονας φαίνεσθαι*. The latter may possibly rather refer to princes and wealthy people. See Curtius below IX 1 § 29.

linteis] linen [or cotton] cloths. See above on § 15. *linteum* is used for a dinner napkin (Catullus 12) or the sail of a ship.

lapilli] compare IX 1 § 30. Mützell quotes Pliny N H XI § 136 (of the ears) *nec in alia parte feminis maius impendium margaritis dependentibus. in Oriente quidem et viris aurum eo loci gestare decus existimatur*. Arrian Indica 16 § 3 says *καὶ ἐνώτια Ἰνδοὶ φορέουσιν ἐλέφαντος, ὅσοι κάρτα εὐδαίμονες· οὐ γὰρ πάντες Ἰνδοὶ φορέουσι*. Strabo XV 1 § 59 reports (after Megasthenes) of the Brahman at a certain stage of his life *καὶ ζῆν ἀδεῶς καὶ ἀνειμένως μᾶλλον, σινδονοφοροῦντα καὶ χρυσοφοροῦντα μετρίως ἐν τοῖς ὠσὶ καὶ ταῖς χερσί*. Elphinstone bk III c 11 p 202 'Both sexes wear many ornaments. Men even of the lower orders wear earrings bracelets and necklaces'.

brachia et lacertos] the fore and upper arm. For the bracelets see last note, and compare IX 1 § 29.

colunt] deck, dress. Compare III 3 § 14 *haec vero turba muliebriter propemodum culta luxu magis quam decoris armis conspicua erat*, and the substantive *cultus*=dress in IX 3 § 11 and elsewhere.

eminent] stand out, are notable. Compare 12 § 13, IX 1 § 28.

§ 22. *capillum*] Strabo XV 1 § 71 (after Klitarchus) *κομᾶν δὲ καὶ πωγωνοτροφεῖν πάντας, ἀναπλεκομένους δὲ μιτροῦσθαι τὰς κόμας*, also §§ 13, 30. Arrian Indica 6 § 9, 7 § 9. The custom seems to have changed, according to Elphinstone bk III c 11 p 201 'The head and beard are shaved, but a long tuft of hair is left on the crown. Mustachios are also worn, except perhaps by strict Bramins'.

mentum] see Arrian Indica 16 § 4 *τοὺς δὲ πώγωνας λέγει Νέαρχος ὅτι βάπτονται Ἰνδοὶ χροιὴν ἄλλην καὶ ἄλλην*, mentioning white, dark blue, scarlet, purple, green as the colours. Strabo XV 1 § 30 gives much the same account.

ad speciem levitatis] 'so that it looks polished'. Compare III 1 § 13 *quae quia continenti adhaeret, sed magna ex parte cingitur fluctibus, speciem insulae praebet*, 'looks like an island'.

§ 23. *regum*] though we find mention elsewhere (see on IX 8 § 4) of communities in India at the time of Alexander's visit living under other institutions, still government by a king is generally assumed by the ancients to have been the normal constitution. See Elphinstone bk I c 2 (on Government) which opens thus; 'The government of the society thus constituted (viz as described by Menu) was vested in an absolute monarch'. Compare Virgil georg IV 210—212.

luxuria......magnificentiam] for the contrast between barbaric gorgeousness and effeminacy on the one hand, and well-judged splendour on the other, compare V 1 § 23 *equites deinde Babylonii, suo equorumque cultu ad luxuriam magis quam ad magnificentiam exacto, ultimi ibant.* Also Cic pro Murena § 76 *odit populus Romanus privatam luxuriam, publicam magnificentiam diligit.* For the former see Milton P L II 1—4 'High on a throne of royal state, which far outshone the wealth of Ormus and of Ind, or where the gorgeous East with richest hand showers on her kings barbaric pearl and gold'. Eastern luxury and pomp was and still is proverbial.

patitur] 'allows', marking condescension. Eastern sovereigns have ever been proverbially difficult of access, far removed from the mass of their subjects. See the account of the Chinese emperors in Marco Polo bk II cc 38, 77. The present passage is especially illustrated in many of its details by Strabo XV 1 § 55.

§ 24. *lectica*] palanquin.

recubat] 'lolls', marking lazy languor.

distincta] 'picked out'='embroidered'. For this use of *distinguo* =mark, set off, throw into relief, compare III § 18 *pallam auro distinctam*, § 19 *caerulea fascia albo distincta*, and below § 26, 13 § 7, IX 1 §§ 29, 30, 4 § 30, 7 § 12, Cic pro Murena § 49.

carbasa] the robes of *carbasus*. See § 21. Pliny N H XIX § 10 says that *carbasa* (=*vela carbasina*, as Mützell rightly remarks) were first invented in Spain.

quae indutus est] the construction is common. Compare V 9 § 1 *pretiosissimam vestem induti*, Tacitus hist II 20 *bracas barbarum tegmen indutus.*

§ 25. *inter quos......pendent*] 'among whose ranks, perched on boughs, are birds which they have taught to interrupt business with their cries'. The construction is bold, but quite intelligible. The matter may be illustrated by what Strabo XV 1 § 69 says of the proceedings at Indian festivals καὶ τῶν ποικίλων ὀρνέων καὶ εὐφθόγγων πλῆθος. ὁ δὲ Κλείταρχός φησιν ἁμάξας τετρακύκλους, δένδρα κομιζούσας τῶν μεγαλοφύλλων, ἐξ ὧν ἀνήρτηται γένη τετιθασευμένων ὀρνέων. It will be well also to quote here the abstract of Menu (on the king's duties) given by Elphinstone bk I c 2 p 24 'He is to rise in the last watch of the night and, after sacrifices, to hold a court in a hall decently splendid, and to dismiss his subjects with kind looks and words. This done, he is to assemble his council on a mountain or a terrace, in a bower or a forest, or other lonely place, without listeners; *from which women and talking-birds are to be carefully removed.* He is then, after manly exercises and bathing, to dine in his private apartments, and this time and midnight *are to* be allotted to the regulation of his family, to considering appointments, and such other public business as is most of a personal nature. He is now also to give some time to relaxation; and then to review his troops, perform his religious duties at sunset, and afterwards to receive the reports of his emissaries. At length he withdraws to his most private apartments to supper; and, after indulging for some time in music, is to retire to rest'.

§ 26. *auro caelata*] in gold-raised work, embossed in gold. Compare Virgil Aen I 640, 641 *ingens argentum mensis, caelataque in auro fortia facta patrum.* Also the Trojan doorways Aen II 504 (*thalami*) *barbarico postes auro spoliisque superbi*, where to treat *auro spoliisque* as a hendiadys is weak.

§ 27. *cum....pectit atque ornat*] 'even when he is combing and dressing his hair'. Through this sense 'even when' comes that of 'though'. Compare Caesar bell Gall II 27 *at hostes etiam in extrema spe salutis tantam virtutem praestiterunt ut, quum primi eorum cecidissent, proximi iacentibus insisterent atque ex eorum corporibus pugnarent;* where *cecidissent* is subjunctive because past tense and in dependent clause. It will too be interesting to turn to Cic de Off III § 74 where *cum potest*='having the power', and compare the parallel *si possunt* and *si potest* in I § 23, the place referred to.

capillum] Strabo XV I § 55, though he does not mention the hairdressing in particular, well illustrates the general sense of this passage; *τῶν δὲ μὴ κατὰ πόλεμον ἐξόδων μία μέν ἐστιν ἡ ἐπὶ τὰς κρίσεις, ἐν αἷς διημερεύει διακούων οὐδὲν ἧττον κἂν ὥρα γένηται τῆς τοῦ σώματος θεραπείας· αὕτη δ' ἐστὶν ἡ διὰ τῶν σκυταλίδων τρῖψις· ἅμα γὰρ καὶ διακούει καὶ τρίβεται τεττάρων περιστάντων τριβέων.*

legationibus] so in Elphinstone bk I c 2 (abstract of Menu) the king is supposed throughout to give personal attention to foreign affairs, though he employs ministers.

iura reddit] gives legal decisions=administers justice, hearing cases. Compare Livy VII I § 6 where *praetorem iura reddentem* is to be explained by VI 42 § 11 *qui ius in urbe diceret*, Tacitus ann XIII 51 *iura adversus publicanos extra ordinem redderent*, VI 11 *qui ius redderet.* Curtius V 7 § 8 speaking of the burning of Persepolis has the corresponding phrase; *hunc exitum habuit regia totius orientis, unde tot gentes antea iura petebant.* For the matter see Elphinstone bk I c 3 (abstract of Menu) 'Justice is to be administered by the king in person, assisted by Bramins and other counsellors', and the note there on p 27. From Strabo XV I §§ 34, 49, 53, 54, Diodorus II 42 we gather that the Indians appeared to the Greeks a people averse to litigation, that the king and his assessors were severe and discouraged litigation, and that the cases brought for judgment were chiefly of a criminal nature, such as murder and personal violence. See Elphinstone appendix III *On the Greek accounts of India.*

odoribus inlinuntur] no doubt after washing.

§ 28. *venatus*] Megasthenes is perhaps the only authority for this statement, as he seems to be for that in Strabo XV I § 55 *τρίτη δ'* (*ἔξοδος*) *ἐπὶ θήραν βακχική τις κύκλῳ γυναικῶν περικεχυμένων, ἔξωθεν δὲ τῶν δορυ-*

φόρων· παρεσχοίνισται δ' ἡ ὁδός, τῷ δὲ παρελθόντι ἐντὸς μέχρι γυναικῶν θάνατος· προηγοῦνται δὲ τυμπανισταὶ καὶ κωδωνοφόροι. κυνηγετεῖ δ' ἐν μὲν τοῖς περιφράγμασιν ἀπὸ βήματος τοξεύων (παρεστᾶσι δ' ἔνοπλοι δύο ἢ τρεῖς γυναῖκες), ἐν δὲ ταῖς ἀφράκταις θήραις ἀπ' ἐλέφαντος· αἱ δὲ γυναῖκες αἱ μὲν ἐφ' ἁρμάτων αἱ δ' ἐφ' ἵππων αἱ δὲ καὶ ἐπ' ἐλεφάντων, ὡς καὶ συστρατεύουσιν, ἠσκημέναι παντὶ ὅπλῳ.

inclusa] followed by dative. See IX 8 § 11.

vivario] a royal park or forest, fenced round (*περίφραγμα*) and full of game. In VIII 1 §§ 11—13 we have an account of a similar enclosure (called a *saltus*) in Sogdiana, of vast size, having walls and towers for the accommodation of the hunters. The beasts in it had enjoyed an unbroken quiet for four generations before they were disturbed by Alexander.

binum cubitorum] Zumpt remarks that distributive numerals commonly have the genitive plural contracted. See in general on the question of form the well-known passage Cic. orator §§ 155—157. Mützell here well compares Pliny N H V § 34 *puteos tamen haut difficile binum ferme cubitorum altitudine inveniunt.* These arrows seem to have been something like the 'cloth-yard shafts' of our English forefathers. Strabo XV 1 § 66 assigns them *οἰστοὺς τριπήχεις* on the authority of Nearchus.

maiore nisu etc] Curtius repeats this in 13 § 6, 14 § 19, but 10 § 6, IX 5 §§ 9, 24 can hardly be reconciled with the statement, which is also set aside by the testimony of Arrian Indica 16 §§ 6, 7 (apparently following Nearchus) *οἱ μὲν πεζοὶ αὐτοῖσι τόξον τε ἔχουσιν ἰσόμηκες τῷ φορέοντι τὸ τόξον, καὶ τοῦτο κάτω ἐπὶ τὴν γῆν θέντες καὶ τῷ ποδὶ τῷ ἀριστερῷ ἀντιβάντες οὕτως ἐκτοξεύουσι τὴν νευρὴν ἐπὶ μέγα ὀπίσω ἀπαγαγόντες· ὁ γὰρ ὀϊστὸς αὐτοῖσιν ὀλίγον ἀποδέων τριπήχεος, οὐδέ τι ἀντέχει τοξευθὲν πρὸς Ἰνδοῦ ἀνδρὸς τοξικοῦ, οὔτε ἀσπὶς οὔτε θώρηξ οὔτε εἴ τι καρτερὸν ἐγένετο.* See also Julian 205 d, Plutarch Alex 63, regum et imper apophth (No 23 of Alex) in which last there is a pretty story of an Indian archer who had rather have been put to death than shame his art by trying to perform feats when out of practice: Virgil georg II 122—125 *aut quos Oceano propior gerit India lucos, extremi sinus orbis, ubi aera vincere summum arboris haut ullae iactu potuere sagittae? et gens illa quidem sumptis non tarda pharetris.*

pondere] Livy would hardly have written such loose stuff as this: see at least VII 23 § 8, IX 19 § 7, XXX 10 § 13, also Virgil Aen IX 704—708.

§ 29. *equo* etc] Arrian Indica 17 §§ 1, 2 *ὀχήματα δὲ τοῖσι μὲν πολλοῖσιν Ἰνδῶν κάμηλοί εἰσι καὶ ἵπποι καὶ ὄνοι, τοῖσι δὲ εὐδαίμοσιν ἐλέφαντες. βασιλικὸν γὰρ ὄχημα ὁ ἐλέφας παρ' Ἰνδοῖσίν ἐστι· δεύτερον δὲ τιμῇ ἐπὶ τούτῳ τὰ τέθριππα, τρίτον δὲ αἱ κάμηλοι· τὸ δὲ ἐπ' ἑνὸς ἵππου ὀχέεσθαι ἄτιμον.* See also Strabo XV 1 §§ 41, 43, and Curtius himself 12 § 8, 14 § 13.

vehunt currum] Curtius seems to be thinking of a howdah; or perhaps, since *elephanti* is in the plural, he may refer to something like *the* Great Kaan's gold-plated litter, borne by four elephants, mentioned in Marco Polo II 20. Nearchus in Strabo XV I § 43 seems to mean a car drawn by elephants, *μέγιστόν τε νομίζεσθαι κτῆμα ἐλεφάντων ἅρμα· ἄγεσθαι δ' ὑπὸ ζυγὸν καὶ καμήλους.*

§ 30. *feminae*] Strabo XV I § 55 *τῷ βασιλεῖ δ' ἡ μὲν τοῦ σώματος θεραπεία διὰ γυναικῶν ἐστιν, ὠνητῶν καὶ αὐτῶν παρὰ τῶν πατέρων.*

vinum] Athenaeus X 434 tells us that among the Indians the king may not get drunk, and Strabo XV I § 55 says *μεθύοντα δὲ κτείνασα γυνὴ βασιλέα γέρας ἕχει συνεῖναι τῷ ἐκεῖνον διαδεξαμένῳ· διαδέχονται δ' οἱ παῖδες.*

omnibus...usus] Strabo XV I § 53 (following Megasthenes) says that though they may manage their affairs by memory without writing *εὐπραγεῖν δ' ὅμως διὰ τὴν ἁπλότητα καὶ τὴν εὐτέλειαν· οἶνόν τε γὰρ οὐ πίνειν ἀλλ' ἐν θυσίαις μόνον, πίνειν δ' ἀπ' ὀρύζης ἀντὶ κριθίνων συντιθέντας*, and in § 45 (after Nearchus) he speaks of their general good health *διὰ τὴν λιτότητα τῆς διαίτης καὶ τὴν ἀοινίαν.* But in § 47 he says, speaking of the military class in time of peace, *οἷς τὸν ἄλλον χρόνον ἐν σχολῇ καὶ πότοις ὁ βίος ἐστίν.* Curtius may have been thinking of some account referring especially to the soldiers. See also Athenaeus X 437 a, b, Aelian var hist II 41, for the love of wine attributed to the Indians. Pratt points out that the report of Megasthenes is not entitled to much respect, and the account of imports into India given in the *periplus maris erythraei* confirms that of Curtius. Strabo in § 43 speaks of *ὁ μέλας οἶνος* as the cure for most of the diseases of elephants.

mero somnoque sopitum] compare 10 § 18, Virgil Aen II 265 *invadunt urbem somno vinoque sepultam.*

noctium deos] Mützell refers this to Indra, the god of the atmosphere. But surely this would require *noctis* or *noctem regentes.* Rather I fear is the sense suggested by the context to be supported by such passages as Cic ad Atticum I 16 § 5.

§ 31. *sapientiae*] 'philosophy' as often. Compare VII 8 §§ 9, 10 *Scythis autem non ut ceteris barbaris rudis et inconditus sensus est: quidam eorum sapientiam quoque capere dicuntur, quantamcumque gens capit semper armata,* Tacitus Agr 4, Cic de off II § 5 with Holden's note, Horace carm I 34. To determine precisely and correctly whether Curtius is in this place thinking of any particular class or classes of Indian sages, and if so to what class or classes he refers, is quite impossible; so faint are the outlines preserved to us in his sketch. Moreover it is not possible to point out with certainty even the parts of the Greek accounts preserved by Strabo and other writers which are to be taken as corresponding to the traces remaining in the meagre sentences of Curtius. It will be best to begin by giving the general references needed to guide the reader to the fragments we possess of the ancient writers on the subject and other useful matter. See Strabo XV I §§ 39, 45, 49, 58—71, Arrian VI 7 § 4, 16 § 5, 17 § 2, and Indica 11 §§ 1—8, Diodorus II 40, Plutarch Alex 59, 64, 65, 69, Pomponius Mela III 7, Aelian var hist II 41, IV 20, Elphinstone appendix III pp 258—261, and bk I cc 1, 4, Prof M Williams' *Hinduism* c 5. It may also be remarked that there were two main openings for error, which may have misled the Greek observers. First, they may have mistaken (and probably did so) the Brahmans at different points of their ordained life for different schools or sects. Second, they may have confounded Brahmans in their ascetic periods with either the Buddhist ascetics or the monastic orders.

unum...genus est] 'there is one rude uncouth class called "wise men" (philosophers)'. Perhaps *agreste* should be rendered strictly 'living in the fields'. In Strabo XV 1 § 59 we find an account of Βραχμᾶνες (Brahmans) living in a grove near their city, who directed most of their austere training to the attaining a readiness for death (πρὸς τὸ ἑτοιμοθάνατον). In § 60 the Γαρμᾶνες (Sramana, Elphinstone p 260) called ὑλόβιοι are described as ζῶντας ἐν ταῖς ὕλαις ἀπὸ φύλλων καὶ καρπῶν ἀγρίων etc (see Arrian Indica 11 §§ 7, 8). In § 63 we have the description of the visit of Onesikritus to the ascetics. In § 70 we are told of a rival school to the Brahmans, called Πράμναι (see index to Williams' *Hinduism* under Pramā, Pramānas, *Prameya*) who seem to have been a logical and metaphysical school. The following words seem to refer to the Brahmans: τούτων δὲ τοὺς μὲν ὀρεινοὺς καλεῖσθαι τοὺς δὲ γυμνήτας τοὺς δὲ πολιτικοὺς καὶ προσχωρίους· τοὺς μὲν ὀρεινοὺς δοραῖς ἐλάφων χρῆσθαι, πήρας δ' ἔχειν ῥιζῶν καὶ φαρμάκων μεστάς, προσποιουμένους ἰατρικὴν μετὰ γοητείας καὶ ἐπῳδῶν καὶ περιάπτων. τοὺς δὲ γυμνήτας κατὰ τοὔνομα γυμνοὺς διαζῆν, ὑπαιθρίους τὸ πλέον, καρτερίαν ἀσκοῦντας ἣν ἔφαμεν πρότερον μέχρι ἑπτὰ ἐτῶν καὶ τριάκοντα.... § 71 goes on τοὺς δὲ πολιτικοὺς σινδονίτας κατὰ πόλιν ζῆν ἢ καὶ κατ' ἀγροὺς, καθημμένους νεβρίδας ἢ δορκάδων δοράς.

quod...vocant] the more common construction is the attraction of the pronoun (*quos...vocant*). See however IX 8 §§ 8, 26, Madvig § 316.

§ 32. *occupare*] to seize in time, hence 'anticipate'. Compare IV 4 § 12 *alii supplices in templa confugiunt, alii foribus aedium obseratis occupant liberum mortis arbitrium*, V 6 § 7 *multi ergo hostium manus voluntaria morte occupaverunt*, Virgil Aen VI 424 *occupat Aeneas aditum*. See below on 14 § 19, IX 1 § 32, 6 § 19, 7 § 22.

fati diem] the hour of destiny. See IX 6 § 26, and compare Virgil Aen X 467 *stat sua cuique dies*. For the matter see Strabo § 65 of the Brahmans αἴσχιστον δ' αὐτοῖς νομίζεσθαι νόσον σωματικήν· τὸν δ' ὑπονοήσαντα καθ' αὑτοῦ τοῦτο ἐξάγειν ἑαυτὸν διὰ πυρὸς νήσαντα πυράν, ὑπαλειψάμενον δὲ καὶ καθίσαντα ἐπὶ τὴν πυρὰν ὑφάψαι κελεύειν, ἀκίνητον δὲ καίεσθαι, and § 68 of the suicide of Calanus at Pasargadae.

pro dedecore vitae] 'as a disgrace to their life'. *vitae* is an objective genitive.

redditur] 'is paid' or given as due. Compare 11 § 25, and *recipit* here below.

inquinari] the notion that the burning of a dead body defiled the fire points to the fire having been looked upon as a sacred element. But Elphinstone bk III c 11 p 206 says 'The Hindus in general burn their dead'. And there is no trace of the feeling described by Curtius in the following passage out of a hymn to Agni (*ignis*, the fire-god in 3 forms, fire lightning and sun) in the Rig-veda, taken from Williams' *Hinduism* c 2. 'Deliver, mighty lord, thy worshippers; purge us from taint of sin and when we die deal mercifully with us on the pyre, burning our bodies with their load of guilt, but bearing our eternal part on high to luminous abodes and realms of bliss for ever there to dwell with righteous men'. Bohlen (*Indien* I p 147), quoted by Mützell, restricts the scruple to the worshippers of Siva.

§ 33. *qui...degunt*] see the quotation from Strabo §§ 70, 71 given on § 31 above. Also § 59, apparently referring to the Brahmans in their second period, that of marriage, after the probationary period; ἔτη δ' ἑπτὰ καὶ τριάκοντα οὕτως ζήσαντα ἀναχωρεῖν εἰς τὴν ἑαυτοῦ κτῆσιν ἕκαστον καὶ ζῆν ἀδεῶς καὶ ἀνειμένως μᾶλλον, σινδονοφοροῦντα καὶ χρυσοφοροῦντα μετρίως ἐν τοῖς ὠσὶ καὶ ταῖς χερσὶ...etc.

publicis moribus] like civilized people. The notion conveyed is the same as that in Strabo's word πολιτικούς.

degunt] live. Compare IX 3 § 8, Horace carm III 29 42. *ago* is also used thus by itself (as though with an ellipse of *vitam*).

siderum motus] Strabo § 70 τοὺς δὲ Βραχμᾶνας φυσιολογίαν καὶ ἀστρονομίαν ἀσκεῖν. Elphinstone bk III c 1.

futura praedicere] Arrian Indica 11 § 4 εἰσὶ δὲ καὶ μαντικῆς οὗτοι μοῦνοι Ἰνδῶν δαήμονες, οὐδὲ ἐφεῖται ἄλλῳ μαντεύεσθαι ὅτι μὴ σοφῷ ἀνδρί. In §§ 5, 6 he goes on to say what Strabo §§ 39, 65 and Diodorus II 40 also relate (no doubt following Megasthenes), that their prophecies concerned chiefly the weather, the crops and other farming matters, and affairs of state. If a Brahman made three false prophecies, he was condemned to strict silence for the rest of his life.

admovere] that is *sibi*.

credunt] the Greek writers on India seem to have come across two different views on the subject of suicide. The common one has been set forth in the note on § 32. Strabo § 68 will supply the other; Μεγασθένης δ' ἐν τοῖς μὲν φιλοσόφοις οὐκ εἶναι δόγμα φησὶν ἑαυτοὺς ἐξάγειν· τοὺς δὲ ποιοῦντας τοῦτο νεανικοὺς κρίνεσθαι. Curtius seems to have treated the two different views as if they were contrary ones, to have heightened the contrast between them by rhetorical touches, and then to have assigned them severally to the two schools of philosophers whom he, following some of the Greeks, has made of the Brahmans in two separate stages of their career. Here we may quote Strabo § 59 (after Megasthenes) πλείστους δ' αὐτοῖς εἶναι λόγους περὶ τοῦ θανάτου· νομίζειν γὰρ δὴ τὸν μὲν ἐνθάδε βίον ὡς ἂν ἀκμὴν κυομένων εἶναι, τὸν δὲ θάνατον γένεσιν εἰς τὸν ὄντως βίον καὶ τὸν εὐδαίμονα τοῖς φιλοσοφήσασι· διὸ τῇ ἀσκήσει πλείστῃ χρῆσθαι πρὸς τὸ ἑτοιμοθάνατον.

interrito] this attracted construction is the common one. See Madvig § 393 c.

§ 34. *colere*] it is most difficult to determine the precise meaning of this word. Perhaps it should not be taken as more than 'cultivate' 'honour' 'value', though the use of the word in the present passage may have been suggested by the sense 'worship'. Compare Horace carm II 14 22 *harum quas colis arborum*, Lucan I 136—143 ending *sola tamen colitur*. See also Curtius IV 7 § 23 *id quod pro deo colitur non eandem effigiem habet quam vulgo diis artifices accommodaverunt: umbilico maxime similis est habitus.*

arbores] that there was among many nations a worship either of trees or of unseen divinities dwelling in or among trees, is well known. See Tacitus Germ 9, 39, 43. Col Sleeman in his 'Rambles and recollections of an Indian official', vol II cc 12, 13, has a description of the extraordinary care bestowed on trees in some parts of India, which reads as if it might be taken to imply a tree-worship. It is known that the Hindus have sacred trees, such as the Pipal.

capital est] for this separate form compare VIII 4 § 17 *illis enim in sella regis consedisse capital foret.* It occurs also in a statute-form in Cic de legibus II § 21. Curtius seems to have taken a fancy to it as archaic.

§ 35. *menses*] Bohlen quoted by Mützell observes that the Indian months are divided into halves of 15 days each. The name for such a half is *paksha;* these as Pratt says commence with the new and full moon respectively and are named accordingly. The year is solar.

§ 36. *non ut plerique*] Curtius evidently means that their 15 day months are reckoned from half-moon, not from new to full and full to new. But what authority he had for this assertion is not so clear.

et idcirco] the argument is most obscure. What difference to the length of the months would the difference of starting-point make?

qui dirigunt] this must surely mean 'those who measure out', being probably a translation of some Greek clause beginning with ὅσοι. One would rather have expected *dirigant*, as the relative proposition expressing the reason of the leading proposition (see Madvig § 366) would be more appropriate here.

§ 37. *haud sane*] 'not at all'. Compare 14 §§ 3, 46, V 3 § 4 *Madates erat regionis praefectus, haud sane temporum homo,* Cic de off II § 5 *cuius studium qui vituperat haud sane intellego quidnam sit quod laudandum putet.*

operae] 'convenient'. For this see Roby's grammar vol II preface p xlix and § 1283. He determines it to be a predicative dative (like *curae odio oneri* etc), rendering it 'matter for attention', and so *mihi non est operae* 'I have not time'. Compare Livy I 24 *multisque id verbis, quae longo effata carmine non operae est referre, peragit.*

CHAPTER X.

§ 1. *igitur*] this conjunction, commonly expressing a reasonable inference (Kennedy § 81), is sometimes used as a simple connecting particle 'so then' in resuming the narrative after a digression. Compare Tacitus Agr 13 *igitur primus omnium......*, where *igitur* points back to the end of chapter 9. Here Curtius refers us to 9 § 1 above. See on 12 § 15 below, and IX 5 § 28.

fines Indiae] Curtius must have followed authorities who reckoned in India some part of the land to the West of the Indus, though that river was held to be the boundary of India proper. Arrian does the same.

facturi] Curtius is much given to the use of the future participle when he wants to express willingness or purpose. Compare §§ 2, 33.

Iove genitum] this expression, like many others in Curtius, has a poetic ring. Compare IX 8 § 22 *Philippo genitum*, Virgil Aen IX 642 *dis genite et geniture deos.* For the construction see Madvig § 269.

ipsos]=*se.* Curtius writes thus often. Compare § 9, 11 § 21, 12 § 17, 13 §§ 20, 24, IX 1 §§ 8, 20, 3 § 11, 4 § 25, 5 §§ 1, 25, 9 §§ 3, 6, 21, 10 §§ 14, 19. See Seneca in appendix A § 6.

fama cognitos] see the beginning of Arrian's Indica generally, in particular 5 § 8 *καὶ πρὸ Ἀλεξάνδρου Διονύσου μὲν πέρι πολλὸς λόγος κατέχει, ὡς καὶ τούτου στρατευσαντος ἐς Ἰνδοὺς καὶ καταστρεψαμένου Ἰνδούς· Ἡρακλέος δὲ πέρι οὐ πολλός.* See Thirlwall c 53 (vol VII p 12).

§ 2. *ceterum*]=*sed.* This is too common in Curtius to need illustration.

amplius nemo] no one more='no others'. He means none of the important *reges*, as opposed to *reguli* the chiefs of small tribes.

parte] a considerable part. Compare Livy I 10 *Caeninenses Crustuminique et Antemnates erant ad quos eius iniuriae pars pertinebat.* Or perhaps *pars* may here as sometimes (see Lucretius I 617, II 200) mean 'half', since Arrian's words IV 22 § 7 are *διελὼν τὴν στρατιάν.*

ad subigendos qui] *qui*=*eos qui.* See on § 10.

§ 3. *iunxere*] 'put together'. Mützell compares VII 8 § 8 *tanta alacritate militum rates iunctae sunt, ut intra triduum ad* XII *milia effectae sint.*

solutae vehi]=*solvi et vehi.* The more important notion is expressed by the participle. The construction is adopted from the Greek.

§ 4. *phalange*] for this famous formation of the best Macedonian infantry and its subdivisions armament etc see Thirlwall c 48 (vol VI p 147).

§ 5. *praecipit*] Arrian IV 23 § 5 does not attribute the massacre to the orders of Alexander, but to the anger of the soldiers at the wounding of their king.

ne] compare VII 1 § 38 *praecepisti igitur mihi ne quem praeter te intuerer.* See Madvig § 456.

parceretur] verbs which govern a dative in the active are generally used impersonally in the passive. See Kennedy § 135 g.

§ 6. *obequitat*] for the dative following verbs compounded with prepositions which themselves govern an accusative see Madvig § 224.

§ 7. *Nysam*] the position of this place is very uncertain. The best authority on the subject is General Cunningham. For the name of the place and mount Meru or Μηρὸς, both probably corruptions of Hindu names to flatter Alexander's vanity, see Strabo XV 1 §§ 7, 8, Arrian V 1 § 6, Indica 5 § 9, Diodorus II 38, Pomponius Mela III 7, Pliny N H VI § 79, and the remarks of Thirlwall c 53 (vol VII pp 11—13).

frigus] it is to be remembered that this was in February or March 326 B C and we know from the reports of our countrymen in those parts that it is quite possible to feel cold in the Panjab. Moreover the place called Nysa was probably in a river valley some thousands of feet above the sea level.

ignis] genitive of more specific definition. We should render in English by an apposition. See Madvig § 286. Compare 14 § 41.

oblatum] compare IX 1 § 12.

§ 8. *igni*] if the true reading be not *lignis* (which the strangeness of the expression leads us to suspect) we must suppose that the notion in Curtius' mind was simply 'the more fire the more flame'. Mützell reads *igni alito.*

alita] this form is certainly found in post-Augustan writers. Whether it should be admitted earlier is sometimes matter of dispute as in Cicero pro Plancio § 81.

cedro] this wood was well known for its power of resisting decay and was consequently employed in cases where a durable material was required see Pliny N H XVI §§ 212—213. It was a resinous wood which would catch easily and burn fiercely.

§ 9. *ipsos*] see on § 1.

§ 10. *hostium*] genitive after *telis*.

qui]=*ii qui*. So frequently in Curtius, but the present instance is a somewhat remarkable one. Compare § 2 *qui aversarentur*, 12 §§ 2, 16, IX 7 § 9, 9 §§ 11, 13.

aliis......aliis] the townspeople are of course meant.

abstineri] this is used impersonally though *circumsideri* has *eos* for its subject. See on 11 § 2.

§ 11. *conditos se*] that is their town. Compare VI 2 § 14 *Scythae qui Parthos condidere* 'who founded the Parthian empire'.

et] see below on IX 8 § 21.

§ 12. *inde*] from that circumstance.

mentiendi] compare Strabo XV 1 § 9 ὅτι δ' ἐστὶ πλάσματα ταῦτα τῶν κολακευόντων Ἀλέξανδρον etc. See Mayor on Juv X 174.

§ 13. *situ*] see on 9 § 20.

hedera] this is generally attested. See Arrian V 1 § 6, 2 §§ 6, 7, Theophrast hist plant IV 4 § 1, Diodorus I 19. The ivy is said to have been found by them in no other part of India.

§ 14. *pomorum*] 'fruits' generally. 'There are various kinds of wholesome juicy fruits'.

fruges] the 'crop' or 'fruits' from chance seeds. Arrian V 2 § 4 speaks of ἄλση παντοῖα, Strabo XV 1 § 13 πυροὶ κριθαὶ ὄσπρια καὶ ἄλλοι κάρποι ἐδώδιμοι, ὧν ἡμεῖς ἄπειροι.

lauri] Arrian V 2 § 5, Strabo XV 1 § 58 speak of δάφνη.

baccaris] See Pliny N H XXI §§ 29, 30, Conington on Virgil ecl IV 19, VII 27.

agrestis] 'wild'. Compare IX 1 § 13.

§ 15. *lascivia*] Arrian V 2 § 6 καὶ τοὺς Μακεδόνας ἡδέως τὸν κισσὸν ἰδόντας, οἷα δὴ διὰ μακροῦ ὀφθέντα (οὐ γὰρ εἶναι ἐν τῇ Ἰνδῶν χώρᾳ κισσὸν οὐδ' ἵναπερ αὐτοῖς ἄμπελοι ἦσαν) στεφάνους σπουδῇ ἀπ' αὐτοῦ ποιήσασθαι καὶ στεφανώσασθαι ὡς εἶχον ἐφυμνοῦντας τὸν Διόνυσόν τε καὶ τὰς ἐπωνυμίας τοῦ θεοῦ ἀνακαλοῦντας.

redimiti fronde] has a poetical ring.

§ 17. *per herbas*] 'all over the greensward' Poetical again. Compare Virgil Aen V 102 *fusi per herbam*.

omnibus] all sorts of provision. For the sense compare Virgil Aen V 61, 62.

operatum] in present signification = busied. See Madvig § 146. The word is commonly used of sacrificial observances.

habuit] 'kept'. For the sense of this passage generally Mützell well compares Tibullus II 5 95, 96 *tunc operata deo pubes discumbet in herba, arboris antiquae qua levis umbra cadit*.

§ 18. *eximiam quoque gloriam*] 'even distinguished glory'. For this *quoque* = the Greek emphatic καὶ compare 12 § 4, 13 § 15, IX 2 § 33, 3 § 8, 6 § 4, 9 § 12, 10 § 9.

sopitos mero] see on 9 § 30.

felicitas] the good fortune of Alexander has become proverbial. See III 4 § 11, 6 § 18, VII 7 § 30, 8 § 24, VIII 13 § 13, IX 9 § 2, X 5 § 35, Arrian VII 29 § 1, Indica 20 § 11, Aelian var hist III 23. Plutarch wrote two declamations περὶ τῆς Ἀλεξάνδρου τύχης ἢ ἀρετῆς, in the second of which he maintained that his hero grew great not through fortune but in fortune's spite.

inter ora] Mützell well compares Virgil Aen II 681 *manus inter maestorumque ora parentum*.

§ 19. *Daedala*] only once mentioned by one other writer, Justin XII 7, where we find *Daedali montes*. Müller in Smith's Atlas of Ancient Geography thinks that the place Ἄνδακα or Ἄνδηλα in Arrian IV 23 § 5 is the same, and that we should there emend Δαίδαλα.

Acadira] this name is found only in Curtius. Müller prefers to read *Candira*, and thinks that the name is connected with that of the Khond mountain. Schneider (quoted by Zumpt) takes the name to stand for the same place as the Ἀριγαῖον mentioned by Arrian IV 24 § 6.

usta] Acidalius conjectured *vasta* as no burning had been spoken of in the former case. But Zumpt now observes that Arrian in the place just referred to says καὶ ταύτην καταλαμβάνει ἐμπεπρησμένην ὑπὸ τῶν ἐνοικούντων καὶ τοὺς ἀνθρώπους πεφευγότας.

§ 20. *rationem*] principle, plan.

oppressi] that is *incolae*. But the text is probably corrupt here. For the word *oppressi* = 'surprised' compare VI 8 § 21 *illum sive securitate animi sive fatigatione resolutum somnus oppresserat: quem Atharrias torpentem adhuc occupat*, and IX 5 § 2 below.

omni] 'of every kind' Compare IV 1 § 10 *coloniasque Graecorum*

Ionias omni clade vastavit, III 11 § 20 *sed iam illa quoque victor intraverat omni quidem opulentia ditia.*

§ 22. *Choaspe*] probably the same river is meant as that called Χόης in Arrian IV 23 § 2. Whatever the river may be, it seems to have been an affluent of the Cabul river (Κωφὴν) in Arrian IV 22 § 5, V 1 § 1.

in obsidione] compare VI 6 § 25 *in quorum obsidione Cratero relicto*... etc.

Beirani] supposed to be the same place as that which Arrian calls Βάζιρα (IV 27 § 5, 28 § 1), which General Cunningham finds at a place now called Bazar.

Mazagas] Curtius seems to treat this as the name of a tribe. But Arrian IV 26 § 1 calls the town Μάσσαγα and the people (IV 25 § 5) Ἀσσακηνοί. St Martin, quoted by M'Crindle p 152, identifies them with the Afghans. Strabo XV 1 § 27 says *εἶθ' ἡ Ἀσσακανοῦ (χώρα), ὅπου Μάσογα πόλις, τὸ βασίλειον τῆς χώρας.* The names seem to be all connected, and the forms in which they appear in various texts are by no means certain. General Cunningham places the town somewhere by Nanglora. For *ad Mazagas* see on IX 4 § 23.

mater] a mistake for wife, according to Cunningham p 66.

§ 23. The following description of the place is the only one that has reached us.

opere] 'work', that is, 'art'. Compare § 24 *operis*, and III 1 § 7 *turrem et situ et opere multum editam.*

spectat] see on 9 § 2.

§ 24. *a meridie*] see on 9 § 5.

voragines] pits, sloughs. Compare 11 § 7, 14 §§ 4, 8, Catullus XVII 26.

iacent] lie spread, extend. Compare IV 7 § 6 *terra caeloque aquarum penuria est, steriles arenae iacent.*

operis] genitive of quality. Compare IV 6 § 7 *muros ingentis operis.*

obiecta est] has been thrown in the way. Curtius has a remarkable way of using a genitive of quality with a verb so as to form part of the predicate. So IX 3 § 22 *firmatae gratiae reliquit* 'he left them with friendship assured', 7 § 16 *saginati corporis sequi* 'was following in his train with a full-fed body'. Here the sense is 'has been put as a defence with great labour'.

§ 25. *stadium*] the regular genitive plural of this word. Here it is a correction of Zumpt's for MSS *stadia*, which we have accepted because (*a*) *urbem* has far better authority than *urbis* and (*b*) *complectitur* is thus used in a more appropriate sense.

saxo] compare the *κρηπὶς λιθίνη* of Xenophon anab III 4 § 7.

crudo latere] unburnt sun-dried bricks. Arrian Indica 10 §§ 2—4 says that the Indian cities on the banks of rivers are built of wood, 'for when constructed of brick they will not last any length of time, by reason of the rains and the rivers overflowing their banks and deluging the plains around them. But those built in commanding and elevated positions are all constructed of bricks and clay' (ἐκ πλίνθου τε καὶ πηλοῦ). This πλίνθος seems to be of the same kind, a sort of 'adobe'.

ut] =*ita ut* as often.

terra humore diluta] =the πηλὸς mentioned by Arrian.

§ 26. *universa*] 'all at once', referring to *materia* both *durior* and *fragilis*.

consideret] settle down, sink. Compare Virgil Aen II 624, IX 145.

impositae etc] 'strong beams had been placed upon it, and on them floors had been laid covering the walls and affording a passage along them'. How this arrangement was to prevent the upper part of the wall from settling down is a mystery as the text stands: and we can only suppose that (*a*) Curtius has not understood his authorities, or (*b*) has left out some important steps in the description, or (*c*) that the text is mutilated so as to conceal his real meaning.

§ 27. *consilii incertum*] here we have the so-called genitive of respect. See Kennedy § 173 D, and compare below 11 § 3, 13 § 17, IX 3 § 18.

aggere] with a bank or mole, as he had done on a grander scale at the siege of Tyre.

aliter] 'otherwise' than by filling up the hollows in the manner just spoken of. Compare 11 § 7.

percussit] Arrian IV 26 § 4 says τοξεύεται μὲν ἀπὸ τοῦ τείχους ἐς τὸ σφυρὸν οὐ χαλεπῶς.

§ 28. *tum forte*] we have kept the old reading here in preference to the conjecture of Jeep adopted by Hedicke. Zumpt explains the *tum* here by referring to the frequent wounds received by Alexander in different parts of his body.

suram] Curtius' account slightly differs from that of Arrian.

iussit] we see that he had previously been on foot, which is also implied by Arrian, who says προσῆγε τῷ τείχει τὴν φάλαγγα.

obligato] 'without even bandaging his wound'. The *ob* implies the putting of a bandage over the place. Compare *obducere* in § 31 and 13 § 25.

destinata] what he had made up his mind to do, 'his plans'. Compare IX 7 § 18 and above 9 § 23.

§ 29. *frigescens vulnus*] 'the gradual cooling of the wound'.

Iovis filium] the son of Ammon, who had greeted him as such when he visited his oracle in the desert, at least so Alexander allowed his flatterers to declare. See Plutarch Alex 27, 28, who says that Alexander was not vain enough to believe in this fiction himself, but countenanced it as a means of impressing the minds of the Orientals. He adds that when shot with an arrow (perhaps on this occasion) he turned in his pain to his friends and said τοῦτο μέν, ὦ φίλοι, τὸ ῥέον αἷμα καὶ οὐκ ἰχώρ οἷός πέρ τε ῥέει μακάρεσσι θεοῖσιν, a quotation from Iliad V 340.

aegri] 'weak', the set epithet of *mortales* in Virgil and Lucretius, a rendering of the Homeric δειλοῖσι βροτοῖσι, meant to contrast man's weakness with divine strength. See Conington on Virgil georg I 237.

vitia] the physical flaws or defects from which the divine nature is presumed to be free.

§ 30. *ante quam perspexit*] *antequam* and other like particles are put with the perfect, not with the pluperfect, of the indicative mood. See Madvig § 338 *b* obs 5.

moliebantur] we have kept the old reading, which the MSS support. For *moliri*=to destroy, 'pull down' compare VII 5 § 33 *tandem, ut deicerent, fundamenta murorum ab imo moliuntur, ne quod urbis vestigium extaret,* Tacitus ann I 39, hist II 22, Livy IX 3, XXV 36. For the matter see IV 2 § 18 of the mole made at the siege of Tyre *magna vis saxorum ad manum erat Tyro vetere praebente: materies ex Libano monte ratibus et turribus faciendis advehebatur.* See on IX 5 § 19.

faciendo aggeri] for the construction see Madvig § 415.

cum ramis] 'boughs and all'. See 11 § 8.

moles saxorum] 'masses of rocks' that is, 'great solid boulders'. Compare *corporum moles* in 13 § 10, IX 2 § 21.

§ 31. *fastigium*] the highest point, top of a slope. Compare Cic de off III § 33 *sed quoniam operi inchoato prope tamen absoluto tamquam fastigium imponimus* and Holden's note, also Mayor on Cic philippic II § 110.

machinas] Arrian IV 26 § 5.

§ 32. *rudes talium operum*] 'unskilled in such works'. Compare IX 8 § 14. See Elphinstone (abstract of Menu in bk I c 2 p 26) 'In another place 100 bowmen in a fort are said to be a match for 10,000 enemies; so far was the art of attack behind that of defence: a siege therefore is out of the question'.

terrebant] according to Arrian the besieged were not terrified by the works, but lost heart when their leader was killed by a bolt (βέλει ἀπὸ μηχανῆς). This may explain the conduct of the *regina* mentioned by Curtius.

adiutas] the MSS give *auditas*, some having also the marginal correction *adiutas*, which Vogel adopts; rightly, it seems.

negabant...mortalibus] this is quite in Curtius' rhetorical manner, and need not be treated as bearing any direct relation to fact.

§ 33. *inde*] *ab arce.*

patebat] we have accepted this conjecture of Eberhard, as *placebat* (the old reading) seems capable of no satisfactory explanation. In § 10 above it suits well enough. For *patebat* compare 11 § 7.

§ 34. *pateris*] compare Virgil georg II 192 *qualem pateris libamus et auro.*

§ 35. *quippe......est*] 'in fact he addressed her as "queen".' *appellata est* implies *ab Alexandro* in the same way as *inpetravit* above does.

§ 36. *certe*] at all events. *quoque*, though confidently rejected by Vogel, seems to have a meaning: 'the boy also' (as well as the conqueror his supposed father) bore the name Alexander.

ex ea utcumque] 'who anyhow was *her* son', and probably Alexander's also. A piece of gossip such as Curtius loves to preserve.

Alexandro] the attraction of the name to the case of the relative is the common construction. See Madvig § 246 obs 2, Kennedy § 141 (8), and compare Virgil georg III 147, Aen I 267. So here with the substantive *puero*.

CHAPTER XI.

§ 1. *Noram*] this name is thought to stand for the same place as that called by Arrian IV 27 §§ 7—9 τὰ Ὦρα. But it is to be noted that the attacking force is there commanded by Alexander himself.

inconditos] 'undisciplined'. Compare IX 1 § 16, 2 § 22.

secutus] Arrian IV 27 § 9 εὐθὺς ἐξ ἐφόδου προσβαλὼν τοῖς τείχεσι τῆς πόλεως ἐκράτησε.

§ 2. *quorum*...etc] Arrian IV 28 § 1 ὡς δὲ καὶ οἱ ἄλλοι βάρβαροι ἔπραττον· ἀπολιπόντες τὰς πόλεις ξύμπαντες ἔφευγον ἐς τὴν πέτραν τὴν ἐν τῇ χώρᾳ τὴν Ἄορνον καλουμένην. This stronghold is placed by General Cunningham at the hill where is now the ruined fortress of Ranigat.

petram] this word borrowed from the Greek is used by Curtius not only often in this book but in other parts of his history, where it is as hard as here to see why he did not use *rupes*. Pliny also uses the word. A glance at Lucan VI 16 will shew how the word *petra* came to mean 'stronghold', and then became in various places a proper name. Perhaps this may give the real reason for Curtius' preference of the word; we might even render 'stronghold'. See Thirlwall c 52 (vol VI p 300).

Aornim] the attack on this place is one of the most celebrated of Alexander's military operations. See Strabo XV 1 § 8 Ἄορνον δέ τινα πέτραν, ἧς τὰς ῥίζας ὁ Ἰνδὸς ὑπορρεῖ πλησίον τῶν πηγῶν, Ἀλεξάνδρου κατὰ μίαν προσβολὴν ἑλόντος, σεμνύνοντες ἔφασαν τὸν Ἡρακλέα τρὶς μὲν προσβαλεῖν τῇ πέτρᾳ ταύτῃ τρὶς δ' ἀποκρουσθῆναι. See too Arrian IV 28 §§ 1, 2, who says just the same as Curtius, save that he makes no mention of an earthquake. Diodorus however does, see XVII 85.

occupaverunt]=seized in time, before Alexander could catch them. See on 9 § 32.

coactum] that is *eum*. The change of subject is remarkable for its abruptness. See 10 § 10, Livy I 50 § 9, II 28 § 5.

§ 3. *inopem consilii*] see on 10 § 27.

si pretium operae esset] 'if there were reward for his labour'='if it were made worth his while'. Diodorus XVII 85 does not mention this stipulation in telling the story, and also does not name the amount of reward, which Curtius here fixes at an incredibly high figure.

§ 4. *constituit*] appointed, agreed. Compare 9 § 19.

§ 5. *circuitu*] by going round, making a detour. Compare IX 3 § 14.

fallerent] Madvig conjectures *falleret*.

§ 6. *crescit*] compare IV 2 § 19 *iamque a fundo maris in altitudinem modicam opus creverat, nondum tamen aquae fastigium aequabat*, and see Conington on Virgil georg IV 122.

sed etc] see Arrian IV 28 § 3, Diodorus XVII 85 who says 'now the rock was 100 stadia in circuit and 16 in height and presented a smooth surface completely circular. On its southern side it was washed by the Indus, the largest river in India, while the other sides were bounded by deep ravines and inaccessible crags'.

metae etc] compare Livy XXXVII 27 *ipse collis est in modum metae in acutum cacumen a fundo satis lato fastigatus*.

erecta est] lifts itself up, rises up straight. Compare IX 1 § 10.

in artius] Compare VII 3 § 9 *ceterum structura latior ab imo paulatim incremento operis in artius cogitur, ad ultimum in carinae maxime modum coit*, and below VIII 13 § 9. 'Come together into a narrower space'='taper off'.

§ 7. *eluvies*] this word is used by Curtius here and in V 4 § 26, VI 4 § 20 to denote a gully formed by the erosive action of a stream. It is therefore the exact equivalent of χαράδρα.

§ 8. *ad manum*] compare IX 3 § 14.

truncam arborem] compare VI 9 § 28 *velut truncum corpus, dempto capite, sine spiritu sine nomine, aliena terra ludibrium hostis futuros*, Virgil Aen III 659.

index] this word properly means a witness who is himself an accomplice, like 'King's evidence'. Here we may say 'betraying their eagerness'. Compare IX 2 § 30, 6 § 17 where *indicium*='demonstration' or 'way of shewing'.

§ 9. *septimum* etc] Diodorus XVII 85 ἔπειτα τῇ πολυχειρίᾳ χώσας τὴν φάραγγα καὶ τὴν ῥίζαν τῆς πέτρας, προσελθὼν ἐνεργῆ πολιορκίαν συνεστήσατο, συνεχῶς ἐφ' ἡμέρας ἑπτὰ καὶ τὰς ἴσας νύκτας ἐκ διαδοχῆς τὰς προσβολὰς ποιούμενος.

Agrianos] these light troops, raised among the Thracian hill tribe of that name, were often employed by Alexander on such services as the present, where agility would be required. See 14 § 24, IX 8 § 18. Arrian IV 28 § 8 also mentions them on this occasion.

per ardua niti] 'to struggle up the steep'. Compare VII 11 § 16 *per aspera nisis duriora restabant, et crescere altitudo petrae videbatur*, Horace carm II 19 21.

iuvenes promptissimos] compare 13 § 14, and below § 17.

ex sua cohorte] that is, from the *regia cohors* of pages or gentlemen in immediate attendance on the king. Curtius VIII 6 § 6 says of this body *haec cohors velut seminarium ducum praefectorumque apud Macedonas fuit: hinc habuere posteri reges, quorum stirpibus post multas aetates Romani opes ademerunt*. See Thirlwall cc 48, 52 (vol VI pp 149, 315).

§ 10. *Alexander*] Plutarch Alex 58 apparently speaking of this same affair says ἑτέρᾳ δὲ ὁμοίως ἀποτόμῳ (πέτρᾳ) προσβαλὼν τοὺς νεωτέρους τῶν Μακεδόνων παρώρμα, καὶ 'Αλέξανδρόν τινα καλούμενον προσαγορεύσας "ἀλλὰ σοί γε" εἶπεν "ἀνδραγαθεῖν προσήκει καὶ διὰ τὴν ἐπωνυμίαν" ἐπεὶ δὲ λαμπρῶς ὁ νεανίας ἀγωνιζόμενος ἔπεσεν, οὐ μετρίως ἐδήχθη.

non placuit] perhaps this may refer to some resolution of a council of war or of a general assembly of the Macedonian troops. In VIII 1 § 18 we are told that after Alexander had exposed himself to great peril in the great hunt in Sogdiana the Macedonians *quamquam prospero eventu defunctus erat Alexander, tamen scivere gentis suae more ne aut pedes venaretur aut sine delectis principum atque amicorum.* See Thirlwall c 52 (vol VI pp 304, 305).

§ 11. *vir audaciae promptae*] see a like passage IX 6 § 10.

corporis custodes] the Greek name for these was σωματοφύλακες. There seem to have been two sorts of them (1) a small picked body of distinguished officers who formed a kind of Staff attached to the king's person, and (2) a larger body of Macedonian youths of high family who formed the *regia cohors* of bodyguards and attendants. See Arrian VI 28 § 4, Curtius IX 6 § 4, 8 § 23, 10 § 26, VIII 6 §§ 21, 22, and §§ 2—6.

relictisque] *que* as often = *sed*. Compare 14 § 35.

§ 12. *miserabilis* etc] for the general sense compare VII 11 § 16 *illa vero miserabilis erat facies, quum ii quos instabilis gradus fefellerat ex praecipiti devolverentur. mox eadem in se patienda alieni casus ostendebat exemplum.*

§ 14. *superne* etc] Diodorus XVII 85 'at first then the barbarians being on higher ground had the advantage and killed many of those who came rashly up to the assault'.

§ 15. *acrius quam cautius*] 'with more spirit than judgment'. For the double comparative see Madvig § 307, Kennedy § 76 B 2.

§ 16. *incesserent*] so IX 5 § 8.

§ 18. *intrepidi*] not in a hurry, cool. The word is somewhat rare, and seems not to be used by Curtius elsewhere.

depulisse contenti] compare IV 10 § 14 *Mazaeus, qui antea per otium vicos incenderat, iam fugere contentus pleraque inviolata hosti reliquit.* See Madvig § 389 obs 3.

§ 19. *statuisset* etc] Arrian and Diodorus give no account of any such intention on the part of Alexander. The former (who is the more worthy of our confidence) says that the Indians terrified at last by the occupation of a cliff commanding their position, while the front attack was pushed on with unflagging vigour, made proposals for a surrender. This was merely a ruse in order to gain time for a retreat under cover of night. Alexander discovered their purpose, left open a way for them to escape, and fell upon them in their retreat, as described below by Curtius. See Thirlwall c 53 (vol VII p 10).

succedere] to take the place of, 'relieve'. *sub* conveys the notion of 'to the help'. Compare *subvenire, succurrere, subsidium.* So in Greek ὑπό, as in ὑπουργεῖν, ὑπηρέτης.

§ 22. *Balacro*] Mützell remarks that a Βάλακρος is mentioned once or twice by Arrian as commanding the ἀκοντισταί.

§ 23. *adesset*] 'were upon them'.

praecipitati] 'flinging themselves headlong'. Arrian says (IV 30 § 4) οἱ δὲ καὶ πεφοβημένως ἀποχωροῦντες κατὰ τῶν κρημνῶν ῥίψαντες σφᾶς ἀπέθανον.

mulcati] hurt, especially of bruises and blows with sharp objects. The word is used again VII 11 § 17 in precisely the same connexion.

§ 24. *speciem*] this word is added by Hedicke from a conjecture of Mützell. We have rather chosen to accept this than read with Zumpt *magnam victoriam*.

§ 25. *quo*] that is, *itinere*. He refers to § 5 above. For construction see note on IX 10 § 1.

cum fide] honourably. Diodorus XVIII 86 says καὶ τῷ μὲν ὁδηγήσαντι τὰς ὡμολογημένας δωρεὰς ἀπέδωκεν.

Sisocosto] Arrian IV 30 § 4 καὶ ἔθνεν ἐπ' αὐτῇ (τῇ πέτρᾳ) Ἀλέξανδρος καὶ κατεσκεύασε φρούριον, παραδοὺς Σισικόττῳ ἐπιμελεῖσθαι τῆς φρουρᾶς.

CHAPTER XII.

§ 1. *Ecbolima*] Arrian IV 28 § 7 has the form Ἐμβόλιμα. General Cunningham places it about Ohind on the upper Indus.

Erice] seems to be the same person as the one named by Diodorus XVII 86 Ἀφρίκης.

§ 2. *per funditores*] the insertion of *per* here is a fine conjecture of Foss. The MSS for the most part have nothing, but two have *fere*. It is better to read *per* than to adopt the old emendation *funditore et sagittario*. For *per* expressing agency compare § 9 below, III 2 § 1 *quippe quae per duces suos acta erant cuncta damnabat* and many other places in Curtius, Tacitus Agr 22 *nec Agricola umquam per alios gesta avidus intercepit*.

§ 3. *inpunitatem*] Diodorus XVII 86 τοῦτον δέ τινες ἀνελόντες καὶ τὴν κεφαλὴν αὐτοῦ πρὸς Ἀλέξανδρον ἐνέγκαντες διὰ ταύτης τῆς εὐεργεσίας περιεποιήσαντο τὰς ἰδίας σωτηρίας.

honorem etc] compare the more decided censure of the Amalekite in II Samuel i. vv 1—16.

§ 4. *hinc*] that is, from the pass whence he had dislodged Erix.

castris] 'day's march'. This is a common Roman expression, arising from the custom of forming a regular encampment at the end of the day. See IX 10 § 5.

repperit] Diodorus XVII 86 αὐτὸς δὲ παρελθὼν ἐπὶ τὸν Ἰνδὸν ποταμὸν καὶ καταλαβὼν τάς τε τριακοντόρους κατεσκευασμένας καὶ τὸν πόρον ἐζευγμένον.... Wherever this bridge may have been, it seems pretty certain that it was above the junction of the Cabul river with the Indus.

Omphis] Diodorus XVII 86 calls him Μῶφις. His account in general corresponds very closely to that of Curtius. The kingdom of this prince was that of which the great and wealthy city Taxila was the capital. It is strange that Curtius should make no mention of this place, which struck the Greek observers so forcibly as a city both populous and well-ordered. See Strabo XV 1 §§ 17, 28, 61, 62, Arrian V 3 § 6, 8 § 2, VII 2 § 2. See the interesting remarks of General Cunningham on this place. He shews that 50 years after Alexander's visit it was very wealthy, and that it remained great down to comparatively recent times. He finds its site near Kalaka Serai.

fuerat auctor] 'had urged'. The preceding *quoque* merely emphasizes *patri*. See on 10 § 18.

§ 6. *permissoque*] this is undoubtedly the right reading. Mützell well cites Livy VI 25 *permissoque ut ex collegis optaret quem vellet*, XXXVIII 10 *permissoque ut et Rhodii et Athenienses deprecatores irent*. See Madvig § 429.

ut regnaret] Diodorus does not mention Alexander's answer.

usurpare] compare III 12 § 16 (of Hephaestion) *libertatis quoque in admonendo eo non alius ius habebat: quod tamen ita usurpabat ut magis a rege permissum quam vindicatum ab eo videretur.*

sustinuit] did not venture or 'make up his mind' to. Compare IX 1 § 34, 10 § 15. In Greek we should probably have οὐκ ἐτόλμησε.

ullius] for this substantival use of *ullus* by the best writers see Madvig § 90, 3. Curtius uses the dative (see IX 3 § 1), which is less common.

experiretur] 'make trial of' the good faith (or protection) of any but Alexander. That is, put himself in the hands of, submit to the authority of. See §§ 9, 10. For *fidem* see IX 1 § 23, 7 §§ 13, 14.

§ 7. *per modica intervalla*] at short intervals. See 14 § 13.

agmini] this word is continually used by Curtius as the equivalent of *acies*. Compare 13 § 19 and chapter 14 *passim*. This usage is almost confined to the poets and silver-age prose authors. An excellent instance is Virgil georg II 280 which Conington's ingenious note cannot be said to have explained away.

castellorum] so Diodorus XVII 87 in the account of Porus' forces before the battle ἡ μὲν οὖν ὅλη σύνταξις αὐτῶν ὑπῆρχε πόλει παραπλήσιος τὴν πρόσοψιν· ἡ μὲν γὰρ τῶν ἐλεφάντων στάσις τοῖς πύργοις, οἱ δὲ ἀνὰ μέσον τούτων στρατιῶται τοῖς μεσοπυργίοις ὡμοίωντο. See below 14 § 13, IX 2 § 15.

§ 8. *ipse concitat equum*] Diodorus says αὐτὸς δὲ μετ' ὀλίγων προϊππεύσας.

§ 9. *vel...vel*] *vel*, probably an old imperative of *volo*, is used in stating such alternatives as the present where the distinction is not the point forcibly insisted on. Here it is especially suitable, since *sive...sive* has just been used above. We may render *vel* here 'perhaps' or 'it might be'. See Madvig § 436, and compare above III 1 § 18 (of the Gordian knot) *gladioque ruptis omnibus loris oraculi sortem vel elusit vel implevit*, below IX 5 § 27, Cic in Catil II § 1.

quod posset intellegi] 'so far as could have been gathered'. The sense is the same as if he had written *quantum potuit*. See Madvig § 364 obs. 2.

vultu] 'expression'. Connected with *volo*.

conseri] joined. That is, conversation could not be held.

eo] that man, the man wanted; namely an interpreter.

§ 10. *gloriae militantem*] 'fighting for fame'.

timere] the position of this word is strange, as *famam* cannot stand where it is by way of emphasis, *perfidiae* being the emphatic word.

§ 11. *pecora*] Mützell argues that this word probably refers to sheep especially, for in Arrian V 3 § 5 among the presents from Taxiles that awaited Alexander at the crossing of the Indus we find mention of βοῦς πρόβατα and ἐλέφαντας. See below 14 § 30, IX 2 § 16, and above VIII 4 § 19 *pecora et armenta*, IX 8 § 29.

magnitudinis] Pliny N H VII § 21 *maxima in India gignuntur animalia*.

acceptum] 'acceptable'. See Mayor on Cic philippic II §§ 32, 65, and compare IX 1 § 18 *invictum*.

§ 12. *agricultores an milites*] this question must have been suggested by the division of the Hindus into classes or castes, which was soon found out by the Greeks, and of which the γεωργοὶ and πολεμισταὶ formed two important divisions. See below IX 1 § 36, Strabo XV 1 §§ 40, 47, Arrian Indica 11 §§ 9, 10 'next to these in the second place come the farmers (γεωργοὶ) who are the most numerous class among the Indians: these have no martial weapons and take no thought for the works of war, but till the ground; and they pay their tributes to the kings or the independent states as the case may be. And in case of a war among the Indians, neither party may lay hands upon the tillers of the land or ravage the land itself: but the soldiers are warring and slaughtering one another while they (the farmers) hard by are ploughing or gathering the vintage or pruning the vines or reaping the corn undisturbed', 12 §§ 2—4. For the Greek accounts of the classes in general (which Curtius has strangely omitted to notice above), and their mistakes, see Elphinstone appendix III.

§ 13. *Abisares*] Mützell cites the remark of the famous geographer Ritter, that this prince probably ruled in the territory of Abhisara, a part of Kashmir bordering on the Panjab. See on 13 § 1. Thus here also the names of king and kingdom correspond. See the medley in note on 10 § 22 *Mazagas*, and compare *Taxiles* and *Taxila*.

eminebat] see on 9 § 21, IX 1 § 2. Perhaps we might simply render 'surpassed his rival in power'. The kingdom of Porus lay between the Hydaspes and the Acesines, Strabo XV 1 § 29, and contained some 300 cities.

§ 14. *permittente*] Diodorus XVII 86 says that Alexander gave him back his kingdom καὶ μετωνόμασεν αὐτὸν Ταξίλην.

sequente nomine] we have seen in note on § 5 that the name of the *capital was* Taxila, and have remarked on § 13 that the name Taxiles corresponds to this name. The principle of giving to the reigning prince a name indicative of his seat of government is known to have existed in India. So in IX 8 § 8 Curtius calls the people Musicani, while Arrian and Diodorus call their king Μουσικανός. See Strabo XV 1 § 36 (speaking of Παλίβοθρα = Pataliputra = Patna) *τὸν δὲ βασιλεύοντα ἐπώνυμον δεῖν τῆς πόλεως εἶναι, Παλίβοθρον καλούμενον πρὸς τῷ ἰδίῳ τῷ ἐκ γενετῆς ὀνόματι καθάπερ τὸν Σανδρόκοττον* (Chandragupta, see Williams' *Hinduism* c 1 p 4) *πρὸς ὃν ἧκεν ὁ Μεγασθένης πεμφθείς. τοιοῦτο δὲ καὶ τὸ παρὰ τοῖς Παρθυαίοις· Ἀρσάκαι γὰρ καλοῦνται πάντες, ἰδίᾳ δὲ ὁ μὲν Ὀρώδης ὁ δὲ Φραάτης ὁ δ' ἄλλο τι.* Porus is probably another name of the same kind. See appendix D. We hear of another Porus contemporary with the more famous one here mentioned, Arrian V 20 § 6, 21 §§ 2, 3, 5, Strabo XV 1 § 30, and there seems to have been one contemporary with the emperor Augustus, Strabo § 73. It is to be noted that Curtius in 13 § 5 gives this Omphis his new and official title of Taxiles. For a name passing down with an office, but with no local connexion, see *Surena* in Tacitus ann VI 42 with Orelli's note. Curtius probably misunderstood the significance of the transmission, as Diodorus seems also to have done.

§ 15. *igitur*] carries us back to the end of § 11. See on 10 § 1.

signati] stamped, that is, coined. Arrian V 3 § 5 says *ἀργυρίου τάλαντα ἐς διακόσια.*

§ 16. *Persicae vestis*] whether this *vestis* be something of the nature of tapestry, as rugs, shawls etc, or 'changes of raiment' is not easy to say. The splendour of Oriental drapery was proverbial. See Propertius III 18 19. In IX 3 § 10 it is merely a rhetorical expression for a foreign dress.

§ 17. *sicut...ita*] this is one of the Latin equivalents for the Greek *μὲν...δέ*, and should be rendered by simply putting 'while' with the former of the two verbs. Compare III 12 § 16 of Hephaestion *et sicut aetate par erat regi ita corporis habitu praestabat.*

obstrinxerat] perhaps the force of this pluperfect is 'bound him for the present'.

offendit] So Plutarch Alex 59, Strabo § 28 of the reception of Alexander at Taxila *ἔτυχόν τε πλειόνων ἢ αὐτοὶ παρέσχον, ὥστε φθονεῖν τοὺς Μακεδόνας καὶ λέγειν ὡς οὐκ εἶχεν, ὡς ἔοικεν, Ἀλέξανδρος οὓς εὐεργετήσει πρὶν ἢ διέβη τὸν Ἰνδόν.*

super cenam] for *super* of time = 'during', see Kennedy § 72, 3 a 4.

§ 18. *occidisset*] VIII 1 § 51.

invidos etc] this is a regular saying, such as the rhetoricians dearly loved. Compare Isocrates Euag § 7 (p 190) *τούτων δ' αἴτιος ὁ φθόνος, ᾧ τοῦτο μόνον ἀγαθὸν πρόσεστιν, ὅτι μέγιστον κακὸν τοῖς ἔχουσίν ἐστιν*, Menander incert 12 and Meineke *ad locum*, Seneca de ira III 30 § 3 *numquam erit felix quem torquebit felicior*, Horace epist I 2 57—59, Virgil ecl VII 26, Martial IX 97, Erasmus adagia (title *ab initio ad finem*).

CHAPTER XIII.

§ 1. *Abisarae*] Arrian V 8 § 3 ἧκον δὲ ἐνταῦθα παρ' αὐτὸν καὶ παρὰ Ἀβισάρου πρέσβεις τοῦ τῶν ὀρείων Ἰνδῶν βασιλέως.

mandatum] by Abisares.

§ 2. *stipendium*] tribute. Compare IX 1 § 14, 7 § 14, Livy II 9.

suorum finium] Mützell in a long and learned note shews that this order of the words is chosen so as to throw stress on *suorum*. Porus was not to cross his own frontier.

occurreret] the word is chosen as being neutral, taking indifferently a friendly or hostile sense, as *praesto esset* below.

regi] 'his sovereign'.

alterum] the one, or more strictly 'the second', as the explanatory clause with *ut* shews.

praesto esset] used again but in friendly sense IX 2 § 24.

§ 3. *quippe* etc] an explanatory clause, suggested by the emphatic *adversus Indos* just above.

§ 4. *regulo*] refers to the obscure Samaxus (or Gamaxus) above.

§ 5. *transitu*] the simple ablative with *prohibere* comes again X 3 § 5 *quum postero die prohibiti aditu regis essent*. In IX 3 § 5 we have the more common construction. Arrian V 8 § 4 says ἐγνωκὼς εἴργειν τοῦ πόρου αὐτὸν ἢ περῶντι ἐπιτίθεσθαι.

§ 6. *ultra eos*] beyond, that is here 'behind' them. Compare 14 § 30 and III 9 § 5 of the Persian array at Issus *Hyrcani deinde Medique equites: his proximi ceterarum gentium ultra eos dextra laevaque dispositi*.

ante] 9 § 28.

apte] readily, conveniently. Compare 14 § 19.

§ 7. *par......corporis*] Mützell compares Justin XII 8 *viribus corporis et animi magnitudine pariter insignis*.

sapientia] 'wisdom' simply here. The passage quoted on 9 § 31 will however illustrate this one well. Alexander's Greek flatterers made the most of Porus in order to enhance the glory of their patron. See 14 § 46.

§ 8. *fluminis magnitudo*] the size of the river would depend on the season of the year. Arrian V 9 § 4 says that when Alexander and Porus faced one another on the Hydaspes it was just the summer solstice. In 19 § 3 he places the battle with Porus in the Athenian month Munychion. One of these two statements must be wrong. Probably the former is, for he says in the same place that it was precisely at the time of the solstice that the rivers would be at their highest, both on account of the melting of mountain-snows and of the rains (of the S W Monsoon). Now Aristobulus in Strabo XV 1 § 17 while agreeing in the statement as to the fullness of the rivers in the summer, says that they did not experience continuous rains till the march from the Hydaspes to the

Hypanis and back again (*καὶ ἐπειδὴ καταβᾶσιν ἐπὶ τὸν Ὑδάσπην καὶ νικήσασι Πῶρον ὁδὸς ἦν ἐπὶ τὸν Ὕπανιν πρὸς ἕω κἀκεῖθεν ἐπὶ τὸν Ὑδάσπην πάλιν, ὕεσθαι συνεχῶς καὶ μάλιστα τοῖς ἐτησίαις*). It would seem then that Alexander reached the Hydaspes early in May and crossed the river and defeated Porus about the middle of that month (end of Munychion). As Mützell remarks, the accounts of modern travellers shew that the river could then be crossed; a month later it would hardly be possible. It seems then that Curtius speaks of the greatness of the river more as a rhetorician than as an historian, though the width assigned (about ½ mile) is no great distance and hardly if at all exaggerated.

diffusus] not *diffusum*, for though he has spoken of *flumen* above he is really thinking of *Hydaspes*. So in 14 § 40 we have *eo* though *belua* has gone before, for he is thinking of *elephantus*. Zumpt. The personification of the river in this passage suits well with this view.

aperiente] compare IV 9 § 21 *tandem qua leniore tractu amnis aperit vadum emersere*, Virgil Aen I 107.

§ 9. *nec*] = yet not. Compare 14 § 10.

pro spatio] pro = 'in proportion to', 'according to'. So *κατά* with accusative in Greek. Compare IX 1 § 6, 4 § 14, and for *spatium* IX 2 § 17.

stagnantium] Mützell remarks that this word (see on 9 § 7) is not appropriately used here. Compare IX 2 § 12.

torrens et elisus] 'boiling and compressed'. *elisus* = throttled, squeezed. For the use of the word in speaking of a river compare IX 2 § 17, and generally IX 2 § 21, 7 § 22. The sense is well illustrated by Pomponius Mela III 5 of the Araxes. Mützell remarks that the name of this river in Sanskrit is Vitasta (*Hydaspes*), which means 'arrow-swift'.

occulta saxa] this mention of hidden rocks in the bed of the Hydaspes has led some observers to fix the point of Alexander's passage somewhere by the village of Jhelam. But General Cunningham rather inclines to the other place of crossing at Jalalpur. Old lines of high road run to both these points. The mention of the rocks by Curtius is not in itself decisive of anything, and the *insulae* in § 12 may come out of another account and be no more than the *saxa* from another point of view.

repercussae] 'beaten back' in eddies. Compare 9 § 8 and VI 4 §§ 4, 5 (*amnis*) *qui tria fere stadia in longitudinem universus fluit, deinde saxo quod alveolum interpellat repercussus duo itinera velut dispensatis aquis aperit. inde torrens et saxorum per quae incurrit asperitate violentior terram praeceps subit.*

§ 10. *vastorum*] Mützell refers to IV 13 § 5 where Parmenio is made to attribute to the Scythians and Bactrians *eximiam vastorum magnitudinem corporum*. Compare IX 2 §§ 19, 21.

inritatae] by their drivers.

aures fatigabant] poetical, and used in a slightly different sense below in IX 10 § 16.

§ 11. *hinc......hinc*] used here of two things both on the same side of the persons considered, for both river and enemy were in the front of the Macedonian army. See on IX 4 § 10, 8 § 6.

se experta] that had proved themselves, and so knew what they could bear. The sense is well illustrated by Odyssey XX 18, Horace sat II 5 20.

inproviso] see on IX 2 § 13.

inhabiles] awkward, unhandy. See IX 9 § 13. We have accepted this conjecture of Mützell in preference to the old reading *instabiles*. The latter would have suited well with *rates* had these been rafts. But that boats or ships are meant is shewn by §§ 26, 27. Probably the boats referred to in 10 §§ 2, 3, 12 § 4 are meant. Arrian V 7 thinks that the Indus had been crossed by a bridge of boats used as pontoons. In 12 § 4 he says that the boats taken to pieces had been brought to the Hydaspes and put together.

§ 12. *insulae*] General Cunningham in his plan of the river by Jalalpur shews plenty such.

parvae......eventum] 'by the decision of small affairs were gauging the issue of the final struggle'. Compare IV 16 § 28 *magno consilio iacturam sarcinarum impedimentorumque contempsit, quum in ipsa acie summae rei videret esse discrimen: dubioque adhuc pugnae eventu pro victore se gessit*, and 14 § 1 below.

§ 13. *perpetua*] compare IX 9 § 2.

partium] often used for 'side' in a contest, and even by itself as here for the side to which the person considered belongs. Compare IV 16 § 4 (*Mazaeus*) *fortuna partium territus.*

felicitate] see on 10 § 18.

accensi] for sense compare Pliny epp IX 33 § 6 *crescit audacia experimento.*

§ 14. *frequens hostis*] 'the enemy in crowds'.

§ 15. *poterant, si......inveniret*] see Madvig § 348 e, Kennedy § 214, 3.

temeritas felix] these words are used by Seneca de benef VII 3 § 1 in speaking of Alexander himself. The position of *felix* here shews that it means 'when fortunate', εὐτυχὴς οὖσα or εὖ φερομένη. For the sense in general compare IV 14 § 19 *licet felicitas adspirare videatur, tamen ad ultimum temeritati non sufficit.*

supervenientes] those coming upon them, coming up to maintain the fight on their own side.

enaverant] had reached (the island) by swimming. See on IX 9 § 18. *occulti* = λάθρα or λαθόντες.

§ 17. *dolum intendit*] the phrase comes again VII 5 § 21. *intendit* = prepares as a trap, net etc. Arrian V 10 § 4 says μηχανᾶταί τι τοιόνδε.

erat insula etc] Arrian V 11 §§ 1, 2 'there was a bluff standing up from the bank of the Hydaspes, at a point where the river made a remarkable bend: this was itself overgrown with all sorts of trees, and over against it lay an island in the river, a wooded untrodden and solitary place. When he observed this island opposite the bluff, two wooded spots suited to cover the attempt at crossing, he decided to take his army over this way. Now the bluff and the island were distant as much as 150 stadia from the great camp'.

tegendis etc] compare VII 7 § 31 *silvestre iter aptum insidiis tegendis erat.*

fossa] comparing Arrian quoted above (ἀνέχουσα) we must infer that this *fossa* is the hollow behind the bluff (ἄκρα). For the sense compare Virgil Aen XI 522 *est curvo anfractu valles adcommoda fraudi armorumque dolis.*

haud procul ripa] compare IX 8 § 3. The construction is common in silver-age Latin.

§ 18. *opportunitatis*] = 'convenient place', the abstract having passed into concrete signification, as in many other words, for instance *cenatio, ambulatio, pensio*. See on IX 2 § 10.

Ptolomaeum] so Hedicke, following the MSS authority, spells the name. Anyhow Curtius seems to have made a mistake here. In 14 § 15 he represents Ptolemy as being in the immediate company of the king, and Arrian writing mainly from Ptolemy's own accounts (V 7 § 1, 14 § 5) says that it was Craterus who was left in charge of the army facing Porus at the ford (V 11 § 3), and adds (§ 4) παρηγγέλλετο δὲ Κρατέρῳ μὴ πρὶν διαβαίνειν τὸν πόρον πρὶν ἀπαλλαγῆναι Πῶρον ξὺν τῇ δυνάμει ὡς ἐπὶ σφᾶς ἢ φεύγοντα μαθεῖν, αὐτοὺς δὲ νικῶντας.

omnibus turmis] a sort of ablative of the instrument.

obequitare] that is, *hostibus*. See on 10 § 6.

quasi] 'making pretence' of attempting the passage. *quasi* and *tamquam* are continually used thus by writers of the Silver Age. Compare IX 7 § 24.

§ 19. *ei parti*] *ripae.*

advertere] Compare Virgil Aen XII 555 *urbique adverteret agmen.*

§ 20. *iam......erat*] 'by this time the island was out of sight of the enemy'. That is, by continual feints at different points Porus had been enticed lower down the stream. Alexander was now free to carry out his plan of turning his enemy's right flank by crossing higher up.

diversa] 'looking the other way'. Compare IX 1 § 35, IV 4 § 6 *forte rex classem in diversam partem agi iusserat*, Virgil Aen V 166 *quo diversus abis?* Tacitus Agr 11 *procurrentibus in diversa terris* (of Britain and Gaul).

§ 21. *Attalum*] Arrian V 12 § 1 mentions Attalus with other officers as detailed off for a third attack between the other two. But his presence in the character of Alexander at the sham headquarters is not as Mützell seems to think inconsistent with the duty assigned to him by Arrian. He might wait there till the time of the intended night-attack and then at once join his detachment in time for action. In fact this is likely, for Alexander would probably choose an officer of rank to take his place, and yet want to employ him in the battle.

speciem] 'the appearance that......' What follows is explanatory.

praesidere] guarding. Compare VII 9 § 6 *ceterum praeter hanc speciem ripis praesidentis exercitus ingens navigantes terror invaserat*, Livy XXII 11 § 9.

§ 23. *in regionem insulae*] into the quarter of the island, that is, to reach the land over against it.

averso in eos] 'was busy watching those' who were with Ptolemy.

obstrepentibus ventis] Arrian V 12 § 3 'and in the night there came on a violent storm of rain. In this way his preparations and attempt to cross were the less exposed to detection by the rattle of arms and the noise of giving orders; for the sound of the thunder and rain drowned them'.

§ 24. *conderent lucem*] the words have a poetical ring.

§ 25. *terruisset*] compare IX 5 § 19.

petebant tenente] the former word was supplied by Aldus. The second is received by Hedicke from the correction of Jeep. The old reading *occupante* had no authority of value.

§ 26. *suam occasionem*] was his opportunity. Compare IV 6 § 13 *recedentibus inferunt signa, cunctationem hostium suam fore occasionem rati.*

expelli] to be run aground. Compare IX 4 § 11. Arrian V 13 § 2 *πρῶτος αὐτὸς ἐκβάς.*

CHAPTER XIV.

Curtius passes on to describe the battle itself, as though after once reaching shore and disembarking his men Alexander had had no further difficulty. But we learn from Arrian, who is manifestly better informed, that on disembarking his men Alexander found that they had not reached the river-bank but only a large island. The channel between this and the bank was not usually deep, but the rain of the preceding night made it very hard to find the ford in the early morning. He goes on (V 13 § 3) *ὡς δὲ ἐξευρέθη ποτὲ ὁ πόρος, ἦγε κατ' αὐτὸν χαλεπῶς· ἦν γὰρ τῶν μὲν πεζῶν ὑπὲρ τοὺς μαστοὺς τὸ ὕδωρ ἵναπερ τὸ βαθύτατον αὐτοῦ· τῶν δὲ ἵππων ὅσον τὰς κεφαλὰς ὑπερίσχειν τοῦ ποταμοῦ.* Either then Curtius did not find this important point noticed in his authorities, or he passed it over as not being striking enough to give opportunity for a fine descriptive passage. The latter view is in itself the less probable, and the silence of Diodorus, who seems to have followed much the same authorities as Curtius, gives great probability to the former. The account given in Plutarch Alex 60 is nearer that of Arrian, but would be of little use if the other versions had not survived.

§ 1. *ripam*] 'the bank' on which he himself was.

Abisaren] in spite of his submission (13 § 1). See 12 § 13, IX 1 § 7.

Diodorus XVII 87, 90 mentions 'Εμβίσαρος as an ally of Porus. See Arrian V 20 §§ 5, 6.

§ 2. *liquidiore*] clearer after the storm. Compare VII 11 § 21 *verum ut liquidior lux apparuit caelo, dubitatio exempta est*, Virgil georg I 404.

Hages frater ipsius] according to Arrian V 14 Ptolemy and Aristobulus, though differing in other details, agreed in stating that this force was commanded by a son of Porus. Whence Curtius got his information we cannot tell.

§ 3. *senos*] Strabo XV 1 § 52 says *δύο δ' εἰσὶν ἐπὶ τῷ ἅρματι παραβάται πρὸς τῷ ἡνιόχῳ*. Mützell thinks that the numbers given in Curtius may be reconciled with the above by supposing that this arrangement was a special one, due to the terror inspired by Alexander.

haud sane] see on 9 § 37.

§ 4. *vix ullus*] see Madvig § 494.

inluvie ac voraginibus] the muddy sloughs formed by the rain on the low grounds. Arrian V 15 § 2 says that the chariots during the action were *ὑπὸ πηλοῦ ἀχρεῖα*.

§ 5. *strenue*] Arrian V 15 § 2 *ἐνταῦθα δὴ ὀξέως ἐπιπεσεῖν αὐτοῖς ξὺν τῇ ἀμφ' αὐτὸν ἵππῳ*.

Scythae et Dahae] Alexander had raised troops among the warlike tribes of Central Asia. Curtius makes Alexander refer to them in his speech IX 2 § 24.

emisit] 'launched'. Compare § 24, V 13 § 19 *Alexander hostium trepidatione comperta Nicanorem cum equitum parte ad inhibendam fugam emittit: ipse cum ceteris sequitur*.

§ 6. *pugna se moverat*] a remarkable expression savouring of poetic licence.

illud] ἐκεῖνο, what follows: namely the desperate charge described.

§ 7. *anceps......erat*] 'the harm done by the charge to both sides could not be told'. That is, it was not clear which suffered the more. The sense would be clearer without *utrisque*, as the context shews who are referred to. See on § 16 below, and IX 4 § 12.

§ 9. *exacti*] driven off, that is, off the field. Compare § 30.

pugnam cientem] poetical and rhetorical, as Mützell remarks.

elephantos] Arrian V 15 § 5: (he drew up) 'the elephants first in front at intervals of at least 100 feet, so as to have his elephants ranged in front before the entire phalanx of his infantry, and so frighten Alexander's cavalry at all points'.

§ 10. *olim*] see on IX 6 § 26.

mitigatis] tamed, hence 'accustomed', 'deadened'.

§ 11. *Herculis*] See IX 4 § 2. Megasthenes according to Strabo XV 1 § 58 reported that the philosophers of the lowlands worshipped Hercules. See Tacitus Germ 3, 7. Mützell says that Bohlen takes this Hercules to mean Vishnu. Others say Siva or Krishna. See Williams' *Hinduism* c 8 p 105, M'Crindle pp 39, 111.

simulacrum] the image of a god (ἄγαλμα) as opposed to *statua* that of a man (ἀνδριάς). See Mayor on Cic philippic II § 110.

incitamentum] Compare IX 5 § 6, Tacitus Germ 7.

flagitium] Tacitus Germ 6 *scutum reliquisse praecipuum flagitium.*

§ 12. *illo hoste*] Hercules, of course.

§ 13. *turrium*] see on 12 § 7.

procul] 'to a distant view'.

excesserat] 'had surpassed'. Compare IX 2 § 28. The description of Porus in Diodorus XVII 88 is like that in Curtius, but more extravagant.

formam] 'outline', hence 'conception'. Compare the use of the word in Cic de Off I § 15 *formam et tamquam faciem honesti* 'the outline and so to speak the shape of moral goodness', § 103 *officii formam* 'the outline of duty'. Here it seems to mean 'standard'.

magnitudinem corpori] this is the clever emendation of Vogel. For construction he compares IV 3 § 8 *latitudinem quoque aggeri adiecit.*

quanto] not *quantum*, for the idea of *praestare* includes only the excess of one thing over others, not that of general comparison of size. This is also marked by the construction after it (*aliis* not *inter alios*).

aliis] *hominibus.*

§ 14. *par......video*] compare Scott's 'stern joy which warriors feel in foemen worthy of their steel'.

egregiis] must be repeated in sense with *bestiis.*

§ 15. *comitatus*] the past participles of many deponent verbs are used also in a passive signification by good writers. See Madvig § 153, and compare X 8 § 3 *sedecim omnino pueris regiae cohortis comitatus.*

dextrum move] 'advance the right wing'. Arrian V 16 § 2 tells us that Alexander was making a flanking movement (παρήλαυνεν) with the bulk of his cavalry to attack the enemy's left wing. He then (§ 3) goes on Κοῖνον δὲ πέμπει ὡς ἐπὶ τὸ δέξιον τὴν Δημητρίου καὶ τὴν αὑτοῦ ἔχοντα ἱππαρχίαν, κελεύσας ἐπειδὰν τὸ κατὰ σφᾶς στῖφος τῶν ἱππέων ἰδόντες οἱ βάρβαροι ἀντιπαριππεύωσιν, αὐτὸν κατόπιν ἔχεσθαι αὐτῶν· a hard passage it is true, but one which need not be unintelligible to any one who bears in mind that Alexander's movement was a flanking one and reads with care the description of his attack in 16 § 4, 17 §§ 1, 2. The situation is this: Alexander was not himself in position on the right wing, but put Coenus there with some of the cavalry while he himself with the main body made the flanking movement. This he did with speed, so as to take the Indian horse in flank before they had time to change their front and meet him. They tried to execute this movement, but had not time; and while they were in the confusion thus brought about Coenus fell upon what had been their front but was now their disordered flank. Whether the Indian horse from their right wing was brought over to succour that on their left or not does not affect the probable position of Coenus. The one difficulty in the way of this explanation is the presence, according to Arrian 15 § 7, of the war-chariots in front of the Indian horse. But it seems easier to suppose that Coenus was able to elude these clumsy adversaries than that Alexander expected him to see from the Macedonian left the right moment for his own charge and then wheel round the rear of the whole Indian army and execute his orders opportunely. Diodorus XVII 88 says *γενομένης δὲ μάχης τὸ μὲν πρῶτον τοῖς ἱππεῦσιν ἅπαντα σχεδὸν τὰ ἅρματα τῶν Ἰνδῶν διεφθάρη*. If this refers, as I think it does, to the beginning of the main battle, the chief objection is removed. [I am solely responsible for this note, which will I think explain the passage of Curtius by that of Arrian. W. E. Heitland.]

Leonnate] Arrian mentions Seleucus here and leaves out Leonnatus. The three were in command of the phalanx of foot.

§ 16. *hastae*] the Macedonian *σάρισα* was over 20 feet long. See IX 7 § 19, Livy IX 19 § 7, XXXVII 42 § 4, Polybius XVIII 29, Lucan X 47, 48, Thirlwall c 48 (vol VI p 147). They seem to have been somewhat like the long pikes of the Scotch Borderers described by Scott.

anceps] 'uncertain'; that is, not to be depended on, as being likely to damage their own side as much as (if not more than) the enemy.

§ 17. *laevum cornu*] that is, the cavalry on the Indian left.

§ 18. *uno impetu*] Arrian V 17 § 3 tells us that the phalanx at first suffered greatly from the charges of the elephants. So Diodorus XVII 88.

qua...iussit] Arrian says *καὶ ἐν τούτῳ οἱ ἐπιστάται τῶν ἐλεφάντων ἀντεπῆγον τῇ ἵππῳ τὰ θηρία, καὶ ἡ φάλαγξ αὐτὴ τῶν Μακεδόνων ἀντεπῄει πρὸς τοὺς ἐλέφαντας.*

§ 19. *statuerent*] 'rested'. For the matter see on 9 § 28, and compare what Xenophon says of the Karduchi in anab IV 2 § 28 *ἄριστοι δὲ καὶ τοξόται ἦσαν (οἱ Καρδοῦχοι)· εἶχον δὲ τόξα ἐγγὺς τριπήχη, τὰ δὲ τοξεύματα πλέον ἢ διπήχη· εἷλκον δὲ τὰς νευρὰς ὁπότε τοξεύοιεν πρὸς τὸ κάτω τοῦ τόξου τῷ ἀριστερῷ ποδὶ προσβαίνοντες. τὰ δὲ τοξεύματα ἐχώρει διὰ τῶν ἀσπίδων καὶ διὰ τῶν θωράκων.* Schneider thinks that crossbows are there meant, but this view is probably wrong.

inponunt] put on the string.

lubrica] from the rain of the night before. But Arrian V 15 § 5 says that Porus drew up his army on sandy ground, which the rain no doubt would make firm; in fact he calls it *ἄπεδον καὶ στερεόν.*

id] the slipperiness of the ground.

molientes] preparing, striving to deliver. Compare IX 10 § 19, Virgil georg I 329, IV 331.

occupantur] see on 9 § 32, and add Ovid fasti I 575 *occupat Alcides (Cacum)*. See also below IX 1 § 32, 7 § 22.

§ 20. *turbatis*] *ταραχῆς δὲ πολλῆς γενομένης*, says Diodorus.

§ 21. *in medium*] compare IX 1 § 21, Virgil Aen XI 335 *consulite in medium et rebus succurrite fessis.*

§ 22. *obvius...iubet*] Diodorus also mentions an effort of Porus to retrieve the fortune of the day by a general attack with his 40 remaining elephants, which succeeded at first. Perhaps this may be another version of the fight described in Arrian V 17 § 3. See below on §§ 25, 26.

§ 23. *pavidum*] Compare Tacitus hist. II 68 (*Vitellius*) *ad omnes suspitiones pavidus.*

ad omnia] so we say 'to shy at everything'. The elephants were well known to cause great terror in horses.

§ 24. *concursatione*] 'running about', hence 'skirmishing' of light troops. Mützell compares Livy XXX 34 of the Carthaginian troops, *concursatio et velocitas illinc maior quam vis.*

§ 25. *ingentem...eos*] Arrian V 17 § 3 (continued from quotation above on § 18) *ἔς τε τοὺς ἐπιβάτας αὐτῶν ἀκοντίζοντες καὶ αὐτὰ τὰ θηρία περισταδὸν πανταχόθεν βάλλοντες.*

constanter] 'firmly', 'steadily'. Not as the light troops who would advance or retire as the Indians retired or advanced.

§ 26. *obtriti* etc] Arrian V 17 § 3 'for the beasts charged the ranks of the foot, and wherever they turned were crushing through the Macedonian phalanx though in close formation'. Diodorus gives a vivid description of the havoc wrought by the elephants in the early part of the battle.

fuere documentum] the nominative is less common in the best writers. See Madvig § 249 note a. We have however § 41 *esset exemplum*, and there are many instances in other writers, but none of these seem to have the following construction with *ut*.

§ 27. *facies*] Compare the passage quoted on II § 12, also IX 7 § 10, 8 § 5. Tacitus Agr 36.

manu] 'trunk'. See Cic de divin II § 122, Lucretius II 537, V 1303.

§ 28. *in multum diei*] Madvig § 285 b obs 1.

§ 29. *copidas*] choppers, something like a Goorka knife. *κοπὶς* from same root as *κόπτω*.

timor] this, remarks Zumpt, must be the fear in which the Macedonian soldiers stood of the elephants. This fear stimulated their ingenuity and ferocity, so that the elephants that fell in the battle were destroyed with a spiteful barbarity worth special notice. *novi* = unheard of, horrible.

omittebat] for the sense generally compare Tacitus Agr. 16 *nec ullum in barbaris saevitiae genus omisit ira et victoria.*

§ 30. *ergo...obterebantur*] Diodorus XVII 88 *μετὰ δὲ ταῦτα τῶν θηρίων συνακοντιζομένων καὶ διὰ τὸ πλῆθος τῶν τραυμάτων περιωδύνων γινομένων, οἱ μὲν περιβεβηκότες αὐτοῖς Ἰνδοὶ κρατεῖν τῆς ὁρμῆς τῶν ζῴων οὐκ ἴσχυον· ἐκνεύοντα γὰρ εἰς τοὺς ἰδίους ταῖς ὁρμαῖς ἀκατασχέτως ἐφέρετο καὶ τοὺς φίλους συνεπάτει*, Arrian V 17 §§ 5, 6.

ab ipsis] that is, *quos rexerant*, 'by the very beasts they had driven' = 'by their own beasts'. The words go in the first instance with *praecipitati.*

itaque] having, that is, now no drivers.

pecorum modo] that is, in wild disorder like a flock of sheep. Arrian V 17 § 5 *καὶ αὐτοὶ οἱ ἐλέφαντες τὰ μὲν τιτρωσκόμενοι τὰ δὲ ὑπό τε τῶν πόνων καὶ ἐρημίᾳ ἡγεμόνων οὐκέτι διακεκριμένοι ἐν τῇ μάχῃ ἦσαν*, 18 § 4.

§ 31. *destitutus*] 'left in the lurch'. Compare IX 4 § 33.

a pluribus] 'by the majority of his men'. So Mützell.

tela] Diodorus says that Porus by reason of his great strength could throw darts almost as hard as a catapult (see Rich's dict of antiquities for these engines).

expositus] compare IX 5 § 9.

petebatur] Diodorus says that Alexander ordered the bowmen and light troops to single out Porus and shoot at him. Mützell observes that this is probably only a distorted version of the movement described by Curtius above in § 24. For the words compare IX 4 31.

§ 33. *fluentibus*] drooping. Compare Virgil Aen X 828 *ad terram non sponte fluens.*

vix compotem] Diodorus XVII 88 'Porus having fought like a hero and lost much blood by reason of his many wounds fainted and sinking helplessly on the beast was borne to the ground'.

§ 34. *eius*] Alexander. See on IX 1 § 6.

effuso] compare Virgil Aen X 893.

§ 35. *frater Taxilis*] Arrian V 18 §§ 6, 7 says that Taxiles himself was sent, and then other and more acceptable messengers.

§ 36. *ad notam vocem*] 'at' or 'by' the well-known voice. Compare IV 15 § 32 *ergo haud secus quam in tenebris errabant, ad sonum notae vocis, ut signum, subinde coeuntes.*

proditoris] 'who gave up' his throne and kingdom. The verb is similarly used in Terence hautont 479, 480 *prius proditurum te tuam vitam et prius pecuniam omnem quam abs te amittas filium.*

quod unum] such is the Latin idiom. In English we should rather say 'the one dart that'.

effluxerat] had fallen or slipped from his hand.

penetravit] Arrian says that Taxiles escaped the javelin by speedy flight.

§ 37. *edito opere*] a regular combination of words. Compare Livy I 16 § 1, III 63 § 3. We have *edita pugna* IX 5 § 16.

exceperat] this is quick work. In § 33 the beast was unwounded.

sistit fugam] stays the flight of his troops.

peditem] his remaining infantry. He had lost the greater part, see Arrian V 18 § 4.

§ 38. *vetabat* etc] this is not stated by Arrian, who is more to be trusted. Diodorus XVII 89 says that there was great slaughter in the pursuit, and that Alexander checked it.

labi] see the passage quoted on § 33.

§ 39. *instituti*] 'trained'.

§ 40. *spoliari iubet*] only Curtius states this.

cum belua...inponere] Plutarch Alex 60 has got hold of a still more wonderful account of the sagacity of this beast. Strabo XV 1 § 42 says of trained battle elephants οἱ δὲ καὶ ἐξαίμους τοὺς ἡνιόχους ἐν τοῖς ἀγῶσι πεσόντας ἀνελόμενοι σώζουσιν ἐκ τῆς μάχης, τοὺς δὲ ὑποδύντας μεταξὺ τῶν προσθίων ποδῶν ὑπερμαχόμενοι διέσωσαν.

§ 41. *malum*] this interjection, common in the comic poets, is also found in Cicero. See the passage de off II § 53 *praeclare in epistula quadam Alexandrum filium Philippus accusat quod largitione benevolentiam Macedonum consectetur. 'quae te, malum' inquit 'ratio in istam spem induxit ut eos tibi fideles putares fore quos pecunia corrupisses?'* Render 'What the plague was the infatuation that drove you'...

Taxilis] the genitive is that of further definition after *exemplum*. See on 10 § 7 *ignis*.

§ 42. *fecisti*] granted, given. So often *facere copiam potestatem licentiam* etc.

§ 43. *rursus...esset*] Arrian V 19 § 2 says that when asked by Alexander how he would like to be treated, Porus replied 'like a king' (βασιλικῶς). Curtius seems to have got hold of something not very different from this, and to have dressed it up after the fashion of the rhetoricians with a sage reflection on the mutability of fortune, in order to point his moral.

§ 44. *infractam*] 'broken down', 'dismayed'. The word is very common. Compare IX 2 § 30, Virgil Aen XII 1.

§ 45. *aegrum curavit*] Diodorus XVII 89 says αὐτὸς δὲ ὁ Πῶρος ἔμπνους ὢν παρεδόθη τοῖς Ἰνδοῖς πρὸς τὴν θεραπείαν, that is probably to some of the Brahman doctors.

haud secus quam] =*haud minus quam*.

confirmatum] when he recovered his strength.

ampliore] so Arrian V 19 § 3 τήν τε ἀρχὴν τῷ Πώρῳ τῶν τε αὐτοῦ Ἰνδῶν ἔδωκε καὶ ἄλλην ἔτι χώραν πρὸς τῇ πάλαι οὔσῃ πλείονα τῆς πρόσθεν προσέθηκε, and again in detail 20 § 4, 29 § 2.

§ 46. *nec sane...gloriae*] 'and in truth his nature had no more essential or more permanent quality than a regard for true merit and renown'. See on IX 2 § 14 *ex solido*.

simplicius...in cive] 'but he took more impartial account of glory in an enemy than in a subject'. Compare IV 14 § 19 *praeterea breves et mutabiles vices rerum sunt, et fortuna numquam simpliciter indulget*, 'never shews favour without reserve'. For *aestimabat* compare IX 1 § 26.

destrui] unbuilt, pulled down.

BOOK IX, CHAPTER I.

§ 1. *soli* etc] Diodorus XVII 89 'and the king buried the dead and gave due honours to those who had distinguished themselves in the battle and sacrificed in person to the sun, as the power that had given him the conquest of the eastern world'. Arrian V 20 § 1 only speaks of τὰ νομιζόμενα ἐπινίκια.

reliqua belli] compare VII 5 § 27 *ceteris gratiae actae quod ad reliqua belli navaturos operam pollicebantur.*

pro contione] 'before the assembled army', 'in a general meeting'. The phrase is common in this connexion.

§ 2. *opimam praedam*] compare V 1 § 4 *praedam opimam paratamque ipsum et milites eius spectare.*

celebratas] 'storied', much told of in the rumours that reached Europe. The Eldorado of those days lay in the East.

eminere] were great, 'abounded'. Compare VIII 12 § 13.

proinde] accordingly, 'then'. Compare the advice of the Scythian to Alexander when contemplating an expedition into Scythia VII 8 § 24 *proinde fortunam tuam pressis manibus tene.*

iam etc] 'had become cheap and common'. See on 6 § 14 below.

obsoleta] so Nepos (Miltiades 6 § 2) opposes *obsoleti* to *gloriosi* (=giving glory), speaking of *honores*. See on 6 § 14.

repletum ire] Madvig § 411. 'They were on their way to fill'.

§ 3. *dimissis*] that is, *iis*.

§ 4. *materia* etc] so Diodorus XVII 89, Strabo XV 1 § 29, and Sir A Burnes (quoted by Mützell) says that the same thing is still done on the Hydaspes, and that on no other of the rivers in the Panjab do such facilities exist for building vessels.

adgressi] the use of this word with a following infinitive is poetical and post-Augustan. Compare 10 § 12, Virgil Aen II 165, VI 584.

serpentes] Diodorus XVII 90 'and the neighbouring hill-country had the following peculiarity. Besides the timber for shipbuilding the country contained a number of snakes of extraordinary size, 16 cubits long', Strabo XV 1 § 28.

§ 5. *rhinocerotes*] see on VIII 9 § 16.

aliud] *nomen.*

§ 6. *urbibus*] Arrian V 19 § 4 'Now Alexander founded cities at the place where the fight befell and at the point whence he started in his passage of the Hydaspes. And he called the one Nikaea in honour of his victory (νίκη) over the Indians, and the other Bukephala in memory of his horse Bukephalas who died there, not that anyone had wounded him, but from work and old age'. See VIII 14 § 34 above, where Curtius reports the story rejected by Arrian, and for the name of the town 3 § 23 below.

aureis] if these were gold Philips (Horace epist II 1 234) they would be worth about 16*s* each, if Persian darics (δαρεικοί) about a guinea. But they may have been neither.

§ 7. *neque enim...captivum*] 'for' said he 'I cannot live without the power of a king and this I should not enjoy as a prisoner'. *captivum* stands where in Greek we should have a present participle.

§ 8. *nuntiari* etc] Arrian says in effect just the same (V 20 § 6), Diodorus XVII 90 only observes καταπληξάμενος ἠνάγκασε ποιεῖν τὸ προσταττόμενον.

porro] 'further on'. It seems better to read thus, than *Poro* with the best MSS; a reading which the commentators have vainly striven to torture at once into Latin and sense.

amne] must refer to the Acesines (Chenab). Perhaps *Acesine* has fallen out before *amne*. Arrian V 20 §§ 8, 9 speaks of the crossing of this river at some length, as it had received special notice from Ptolemy. But Diodorus XVII 90 goes on in the same way αὐτὸς δὲ μετὰ τῆς δυνάμεως περάσας τὸν ποταμὸν προῆγε διὰ χώρας ἀρετῇ διαφερούσης. It seems probable therefore that he and Curtius are both here depending on the same writer whose handling of the matter somehow led them into the grave blunder of omitting an important name.

§ 9. *silvae* etc] so Diodorus goes on δένδρων γὰρ εἶχε γένη διαλλάττοντα καὶ τὸ μὲν ὕψος ἔχοντα πηχῶν ἑβδομήκοντα τὸ δὲ πάχος μόγις ὑπὸ τεττάρων ἀνδρῶν περιλαμβανόμενα τριῶν δὲ πλέθρων σκιὰν ποιοῦντα.

prope in inmensum spatium] = *in spatium prope inmensum*, over an almost boundless tract of country.

§ 10. *plerique rami* etc] the tree here described is the Banyan, one of the most celebrated Indian trees, as well known to the ancients as it has been in modern times. Strabo XV 1 § 21 gives a description from Onesikritus and also Aristobulus. See also Theophrast hist plant IV 4 § 4, Pliny N H XII §§ 22, 23, Arrian Indica 11 § 7.

instar] Madvig § 280 obs 6, Kennedy § 166, 2.

rursus] goes of course with *erigebantur*.

qua se curvaverant] at the point where they had bent themselves; at any point, that is, where they took an upward bend from the ground. The clause is obscurely put in, but the sense is pretty certain in itself, and is established by the words in Strabo (δένδρα) ὧν τοὺς κλάδους αὐξηθέντας ἐπὶ πήχεις καὶ δώδεκα ἔπειτα τὴν λοιπὴν αὔξησιν καταφερῆ λαμβάνειν ὡς ἂν κατακαμπτομένους, ἕως ἂν ἅψωνται τῆς γῆς· ἔπειτα κατὰ γῆς διαδοθέντας ῥιζοῦσθαι ὁμοίως ταῖς κατώρυξιν, εἶτ' ἀναδοθέντας στελεχοῦσθαι.

erigebantur] would shoot up straight again. Compare VIII 11 § 6.

§ 11. *caeli...fontibus*] compare IV 7 §§ 16, 17 (of the temple of Ammon) *tandem ad sedem consecratam deo ventum est. incredibile dictu, inter vastas solitudines sita undique ambientibus ramis, vix in densam umbram cadente sole, contecta est; multique fontes dulcibus aquis passim manantibus alunt silvas. caeli quoque mira temperies verno tepori maxime similis omnes anni partes pari salubritate percurrit.*

§ 12. *hic quoque*] see § 4. So Diodorus XVII 90 says εἶχε δὲ καὶ ἡ χώρα ὄφεων πλῆθος μικρῶν μὲν τοῖς μεγέθεσι ταῖς δὲ ποικιλίαις ἐξηλλαγμένων· οἱ μὲν γὰρ χαλκοειδεῖς ῥάβδους ἐπέφαινον etc.

reddentibus] 'sending out', 'giving'. The notion of 'back from' soon passes into that of 'out from', and so *reddere* is really = *praebere*. Compare III 2 § 5 *scutis cetrae maxime speciem reddentibus*, and see on 4 § 23 below.

virus etc] Diodorus says διὰ δὲ τῶν δηγμάτων ὀξεῖς θανάτους ἀπειργάζοντο and so on; Strabo speaking of some small venomous snakes says XV 1 § 45 τοὺς δὲ πληγέντας αἱμορροεῖν ἐκ παντὸς πόρου μετὰ ἐπωδυνίας, ἔπειτα ἀποθνήσκειν εἰ μὴ βοηθήσει τις εὐθύς.

praesens] we have now in English dropped the correct usage of this word, and use 'instant' or 'immediate'. Compare 2 § 19.

remedium etc] Diodorus says μετὰ δὲ ταῦτα παρὰ τῶν ἐγχωρίων μαθόντες τὴν ἀντιφάρμακον ῥίζαν ἀπελύθησαν τῶν δεινῶν. Strabo goes on τὴν δὲ βοήθειαν ῥᾳδίαν εἶναι διὰ τὴν ἀρετὴν τῶν Ἰνδικῶν ῥιζῶν καὶ φαρμάκων. See also Arrian Indica 15 § 11. The *incolae* are probably some of the local Brahmans.

§ 13. *iunctum*] that is, on the banks of the river. The order of the sense is *erat nemus iunctum flumini*. The last two words are an epithet = παραποτάμιον or some such word.

arboribus] Strabo XV 1 § 21 πολλὰ γὰρ δὴ δένδρα παράδοξα ἡ Ἰνδικὴ τρέφει.

pavonum] Elphinstone intr p 10 says 'the peacock also is common in a wild state'.

frequens] 'crowded', 'filled'. Compare V 4 § 6 *fertilis terra multisque vicis atque urbibus frequens*.

§ 14. *oppidum*] Mützell refers this to the same place as that spoken of by Arrian V 22 § 3 καὶ δευτεραῖος μὲν ἀπὸ τοῦ ποταμοῦ τοῦ Ὑδραώτου πρὸς πόλιν ἧκεν ᾗ ὄνομα Πίμπραμα· τὸ δ' ἔθνος τοῦτο τῶν Ἰνδῶν Ἀδραϊσταὶ ἐκαλοῦντο. If this be right, then Curtius must have had a very different account of the affairs before him, for Arrian goes on οὗτοι μὲν δὴ προσεχώρησαν ὁμολογίᾳ Ἀλεξάνδρῳ. See also Diodorus XVII 91, Arrian 21 § 6.

corona] by a general attack all round the walls. Compare 4 § 4, VII 6 § 19 *urbem corona circumdedit munitiorem quam ut primo impetu capi posset*.

magnam etc] Diodorus XVII 91 says that Alexander took τὴν μεγίστην καὶ ὀχυρωτάτην πόλιν of the Kathaeans, but whether this corresponds to the present notice of Curtius is not certain. Strabo XV 1 § 33 says that between the Hypanis (= Hyphasis) and Hydaspes were 9 tribes and 5000 πόλεις οὐκ ἐλάττους Κῶ τῆς Μεροπίδος, and in XIV 2 § 19 he says that Kos was οὐ μεγάλη. We may therefore infer that the words of Curtius *ut in ea regione* are not without authority.

urbem] probably the place called by Arrian τὰ Σάγγαλα the most important town of the Kathaeans. General Cunningham finds this at a hill still bearing the same name, between the Hyarotis (Hydraotes) and Acesines. Alexander must then have turned back for a space, as he had according to Arrian V 21 § 6 already crossed the former river.

palude] Arrian V 23 § 4 *ἵνα καὶ λίμνη οὐ μακρὰν τοῦ τείχους ἦν.* He goes on to say that it was not deep.

§ 15. *vehiculis*] in three rows, according to Arrian 22 § 4 *κύκλῳ δὲ τοῦ γηλόφου ἁμάξας περιστήσαντες ἐντὸς αὐτῶν ἐστρατοπέδευον, ὡς τριπλοῦν χάρακα περιβεβλῆσθαι τῶν ἁμαξῶν.*

tela] weapons of offence. Compare 4 § 3.

transiliebantque] there is here a change of subject. The sentence goes on as if *tela alii hastas alii secures habebant* had been written above. The word seems to denote the jumping from one waggon to another.

§ 16. *incondito*] 'undisciplined'.

auxilio] 'means of warfare', 'force'. Compare IV 9 § 4 *falcatae quadrigae, unicum illarum gentium auxilium*, and VIII 14 § 6.

ab utroque latere] this can hardly refer to the same move as that mentioned below *quo...circumvenirentur.* It would seem then that Curtius is following some account in which the waggons were not ranged round the town, but in a line so as to serve as a rampart to an army covering the town.

§ 17. *vincula* etc] this account does not correspond with that of Arrian V 23 § 2 who mentions gaps between the waggons and says nothing of any means of binding them together.

quo facilius] Madvig § 440 b obs 1, Kennedy § 208.

VIII *milibus*] it is impossible to compare the numbers given by Curtius and Arrian 24 §§ 3, 5, as neither gives the total of killed and the details of the numbers who fell in the separate operations of the siege are not so stated as to admit of comparison.

§ 18. *scalis*] Arrian 24 § 4 says that they also weakened the walls by mining.

paucis] emphatic.

qui] = *ii qui.*

profecto] goes closely with *deorum.* Compare 8 § 18.

§ 19. *Eumeni*] Arrian V 24 §§ 6, 7 has a similar but slightly different account.

ad urbem] see on 4 § 23.

§ 20. *deprecarentur*] to win over, appease. Compare VII 2 § 7 *amici quoque data misericordiae occasione consurgunt flentesque regem deprecantur.* So *παραιτεῖσθαι* in Greek. Compare Aristoph vespae 1257 *ἢ γὰρ παρῃτήσαντο τὸν πεπονθότα.*

§ 21. *imminebant*] were inclined to, bent on. Compare V 11 § 2 *ipse currum regis sequebatur, occasioni imminens adloquendi eum*, VI 10 § 22 *sic ergo imperio, quod dedignor, immineo.*

recipiunt] admit, 'welcome'. The force of the word is 'take in as due', because they had for some time made up their own minds to do so. Compare *recipit* in VIII 9 § 32.

§ 23. *convocaverunt*] called them to a conference. The *con* has the force of 'to', 'to meet'.

vim] Eichert in his lexicon takes this as 'strength', that is, as equivalent to *vires*. But perhaps it may more strictly mean 'violence', 'severity'. Arrian V 24 § 6 says that Eumenes was to tell the people of some hostile towns 'that they would have no harsh treatment from Alexander if they remained and received him as a friend; for neither had any of the other independent Indians who surrendered themselves willingly'. So here we may have just the reverse meant, speaking of those who resisted. But see below § 32.

in fidem accepit] took under his protection. Compare 7 § 14.

§ 24. *regnum Sopithis*] According to Arrian VI 2 § 2 the kingdom of Sopithes lay on the left bank of the Hydaspes. Strabo XV 1 § 30 also says that some place it between that river and the Acesines, but adds that others put it beyond the Acesines and Hyarotis, which view is evidently that followed by Curtius (see § 35) and Diodorus XVII 91. See M'Crindle p 154, who points out that Lassen has identified the name Sopithes with Sanskrit *Asvapati* 'lord of horses'. According to Strabo Sopithes was king of the Kathaei.

ut barbari credunt] 'in the opinion of the natives'.

sapientia] see on VIII 13 § 7.

bonis moribus] so Diodorus XVII 91 *μετὰ δὲ ταῦτ' ἐστράτευσεν ἐπὶ τὰς ὑπὸ Σωπείθην τεταγμένας πόλεις, εὐνομουμένας καθ' ὑπερβολήν.*

regitur] is ruled or directed by. Hence = 'lives under' as in 8 § 4.

§ 25. *genitos* etc] Diodorus says *τὸ κάλλος παρ' αὐτοῖς τιμιώτατον νενόμισται. διόπερ ἐκ νηπίου παρ' αὐτοῖς τὰ βρέφη διακρίνεται, καὶ τὰ μὲν ἄρτια καὶ τὴν φύσιν ἔχοντα πρὸς εὐπρέπειαν καὶ ἰσχὺν εὔθετον τρέφεται, τὰ δὲ καταδεῆ τοῖς σώμασιν ἀνάξια τροφῆς ἡγούμενοι διαφθείρουσιν.* Strabo XV 1 § 30 tells the same story, but only on the authority of Onesikritus. For some remarks on these customs see Wheeler's History of India III 4 (pp 24, 173).

tollunt] this word is strictly applied only to the Roman custom of placing a newborn child on the ground at the feet of the father, who by raising it in his arms signified that he acknowledged the child as his own and was prepared to rear it. Here *tollunt aluntque* is really one notion. Perhaps we may render 'acknowledge and rear'.

eorum etc] 'the commissioners entrusted with the medical inspection of the babies'. So Strabo says *κριθέντα δ' ὑπὸ τοῦ ἀποδειχθέντος ἄρχοντος.*

habitum] 'condition', hence bodily form, 'looks'. Compare 2 § 6, 7 § 12.

insignes] 'remarkable', hence 'deformed'. Compare Suetonius Calig 26 *insignes debilitate aliqua corporis.*

§ 26. *nuptiis* etc] Diodorus says ἀκολούθως δὲ τούτοις καὶ τοὺς γάμους ποιοῦνται προικὸς μὲν καὶ τῆς ἄλλης πολυτελείας ἀφροντιστοῦντες, κάλλους δὲ καὶ τῆς τοῦ σώματος ὑπεροχῆς μόνον φροντίζοντες. For the Spartan custom see Plutarch Lykurg 14.

genere ac nobilitate] a hendiadys, =*generis nobilitate.* The ablative is that of cause.

coniunctis] joined together, 'contracted'. Compare IV 7 § 9 *donis acceptis amicitiaque coniuncta.*

electa specie] =*electione speciei*, through choice of appearance = 'choosing by looks'.

aestimatur] 'is taken account of'.

§ 28. *eminens* etc] so Diodorus XVII 91 παρὰ δὲ πάντας ὁ βασιλεὺς Σωπείθης περίβλεπτος ὢν ἐπὶ τῷ κάλλει, καὶ τῷ μήκει τοὺς τέτταρας πήχεις ὑπεράγων, προῆλθε μὲν ἐκ τῆς πόλεως τῆς ἐχούσης τὰ βασίλεια, παραδοὺς δ' αὑτὸν καὶ τὴν βασιλείαν Ἀλεξάνδρῳ πάλιν ταύτην ἀπέλαβε διὰ τὴν τοῦ κρατοῦντος ἐπιείκειαν.

§ 30. *candore*] 'lustre'. Pliny NH IX § 112 (referred to on VIII 9 § 19) counts *candor* and *magnitudo* as the two merits of pearls.

baculum aureum] sceptre.

precatus etc] 'with the wish that it might bring him good luck'. Some customary Oriental phrase of compliment is no doubt represented by this expression. Zumpt compares the wish to the bride in Plautus casina 4 41 *sospes iter incipe hoc.*

§ 31. *canes*] we have much the same account of these wonderful hunting dogs in Diodorus XVII 92, Strabo XV 1 § 31, and their great size is noted by Pliny NH VII § 31.

viderunt] emphatic, according to Pratt. 'On sighting the game'.

leonibus] Plutarch de solertia animalium 15 tells of an Indian dog who would not notice a stag boar or bear, but at once assailed a lion.

§ 32. *in conseptum*] this is Mützell's excellent emendation of MSS *conseptu.* Diodorus says εἰσήγαγεν εἴς τι περίφραγμα λέοντα τέλειον.

IIII *omnino*] '4 in all'. Strabo and Diodorus say that first two dogs were slipped at the lion and then two more.

occupaverunt] see on VIII 9 § 32. Render 'fastened on' or even our technical slang word 'tackled'.

ex iis...unus] one of the royal huntsmen.

non sequebatur] 'it (the leg) would not come away'. Compare Virgil Aen VI 146 (of the golden bough) *carpe manu, namque ipse volens facilisque sequetur.*

§ 33. *institit*] 'went on to'. Compare *institit quaerere* in IV 7 § 27, VI 7 § 25.

inde] of time, as in 10 § 22.

subinde] over and over again. Diodorus says ἔτεμνεν ἡσυχῇ κατ' ὀλίγον.

[*in*] *illis*] *in* is bracketed by Mützell, following Halm.

§ 34. *transcribo*] 'copy' out of the books of other authors into my own.

adfirmare] 'guarantee'.

subducere] withdraw, 'suppress'. Compare 7 § 24.

§ 35. *Hypasin*] Strabo and Diodorus call the river Ὕπανις, Arrian Ὕφασις. Pliny agrees with the above spelling supported by the MSS of Curtius. Mützell compares the Sanskrit form of the name *Vipasa*.

Hephaestione] Diodorus XVII 93 ἅμα δὲ τούτοις πραττομένοις ἧκεν Ἡφαιστίων μετὰ τῆς συναπεσταλμένης δυνάμεως πολλὴν τῆς Ἰνδικῆς καταπεπολεμηκώς. In 91 he tells us that the expedition had been directed against the younger Porus, a statement found also in Arrian V 21 § 5. Curtius treats this as merely a subordinate operation to the main campaign, and such indeed it is.

diversam regionem] a district in another direction.

§ 36. *Phegeus* etc] Diodorus XVII 93 has this in almost the very same words.

iussis] this is probably no more than Curtius' way of accounting for a circumstance which he found somehow mentioned in his authorities, and the bearing of which he did not fully understand. See on VIII 12 § 12.

CHAPTER II.

§ 1. *superare*] Ritter and Thirlwall argue that this crossing took place below the junction of the Hypasis (Beyas) with the Hesudrus (Sutlej), because the mention of deserts to the east is only true of the part more to the south. Pratt quotes from Elphinstone's *Caubul* to the same effect. See on VIII 9 § 8. Diodorus says XVII 93 τὸν Ὕπανιν ποταμόν, οὗ τὸ μὲν πλάτος ἦν σταδίων ἑπτὰ τὸ δὲ βάθος ἓξ ὀργυιῶν τὸ δὲ ῥεῦμα σφοδρὸν καὶ δυσδιάβατον, and we learn from Strabo XV 1 §§ 17, 27 that this part of the campaign fell in the rainy season. See on VIII 13 § 8.

non spatio...etc] the construction is changed suddenly, for *non spatio* has *sed inpeditum* parallel to it. *spatio* is an ablative of cause.

§ 2. XI *dierum*] So Diodorus goes on ἀκούσας δὲ τοῦ Φηγέως περὶ τῆς πέραν τοῦ Ἰνδοῦ ποταμοῦ [? τοῦ ποταμοῦ simply] χώρας ὅτι δώδεκα μὲν ἡμερῶν ἔχει δίοδον ἔρημον, μετὰ δὲ ταύτην εἶναι ποταμὸν τὸν ὀνομαζόμενον Γάγγην, τὸ μὲν πλάτος τριάκοντα καὶ δυοῖν σταδίων τὸ δὲ βάθος μέγιστον τῶν κατὰ τὴν Ἰνδικήν, ... etc. But Arrian V 25 § 1 says τὰ δὲ δὴ πέραν τοῦ Ὑφάσιος ποταμοῦ εὐδαίμονά τε τὴν χώραν εἶναι ἐξηγγέλλετο... etc.

excipere] meets one advancing, 'comes next'. Compare 10 § 6.

§ 3. *ulteriorem* etc] Diodorus goes on πέραν δὲ τούτου κατοικεῖν τό τε τῶν Πραισίων καὶ Γανδαριδῶν ἔθνος, τούτων δὲ βασιλεύειν Ξανδράμην, ἔχοντα δισμυρίους μὲν ἱππεῖς πεζῶν δὲ εἴκοσι μυριάδας ἅρματα δὲ δισχίλια ἐλέφαντας δὲ πολεμικῶς κεκοσμημένους τετρακισχιλίους. The names of the nations mentioned are according to Captain Wilford (quoted by Pratt) merely corruptions of Indian names denoting the peoples to the eastward generally. See however M'Crindle pp 9, 57, 134, who also identifies Aggrammes with the famous Sandrokottos (*Chandragupta*) who drove the Greeks out of India about 312 B C.

obsidentem vias] that is, he had so many in the field (as we now say 'mobilized') to hold the approaches to his country.

§ 4. *ad hoc*] 'moreover', = *praeterea*. Common in the historical writers. Compare 10 § 13. See Kennedy § 70.

§ 5. *incredibilia* etc] this account is almost word for word the same as that of Diodorus XVII 93.

cum eo] that is, *cum Poro*.

§ 6. *haud falso iactari*] were not falsely represented by report, that is, were not exaggerated.

ignobilem] compare Horace sat I 6 9 *ante potestatem Tulli atque ignobile regnum*. For the sense of this passage see appendix D (*f*).

ultimae sortis] 'of the meanest condition'. Compare III 2 § 11 *ille et suae sortis et regiae superbiae oblitus*, Horace carm IV 11 22 *non tuae sortis* (*puella*).

propulsantem] 'staving off' hunger by his daily earnings. That is, living from hand to mouth.

§ 7. *in propiorem* etc] he had been advanced to a higher place in the confidence of the reigning monarch. *propiorem* = nearer, more intimate.

qui tum regnasset] 'who had then been king' = 'who was then on the throne'.

eo] the king his master.

per insidias] treacherously. Compare 7 § 16, and see Kennedy § 70.

liberum] the regular form of the genitive of this word.

qui nunc regnat] this is put in as a dependent clause in the *oratio obliqua*, but constructed as though meant to represent the very words of the speaker. So we have *dum est* 10 § 21 in a clause really dependent on *voluisse* just above.

invisum etc] Diodorus says εὐτελῆ παντελῶς καὶ ἄδοξον.

vilem] compare Livy II 41 § 8 *vilior civibus* 'cheaper in his fellow-citizens' eyes'.

memorem] that is, he rather 'took after' his father (a low adventurer) than conducted himself as one born to a throne (as Porus himself was).

§ 8. *multiplicem* etc] caused the king manifold anxiety. That is, made him feel anxious on many grounds.

spernebat] see § 21.

situm locorum] the lie of the ground, that is, the natural obstacles that would present themselves to an invader.

vim fluminum] this would probably be the main difficulty with which he would have to contend: *et* therefore should be taken (as *καὶ* often in Greek) = 'and in particular'.

§ 9. *relegatos* etc] 'to follow up and unearth men removed almost to the uttermost bound of the world seemed too hard a task'. Compare V 5 § 14 of the Greek prisoners in Persia, *procul Europa in ultima orientis relegati*, Cic Tusc II § 20 *non saeva terris gens relegata ultimis*. In these passages all notion of banishment has disappeared.

eruere] compare 3 § 8.

rursus] 'on the other hand'.

avaritia gloriae] compare Horace de arte poet 324 (*Graiis*) *praeter laudem nullius avaris*.

insatiabilis etc] Alexander's ambition is proverbial.

§ 10. *tot spatia terrarum*] 'all those broad lands'. Compare IV 14 § 7 *tot terrarum spatia emensis*, and see below on 4 § 19.

senes] Mützell remarks that this would be literally applicable to the old soldiers of Philip who had accompanied Alexander into Asia, but that it must really refer to the Macedonian troops generally who were for the most part men sent afterwards to reinforce the army. Of such it could only be said in a figurative sense, which is well illustrated by 3 § 10. *senes facti* means in truth little more than 'worn out'. See on 3 § 5.

difficultates] 'difficulties' of nature, such as mountains rivers storms floods heat cold etc. Compare for the use of word as concrete VII 11 § 17 *per has tamen difficultates enituntur in verticem montis*.

parta frui] *praeda*, that is, 'Overflowing and laden with booty, they would rather (he judged) enjoy what they had won than wear themselves out by getting more'. We find also *frui parto* (neuter) in much the same sense. See Virgil georg I 300.

velle etc] these infinitives depend on the notion 'he thought' easily to be supplied from what precedes. See Madvig § 403 a.

§ 11. *non idem animi esse*] 'his men were not of the same mind as himself'. For the construction compare VIII 8 § 19 *quem, si Macedo esset, tecum introduxissem,.........nunc Olynthio non idem iuris est*.

mente complexum] had grasped in mind, 'formed the conception' of universal empire.

adhuc] in silver-age Latin this word means not only 'hitherto', but also 'even', 'still'. Compare 3 § 13.

primordio] at the first beginning. Curtius uses the word again 6 § 17.

§ 12. *ergo*] 'so then'. The particle refers back to the end of § 9.

ad hunc maxime modum] 'very much to this effect'. *maxime* is often used like the Greek *μάλιστα* as 'about', 'pretty much', and more particularly with numerals.

disseruit] he who will compare the following brilliant speech with the wearisome harangue supplied to his readers by Arrian V 25, 26, will see the great superiority of Curtius both in imagination and expression.

per hos dies] 'during these last days'. That is, the two days of rest and part of the day on which he is speaking. See § 1.

§ 13. *inprovisa*] unexperienced, unknown. Compare VIII 13 § 11. Such is perhaps also the meaning in 9 § 11, but the common one is 'unexpected', 'unforeseen'.

vanitas] falsehood, lying. So below § 17. See Holden on Cic de off III § 58.

fauces] these are the 'gates' (πύλαι) or 'passes' from Cilicia into Syria. See III 4 §§ 11, 12 *Alexander fauces iugi, quae Pylae appellantur, intravit. contemplatus locorum situm non alias magis dicitur admiratus esse felicitatem suam: obrui potuisse vel saxis confitebatur, si fuissent qui in subeuntes propellerent. iter vix quaternos capiebat armatos: dorsum montis inminebat viae non angustae modo sed plerumque praeruptae, crebris oberrantibus rivis, qui ex radicibus montium manant.* This was on the way to the battle of Issus.

campos] where the battle of Gaugamela or Arbela was fought.

vado] namely the Tigris, of which Curtius says IV 9 § 15 *paucos equitum ad temptandum vadum fluminis praemisit.*

ponte] namely the Euphrates, of which he says IV 9 § 12 *ad Euphratem pervenit quo pontibus iuncto*......etc.

§ 14. *ad liquidum*] to the clear, to clearness. That is, to a state of transparency so that one can look through and see what the fact is which underlies these obscure and distorted statements. Compare Velleius I 16 § 1 *res ad liquidum ratione perducta*, Quintilian V 14 § 28.

illa tradente] when she hands them on, that is, when she is the medium through which they are conveyed.

cum sit ex solido] 'though resting on a real foundation'. That is, a foundation of fact. Compare *solidius* VIII 14 § 46, and Virgil Aen XI 426, 427, *multos alterna revisens lusit et in solido rursus fortuna locavit.*

nominis quam operis] here we have probably no more than an attempt to express the common Greek antithesis between ὄνομα and ἔργον, 'name' and 'reality'.

§ 15. *sustineri*] compare § 22, IX 5 § 18.

§ 16. *armentorum*] cattle. See VIII 12 § 11. The word is connected with the root of *aro*.

difficilius] Strabo however XV 1 § 42 says 'and they are seldom hard to tame; for they are naturally of a mild and gentle disposition, so as closely to resemble a rational animal (λογικῷ ζώῳ)'.

§ 17. *nam flumen* etc] the connexion of the sense seems to be this. [The other obstacles are exaggerated, and so is the breadth of the rivers: but this even if taken for granted would afford no proof of their being hard to cross] 'For a river' etc. Alexander seems to be pointing out that the croakers have for once overshot their mark.

spatio alvei] by reason of the breadth of channel, that is, when the channel is broad.

§ 18. *in ripa*] emphatic.

§ 19. *sed...fingamus*] 'but suppose for the sake of argument that all those stories are true'. Compare Juvenal II 111 *sed tu vera puta.*

praesens] 'before our eyes'. That is, in the battle with Porus.

§ 20. *quot Porus*] VIII 13 § 6.

declinari in fugam] 'turn themselves away into flight'='swerve aside and fly'. See 4 § 20.

§ 21. *elidunt*] 'squeeze out', 'nip': hence 'hamper'.

inhabiles] for the matter see VIII 14 § 18.

opposuerim] did not set them in line.

§ 22. *at enim*] as usual, introducing an objection to be immediately answered. Madvig § 437 c, Kennedy § 79, 6 b.

paucis] emphatic.

enim] ironical.

sustinebitis] endure, support, 'bear the shock of'.

§ 23. *invicti*] goes with *adversus multitudinem.* 'Unconquered in fighting against odds'. But the battle of the Granicus was not a striking instance of this.

Cilicia] this refers to the battle of Issus, in which according to Curtius III 11 § 27 Darius lost 110,000 men.

inundata] 'deluged'. Compare Virgil Aen X 24 *inundant sanguine fossae* (al *fossas*). So Lucan X 32, 33 says of Alexander *ignotos miscuit amnes, Persarum Euphraten Indorum sanguine Gangen.* Compare Horace carm II 1 34—36.

Arbela, cuius] yet *Arbela* is neuter plural.

ossibus strati] Compare the description of the finding the remains of the army of Varus, Tacitus ann I 61.

§ 24. *solitudinem* etc] 'now that you have depopulated Asia by your conquests'. Compare Tacitus Agr 30 (of Roman conquest) *ubi solitudinem faciunt, pacem appellant.*

§ 25. *illi turbae*] that crowd, 'a throng like that' of Scythians Bactrians etc. *turba*, as in § 22, is contemptuous, and denotes mere numbers as opposed to effective strength. See III 3 § 27 (of the Macedonian army) *agmen et stare paratum et sequi, nec turba nec sarcinis praegrave.*

gesturus sum] 'I mean to do'.

vadem praedemque] 'bail and surety'. *vas* was a surety in general, and particularly for the appearance of a person to answer a criminal charge. *praes* was a surety in civil matters, such as the disputed possession of land; he would guarantee that the property should not be damaged before the right of ownership was settled. Ausonius idyll 12 *quis subit in poenam capitali iudicio? vas. quid si lis fuerit nummaria, quis dabitur? praes.*

mei] for this use of the genitive see Madvig § 297 b obs 2. Mützell remarks that the opposition is brought out more strongly thus than if he had written *meos.*

mihi] the so-called *dativus ethicus.* 'I beg'. See Madvig § 248.

§ 26. *in limine*] 'on the threshold', that is, just about to begin. Compare VI 3 § 17 *in ipso limine victoriae stamus.* Arrian V 26 § 6 makes him say ὑμεῖς δὲ καὶ τὰ ἔτι ὑπόλοιπα τῆς Ἀσίας πρόσθετε τοῖς ἤδη κεκτημένοις καὶ τὰ ὀλίγα τοῖς πολλοῖς.

solis ortum] see on 4 § 18.

oceanum] see 4 § 17. Arrian V 26 § 1 makes him say that it is not far to the Ganges and the Eastern sea, which the Hyrcanian sea (Caspian) will be found to join, ἐκπεριέρχεται γὰρ γῆν περὶ πᾶσαν ἡ μεγάλη θάλασσα. See on 3 § 14.

fine terrarum] Arrian V 26 § 2 makes him say that after a voyage pretty well round the earth they will have as theirs all Africa and Asia, καὶ ὅροι τῆς ταύτῃ ἀρχῆς οὕσπερ καὶ τῆς γῆς ὅρους ὁ θεὸς ἐποίησε.

§ 27. *dives et inbellis*] a statement made merely to entice his hearers on.

§ 28. *per vos* etc] *vos* does not go with *per*, but follows *oro quaesoque* below. *per* governs the *gloriam* and *merita* by which he is adjuring them. For this order of words compare V 8 § 16 *per ego vos decora maiorum...oro et obtestor*, Horace carm I 8. Sometimes the verbs of entreaty are left out, to be supplied in sense, as IV 14 § 24 *per ego vos deos patrios aeternumque ignem...vindicate ab ultimo dedecore nomen gentemque Persarum.*

fastigium] the 'pinnacle' of human greatness. Compare 10 § 24, and IV 7 § 8 *haud contentus mortali fastigio.*

invicti] we adhere to the old reading. Compare VII 10 § 8 *si quis ipsos beneficio quam iniuria experiri maluisset, certaturos fuisse ne vincerentur officio.* Vogel adds Cic pro Mil § 96. There is a similar expression in Greek. Plut Alex 59 illustrates it well.

§ 29. *nihil umquam praecepi, quin*] for *quin* = 'in such a way that not' = 'without' see Madvig 440 a obs 3, and below 9 § 23.

infregeritis etc] 'do not break the palm already in my grasp', that is, do not break off my hitherto unbroken career of victory. Mützell compares Seneca Phoenissae 536 foll *exultes licet victorque fratris spolia deiecti geras; frangenda palma est.*

si invidia afuerit] = εἰ ἀνεπίφθονον εἰπεῖν, 'if I may speak thus without incurring the ill-will of heaven'.

§ 30. *pulso*] 'knock at'. Compare Claudian de bell Getico 625 *pulsaretque tuas ululatus coniugis aures.*

§ 31. *tacere perseverarent*] 'still suppressed what they felt'. *tacee* is used of keeping back something: compare VI 10 § 35 *si et quum indicamus invisi et quum tacemus suspecti sumus, quid facere nos oportet?*

The use of the word to denote (as here) the suppression of a feeling is particularly elegant. Compare Virgil Aen IV 67 *tacitum vivit sub pectore volnus.*

deliqui etc] 'I must have inadvertently given you some offence, that you will not even look at me'.

quod...vultis] this clause with *quod* is not dependent on the leading proposition, but rather contains the circumstance that suggested that proposition. The argument then is 'as to [the circumstance of] your being unwilling to look at me, [I infer that] I must have offended you'. See Madvig 398 b obs 2, and compare Virgil Aen II 180, 181 *et nunc quod patrias vento petiere Mycenas, arma deosque parant comites.* Munro's note on Lucretius IV 885 will supply ample information on this point.

in solitudine] compare 4 § 33.

nemo saltem negat] 'no one so much as refuses', that is, to go on with me. *saltem* is used in silver-age Latin after a negative in much the same way as *quidem*. Here he might have written *nemo ne negat quidem.*

§ 32. *quos adloquor*] that is, are you some strangers?

quid autem postulo?] that is, am I claiming something utterly absurd and beyond bearing? *postulo*=ἀξιῶ. *autem*='aye, and', does not set aside what goes before. See Madvig § 437 b.

vestram] emphatic.

vindicamus] note the plural 'that *we* are upholding'. For *vindico* compare X 7 § 15 *in eadem domo familiaque imperii vires remansuras esse gaudebant: hereditarium imperium stirpem regiam vindicaturam: adsuetos esse nomen ipsum colere venerarique, nec quemquam id capere nisi genitum ut regnaret,* Caesar bell gall VII 76.

vulnerati] perhaps this refers to the wound in VIII 10 §§ 27—30.

hostibus deditus] this, the most stinging expression of the three, because most clearly implying the agency of the army, is carefully reserved to the end of the sentence. Compare Cic pro Sulla § 79 *obicere invidiae, dedere suspitioni.*

§ 33. *gentibus, quarum* etc] see 2 § 3.

nomina] the mere names. Compare IV 12 § 9 *Indi ceterique rubri maris accolae, nomina verius quam auxilia, post currus erant,* Tacitus hist IV 14 *attollerent tantum oculos et inania legionum nomina ne pavescerent.*

erunt mecum etc] compare Caesar bell gall I 40 *quod si praeterea nemo sequatur, tamen se cum sola decima legione iturum, de qua non dubitaret, sibique eam praetoriam cohortem futuram.*

§ 34. *precario* etc] to be commander on sufferance. Compare X 2 § 15 *palam certe rupistis imperium, et precario rex sum,* Tacitus Agr 16 *Trebellius fuga ac latebris vitata exercitus ira indecorus atque humilis precario mox praefuit.*

deserto rege etc] Arrian V 28 § 2 says that after Coenus had spoken

Alexander broke up the meeting and on the morrow assembled them again and *αὐτὸς μὲν ἰέναι ἔφη τοῦ πρόσω, βιάσεσθαι δὲ οὐδένα ἄκοντα Μακεδόνων ξυνέπεσθαι· ἕξειν γὰρ τοὺς ἀκολουθήσοντας τῷ βασιλεῖ σφῶν ἑκόντας· τοῖς δὲ καὶ ἀπιέναι οἴκαδε ἐθέλουσιν ὑπάρχειν ἀπιέναι καὶ ἐξαγγέλλειν τοῖς οἰκείοις ὅτι τὸν βασιλέα σφῶν ἐν μέσοις τοῖς πολεμίοις ἐπανήκουσιν ἀπολιπόντες.*

a vobis etc] 'for the victory that you have given up hope of'. *locum inveniam* goes somewhat awkwardly with this, but is natural enough with *morti*.

CHAPTER III.

§ 1. *expectabant ut* etc] this construction is rare, but found in Caesar bell civ I 66 *neque expectant ut de eorum imperio ad populum feratur*. Render 'wait for'.

perferrent etc] 'report [the news] that'.... The construction is like that with *nuntio* (see VIII 14 § 1) and other words.

illi] that is, the *duces principesque*.

§ 2. *sua sponte*] 'of its own accord', that is, no one knew how.

liberius] compare VI 2 § 4 *secessio militum et liberior inter mutuas querellas dolor*.

erigi] to raise itself, arise.

temperare oculis] to refrain from tears. Compare Livy XXI 22.

§ 3. *propius tribunal*] compare VII 7 § 9 *propius ipsum considere amicos iubet*, and see Madvig § 172 part III obs 4.

§ 5. *tum Coenus*] this speech put into the mouth of Coenus has a peculiar literary interest beyond the ordinary run of orations written for their leading characters by the rhetorical historians of antiquity. In the remaining works of the elder Seneca we have a *suasoria* or hortatory oration (see Mayor on Juvenal I 16) on this very subject, in which are arranged all the telling sentences that some of the most famous Roman rhetoricians could compose to suit the situation. The remarkable parallels found in this collection to the present speech of Curtius illustrate in a very striking way the artificial nature of these harangues, and shew what a vast amount of labour this spirited and polished specimen probably took to produce. The corresponding speech in Arrian V 27, though less pointed than that in Curtius, is more natural and easy, and certainly far superior to that put into the mouth of Alexander. See appendix A.

inpias mentes] 'disloyal thoughts'. So Virgil georg I 511 *Mars inpius*, Aen VI 612 *arma impia*, speaking of civil wars.

profecto] one may be sure, 'assuredly'. For the general form of the sentence compare V 8 § 9 *dignissimi quibus, si ego non possim, dii pro me gratiam referant. et mehercule referent.*

idem animus etc] Arrian V 27 § 4 on the contrary *ὀλίγοι δὲ ἐκ πολλῶν ὑπολείπονται, καὶ οὔτε τοῖς σώμασιν ἔτι ὡσαύτως ἐρρωμένοι, ταῖς τε γνώμαις πολὺ ἔτι μᾶλλον προκεκμηκότες.*

animus est...ire] compare Virgil Aen IV 639 *perficere est animus*, Horace epod XVI 17—21 *nulla sit hac potior sententia......ire pedes quocumque ferent.*

commendare etc] 'to give your name in keeping to after ages'. Compare Cic ad fam X 12.

posteritati] Ovid heroid XVI 374 *nomen ab aeterna posteritate feres.*

proinde] 'so then'.

exangues] Lucan I 343 (of the veterans of Caesar) *conferet exanguis quo se post bella senectus?* Sallust Cat 39 § 4, Cic pro Sest § 24.

§ 6. *auspicium*] a very Roman notion, which comes again 6 § 9, VI 3 § 2 (enumerating a list of conquests) *quorum alia ductu meo, alia imperio auspicioque perdomui.* See Horace carm I 7 27, IV 14 33, Suetonius Aug 21, Tacitus ann II 41.

§ 7. *implevimus*] 'have filled up the measure of'. The metaphor is shewn by *capere* (*χωρεῖν*) 'to contain'. Compare Tacitus Agr 44 *vera bona, quae in virtutibus sita sunt, impleverat.*

§ 8. *fine*] Tacitus Agr 33 *nec inglorium fuerit in ipso terrarum ac naturae fine cecidisse.* See also 4 § 18 below.

eruere expetis] Curtius uses this construction elsewhere. Compare VI 11 § 17 *dicturum se quae scire expeterent pollicetur.* See Munro on Lucr I 418.

sol] see on 4 § 18.

victoria lustres] 'may traverse as conqueror'. Compare Virgil Aen IV 607 *sol qui terrarum flammis opera omnia lustras.*

§ 9. *in incremento erit*] 'will be ever growing'. Compare IV 2 § 21 *molis, cuius incrementum eos antea fefellerat.*

§ 10. *putria*] this word seems to mean 'broken', 'cloven', that is, cut up with badly-healed or sloughing wounds. In Livy XXI 37 (of Hannibal's passing the Alps) we are told *ardentiaque saxa infuso aceto putrefaciunt:* the same operation is spoken of by Juvenal X 153 *diducit scopulos et montem rumpit aceto*, and Pliny XXIII § 57 uses *rumpit* in the same way of the effect of vinegar on rocks; while in Virgil Aen IX 432 we have (*ensis*) *candida pectora rumpit.*

iam tela etc] so Diodorus XVII 94 says of the army *καὶ τῶν μὲν ἵππων διὰ τὴν συνέχειαν τῆς ὁδοιπορίας τὰς ὁπλὰς ὑποτετρῖφθαι συνέβαινε, τῶν δὲ ὅπλων τὰ πλεῖστα κατεξάνθαι καὶ τὸν μὲν Ἑλληνικὸν ἱματισμὸν ἐκλελοιπέναι συναναγκάζεσθαι δὲ βαρβαρικοῖς ὑφάσμασι χρῆσθαι, συντεμόντας τὰ τῶν Ἰνδῶν περιβλήματα.*

tela...arma] offensive and defensive respectively.

subvehi] cannot be brought up to supply us. *sub* conveys the notion of 'up' to the place required.

degeneravimus] so VIII 5 § 14 *in peregrinos externosque ritus degenerare.*

§ 11. *quam multos*] that is, how few. The slaves had taken every opportunity of escaping.

laboramus] are straitened, in difficulties. Compare 1 § 5.

§ 12. *nudum*] a supply of arms soon came; see § 21.

ut augeant] for *ut* concessive see Madvig § 440 a obs 4, and compare 4 § 18, 6 § 6 below.

intellego] Coenus speaks in his own person as in § 15.

§ 13. *adhuc*] 'still further'.

decurrere] compare 4 § 2.

§ 14. *hic quoque*] that is, it is not necessary to cross India to find the ocean. See on 2 § 26.

errare] to go wandering about.

§ 15. *non uti* etc] Arrian V 27 § 2 makes Coenus say *οὐδὲ ὑπὲρ ταύτης (τῆς στρατιᾶς τῆς πολλῆς) τὰ καθ' ἡδονὴν ἐκείνοις ἐρῶ, ἀλλ' ἃ νομίζω ξύμφορα......*etc.

§ 16. *ploratu* etc] Arrian V 28 § 1 *τοιαῦτα εἰπόντος τοῦ Κοίνου θόρυβον γενέσθαι ἐκ τῶν παρόντων ἐπὶ τοῖς λόγοις· πολλοῖς δὲ δὴ καὶ δάκρυα προχυθέντα ἔτι μᾶλλον δηλῶσαι τό τε ἀκούσιον τῆς γνώμης ἐς τοὺς πρόσω κινδύνους καὶ τὸ καθ' ἡδονὴν σφισιν εἶναι τὴν ἀναχώρησιν.*

§ 17. *excusatio*] 'begging off' further campaigning.

§ 18. *poterat* etc] 'could not have chidden them for their stubbornness'. That is, the feeling of the army was so strong and unanimous that he could not see his way to giving them a lecture on their misbehaviour.

obstinatos] compare 2 § 30.

itaque etc] Arrian V 28 §§ 1—3 *Ἀλέξανδρος δὲ τότε μὲν ἀχθεσθεὶς τοῦ τε Κοίνου τῇ παρρησίᾳ καὶ τῷ ὄκνῳ τῶν ἄλλων ἡγεμόνων διέλυσε τὸν ξύλλογον·* (on the morrow he spoke as quoted above on 2 § 34) *ταῦτ' εἰπόντα ἀπελθεῖν ἐς τὴν σκηνήν, μηδέ τινα τῶν ἑταίρων προσέσθαι αὐτῆς τε ἐκείνης τῆς ἡμέρας καὶ ἐς τὴν τρίτην ἔτι ἀπ' ἐκείνης.* Diodorus XVII 94 says that Alexander tried to reconcile his soldiers to a further march by giving up the rich river valley-lands to plunder; after which he addressed them in a set speech, but found the Macedonians immoveable, and so abandoned his project.

§ 19. *irae*] Arrian V 28 § 3 says that he was not merely angry but waiting for the chance of a change in the minds of the men, which however did not take place.

erigique etc] Arrian Diodorus and the rest give much the same account, the latter with more detail. Pliny N H VI § 62 says of the Hypasis *qui fuit Alexandri itinerum terminus, exsuperato tamen amne arisque in adversa ripa dicatis.* This statement is not supported by any other writer, and from what we know of the tendency of the Panjab rivers to destroy their banks and change their channels we can hardly expect that the research of travellers will ever settle the point. The account of Pliny is probable enough and is not contradicted.

extendi] 'to be drawn out wide'. Compare Ovid metam I 43 *iussit et extendi campos (deus).* The lines were to be on a larger scale than ordinary.

fallax miraculum] so Plutarch Alex 62 says πολλὰ πρὸς δόξαν ἀπατηλὰ καὶ σοφιστικὰ μηχανώμενος.

§ 20. *repetens*] 'retracing'. Compare Livy XXXV 28 *utrum pergere qua coepisset ire via, an eam qua venisset repetere melius esset.* Diodorus XVII 95 ταῖς αὐταῖς ὁδοῖς πορευθεὶς ἀνέκαμψεν ἐπὶ τὸν Ἀκεσίνην ποταμόν.

Coenus] Arrian's account makes Coenus die by the Hydaspes not at the Acesines, V 29 § 3, VI 2 § 1.

morte] 'at' or 'by reason of' the death of Coenus. The use of the ablative here is very remarkable; in IV 10 § 30 we have *ingemuisse etiam Alexandrum morti* 'over the death'.

propter paucos dies etc] *paucos* and *longam* are in emphatic opposition to each other. 'That it was but for the sake of a few days that he had opened a long-winded speech as though he alone were destined to see Macedonia again'. *visurus*=ἐποψόμενος 'to live to see'. Arrian V 27 § 6 makes Coenus use the word ἐπιδεῖν.

§ 21. *in aqua stabat*] 'was riding [at moorings] in the stream'. Compare 9 § 19. That is, it was completed and ready for service. Diodorus also says that it was in the Acesines, Arrian with much more probability that it was in the Hydaspes. Arrian V 29 § 3 tells us that a city was founded on the Acesines.

inter haec]=*interea.*

in supplementum etc] Diodorus XVII 95 κατὰ δὲ τοῦτον τὸν χρόνον ἧκον ἐκ τῆς Ἑλλάδος σύμμαχοι καὶ μισθοφόροι διὰ τῶν στρατηγῶν ἡγμένοι πεζοὶ μὲν πλείους τρισμυρίων, ἱππεῖς δ' οὐ πολὺ λείποντες τῶν ἑξακισχιλίων, ἐκομίσθησαν δὲ καὶ πανοπλίαι διαπρεπεῖς πεζοῖς μὲν δισμυρίοις καὶ πεντακισχιλίοις, φαρμάκων δ' ἰατρικῶν ἑκατὸν τάλαντα.

milibus] Madvig emends thus, remarking that *arma*='suits of armour', and that we ought thus to have *armorum...caelatorum*, but without any reference to the words of Diodorus, which so strongly support his view.

§ 22. *mille*] Diodorus also makes the total 1000. Arrian VI 2 § 4 says (following Ptolemy) that counting in all the smaller craft there were not far short of 2000, and in the Indica 19 § 7 he gives the total more precisely at 1800. There is however some doubt about the reading in these two passages.

discordesque et...retractantes] 'disagreeing and raking up old-standing feuds'. The *que...et* is one of the quasi-poetical mannerisms of Curtius, and =τε...καὶ in Greek.

Porum et Taxilen] Arrian speaking of the time just after the battle on the Hydaspes says (V 20 § 4) καὶ Ταξίλῃ δὲ διαλλάττει Πῶρον καὶ Ταξίλην ἀποπέμπει ὀπίσω εἰς τὰ ἤθη τὰ αὑτοῦ. This may refer to the same circumstance.

firmatae...relinquit] the construction of *relinquit* here with a genitive of quality following is very remarkable. See however note on VIII 10 § 24 *obiecta est*, and compare the passage quoted on § 23 *dedicans*, Horace sat I 4 17, 18 *di bene fecerunt inopis me quodque pusilli finxerunt animi*, and see Madvig § 287. Render 'left them with friendly relations strengthened by a marriage alliance'. For the word *adfinitatem* see Holden on Cic de off I § 54, where a list of *adfines* is given.

§ 23. *Nicaeam*] General Cunningham finds the site of this at Mong on the left or eastern bank of the Hydaspes. It will be remarked that Curtius speaks as though these towns were on the Acesines, yet he cannot have meant this as he makes the great battle (VIII 14) take place on the Hydaspes.

Bucephala] the name is given thus by Arrian and Diodorus, though the former makes it neuter plural, the latter feminine singular. Strabo and Plutarch call it Βουκεφαλία. General Cunningham finds the site of this place at Jalalpur on the right or western bank of the Hydaspes. For the death of Alexander's favourite horse Bucephalus see VIII 14 § 34.

memoriae ac nomini] a hendiadys, 'to commemorate'.

dedicans] 'dedicating' in the metaphorical sense in which the silver-age writers use the word. Compare Pliny NH praef § 12 *meae quidem temeritati accessit hoc quoque, quod levioris operae hos tibi dedicavi libellos.*

§ 24. *elephantis* etc] this account is neither clear nor correct. We know from Arrian VI 2 § 2 that the bulk of the army marched along the banks of the river, Craterus commanding the division on the right bank, Hephaestion the larger one on the left bank: the elephants were with the latter. With this Diodorus XVII 96 agrees in general terms.

secundo amne] 'down stream', as we say. Compare 6 § 2, 8 § 3, 9 § 27, Virgil georg III 447 *missusque secundo defluit amni.*

quadraginta stadia] that is, about 5 miles. Alexander did not hurry for the reason here given, that he might take every good opportunity of landing. This was not only for the benefit of the armament, but (as we learn from Arrian VI 4 § 2) to receive or compel the submission of the native tribes along the river. Strabo XV 1 § 17 following Aristobulus tells us that the voyage down to Patala at the head of the Indus delta took ten months.

exponi] disembarked, put ashore. See 9 § 11.

subinde] 'from time to time'.

CHAPTER IV.

§ 1. *committitur*] 'joins', 'falls into'. The words seem to imply that the Hydaspes was an affluent of the Acesines, and not *vice versa*, which we know from Arrian VI 1 § 5. It is to be remembered that Curtius supposes the fleet to have been built and the voyage begun on the Acesines. Compare VII 3 § 20 *Taurus secundae magnitudinis mons committitur Caucaso.* See below § 8.

§ 2. *Siborum*] Diodorus also calls them Σίβοι, but Arrian and Strabo have the form Σίβαι. It is generally supposed that a tribe devoted to the worship of Siva are meant. See M'Crindle p 111 and VIII 14 § 11.

Herculis] this same story is preserved by Strabo XV 1 § 8, Diodorus XVII 96, Arrian Indica 5 § 12. The last cites it as an instance of the inventions that were occasioned by Alexander's expedition. Hercules was generally represented with a lion's skin and a club.

§ 4. *hinc*] from the land of Sibi. The word goes with *excessit.* We learn from Diodorus that the Sibi received Alexander kindly and that he in return treated them well.

§ 5. *milia gens*] the reading *alia* is found only in the Paris MS. It seems better to keep the old reading than to insert *alia* before *gens* and then to emend this assumed reading into *Agalasses* as Vogel does in his text merely because Diodorus names the people thus XVII 96 *καταλαβὼν δὲ τοὺς ὀνομαζομένους Ἀγαλασσεῖς ἠθροικότας πεζοὺς μὲν τετρακισμυρίους ἱππεῖς δὲ τρισχιλίους, συνάψας αὐτοῖς μάχην καὶ νικήσας τοὺς μὲν πλείστους κατέκοψε τοὺς δὲ λοιποὺς συμφυγόντας εἰς τὰς πλησίον πόλεις ἐκπολιορκήσας ἐξηνδραποδίσατο.* We must observe that only one *gens* (those of the *regio* and *oppidum* above) seem to be meant here.

fluminum] either the stream formed by the junction of the Hydaspes with the Acesines, or perhaps, the Hydaspes and some small tributary stream (the name of which Curtius has not recorded) are referred to.

quae] that is, the *milia peditum.*

amne] probably a tributary stream.

inclusos] that is the whole population, not merely the remains of the *milia peditum.*

expugnat] *eos.* For this word used with the people (not the place) for its object see VI 6 § 25 *ad expugnandos eos, qui edita montium occupaverant, redit,* Tacitus hist V 12, Agr 41.

§ 6. *alteram...amisit*] Diodorus XVII 96 says just the same.

sed...cremant] Diodorus says, 'and having in his anger set fire to the city he burnt in it most of the inhabitants: but some of the surviving natives took refuge in the citadel and addressed him as suppliants, bearing olive-branches. These he let go free, to the number of 3000'. The account in Curtius is quite as probable as that in Diodorus, and similar instances of desperation have been known in later times. But it must be confessed that Curtius seems here to be straining after effect.

§ 7. *adeo* etc] 'so completely does war invert natural relations'. For *adeo* = 'so true is it that', 'so remarkably', compare 10 § 30, Livy praef § 11, 1 9, Quintilian XII 11 § 16.

naturae iura] the natural rights or relations of men to each other, or to some other object, as a person or place. Compare VII 8 § 28 *quos viceris, amicos tibi esse cave credas: inter dominum et servum nulla amicitia est: etiam in pace belli tamen iura servantur,* where *belli iura* = hostile relations. Compare 8 § 10, 10 § 8.

§ 8. *arx*] emphatic. The town was burnt.

dereliquit] 'left behind'. The word generally means to abandon or forsake, and its use here is very strange.

circumvectus est] the geography of this passage is so utterly confused that it is well-nigh useless to attempt any rational explanation. How he can have sailed round the citadel strictly speaking is very hard to see; and we can only be certain that there is some confusion below between the two confluences (*a*) of the Hydaspes and Acesines and (*b*) of the Acesines and Indus. Diodorus does not confuse these but makes the armament reach the former confluence before these operations and then sail on to the latter, XVII 97 *αὐτὸς δὲ πάλιν μετὰ τῶν φίλων ἐμβὰς εἰς τὰς ναῦς διὰ τοῦ ποταμοῦ τὸν πλοῦν ἐποιεῖτο μέχρι τῆς συμβολῆς τῶν προειρημένων ποταμῶν καὶ τοῦ Ἰνδοῦ.*

munimento] Curtius uses the singular of this word in the same sense 'line of fortification' as the plural. See VIII 2 § 20 *fauces regionis qua in artissimum cogitur valido munimento sepserat*, V 1 § 31.

a septentrione] the meaning of *septentriones* or *septentrio* is discussed by Conington on Virgil georg III 381.

confunditur] 'unites with'. The notion of blending is more prominent in 9 § 7.

§ 9. *coetus*] the meeting (*συμβολή*) of the rivers.

multoque...cogitur] 'and the navigable way is compressed into a narrow channel by mud banks kept continually shifting by the force of the meeting waters'.

turbatur] compare III 4 § 8 *Cydnus non spatio aquarum sed liquore memorabilis: quippe leni tractu e fontibus labens puro solo excipitur, nec torrentes incurrunt qui placide manantis alveum turbent.*

meant] we are unable to follow Hedicke here in adopting the conjecture of Heinsius *meatur navigiis.*

§ 10. *itaque* etc] Arrian VI 4 §§ 4—5. § 3 gives a vivid and detailed account of this violent confluence (according to him that of the Hydaspes and Acesines), but says nothing of Alexander's personal danger. In this however as in other respects the account of Diodorus XVII 97 agrees with that of Curtius. The story of Alexander's upset was probably preserved in some accounts of the incident and Curtius has of course eagerly seized upon it as affording a more dramatic situation for the display of his rhetorical powers.

hinc...hinc] occurring twice here close together should perhaps be taken as 'partly'...'partly', 'both'...'and' in both places. See on VIII 13 § 11. But it is true that *hinc proras hinc latera* may be rendered (beating) 'from the one side on the prows, from the other on the broadsides of the vessels'.

subducere vela] to furl or take in sail. The expression is found also in the account of the Alexandrine war 45.

metu] the MSS give *cetu*. Of the various readings proposed we prefer this of Junius accepted by Mützell, who well refers to the words 9 § 15 which occur in a passage descriptive of a similar scene of confusion.

occupantur] are forestalled: that is, their own flurry and the speed of the current prevented them from executing their orders in time. We may render 'are hindered'. For the sense of *occupare* compare 5 § 24, and for *celeritate* VIII 14 § 19.

§ 11. *in oculis*] = ἐν ὄμμασιν 'before the eyes of'.

maiora] Diodorus says δύο μακραὶ ναῦς. Arrian explains that the shorter and rounder vessels came off safe and sound, while the longer vessels came off badly for the most part, and two sank in consequence of a collision. See below 9 § 2.

cum et ipsa etc] 'though they too were unmanageable'. Arrian tells us VI 5 § 1 that the sailing-masters so soon as they saw the rapids near at hand called on their men to row hard in order to keep some steerage-way on the vessels in the whirling current ahead of them. Curtius implies (and so does Arrian) that any efforts of this kind were not wholly successful.

innoxia] 'unhurt'. This passive use is not uncommon in the writers of the silver age. Compare Lucan IX 892 (*gens*) *a saevo serpentum innoxia morsu*.

expulsa sunt] ἐξέπεσε, says Diodorus.

§ 12. *amici......nabant*] so says Diodorus, and it is a touch that makes one suspect him as well as Curtius of having made the most of the danger.

§ 13. *ergo*] seeing the danger threatening from both sides, that is, in either case.

certamine] compare Virgil Aen III 128, 290, V 778.

concitant] the crew, that is.

everberarentur] 'might be beaten out', that is, forced to give place by the impulse of the vessel's bow. In fact they rowed their very hardest in order to get some steerage-way on the ship even at the eleventh hour. Compare IV 3 § 18 (at the siege of Tyre) *tandem remis pertinacius everberatum mare veluti eripientibus navigia classicis cessit, appulsaque sunt litori, lacerata pleraque*.

§ 14. *crederes*] Madvig § 370. Compare 9 § 16 below.

inliditur] εἰς τὴν γῆν ἐξέπεσε, says Diodorus.

bellum etc] this is sad stuff indeed. Some take *ergo* to refer back to this.

sacrificio] Diodorus says that he compared this affair to Achilles' struggle with the river in Iliad XXI. σωθεὶς δὲ παραδόξως τοῖς θεοῖς ἔθυσεν ὡς μεγίστους ἐκπεφευγὼς κινδύνους καὶ πρὸς ποταμὸν ὁμοίως Ἀχιλλεῖ διαγωνισάμενος. It is possible. But it is very doubtful whether any echo of this statement, however faint, is to be found in *cum amni bellum* etc.

§ 15. *Sudracarum*] we have here retained the form found in the MSS and supported by Justin XII 9 § 3. The Greek writers generally call them Oxydrakae. From Strabo XV 1 § 33 we learn that they lay to the south of the tribes between the Indus and Hydaspes. Meineke's text there has Συδράκαι.

Mallorum] this tribe were neighbours of the Sudracae, and their chief town seems to have occupied the site of the present Multan. See below on 8 § 3.

alias......iunxerat] Diodorus XVII 98 says the same, and adds that they soon got to loggerheads again and never fought together against Alexander.

nonaginta etc] Diodorus says 'more than 80000 infantry, 10000 cavalry and 700 chariots'.

§ 16. *integrum*] a war, that is, no part of which had been got over.

ferocissimis] the most high-spirited nations. Arrian Diodorus and Plutarch all use the epithet μάχιμοι of them, and Strabo calls them μεγάλα ἔθνη.

§ 17. *transmittere*] to let go by, hence to 'give up'. In silver-age Latin we find many of these pregnant words used with a certain archness. Compare Tacitus hist IV 9 *eam sententiam modestissimus quisque silentio deinde oblivio transmisit: fuere qui et meminissent*, also I 13, and Juvenal VII 190 *exempla novorum fatorum transi*, also III 114, X 273, VI 602. Render 'though he had been driven to give up the river Ganges and the regions beyond, he had not ended the war but only shifted it'.

§ 18. *extra sidera*] outside the range of the constellations they had been used to see in their own zone. Curtius is in this place probably thinking of Virgil Aen VI 794—796 (of Augustus) *super et Garamantas et Indos proferet imperium—iacet extra sidera tellus, extra anni solisque vias*, with which georg I 231—251 should be compared.

novis......existere] perhaps Curtius has in his head the story of the serpent's teeth and Jason; perhaps even the very lines of Ovid heroid XII (Medea Jasoni) occurred to him, as for instance 45—47 *semina praeterea populos genitura iuberis spargere devota lata per arva manu, qui peterent secum natis tua corpora telis*, and 95, 96 *arva venenatis pro semine dentibus imples: nascitur et gladios scutaque miles habet*.

identidem] 'over and over again'. The word should be taken closely with *novis*. 'New enemies were ever springing up with arms ever new'. See 9 §§ 10, 21.

existere] for the word compare Lucretius II 871 *quippe videre licet vivos existere vermes stercore de taetro*.

quod...manere] for these questions in *oratio obliqua* see Madvig § 405 a.

caliginem] there was a very old notion that to go far on the earth would surely land the voyager at length in a region of eternal darkness. Racine (*Alexandre* V 1) imitating the present passage says *des déserts que le ciel refuse d'éclairer, où la nature semble elle-même expirer*.

perpetuam] continuous, 'unbroken'.

incubantem] compare Virgil Aen I 88, 89 *eripiunt subito nubes caelumque diemque Teucrorum ex oculis; ponto nox incubat atra.*

beluarum] compare Horace carm III 27 26, 27 *scatentem beluis pontum.*

inmobiles undas] one of the fabled marvels of distant seas. Compare Tacitus Agr 10 *sed mare pigrum et grave remigantibus perhibent ne ventis quidem perinde attolli; credo quod rariores terrae montesque, causa ac materia tempestatum, et profunda moles continui maris tardius impellitur.*

defecerit] for this expression and indeed for the whole of § 18 compare the *suasoria* of Seneca spoken of on 3 § 5 above, and printed in appendix A. We may render 'gave way in despair' or 'broke down'. See below 6 § 20 *aliam naturam*, and 9 § 4.

§ 19. *nihil deinde* etc] 'after that there was nothing in their way beside these tribes'. The *deinde* means 'after the conquest of the tribes spoken of', and *praeter has gentes* is really superfluous.

terrarum spatia] the breadth of the lands, that is, the distance from the place where they stood to the great sea or *oceanus.*

§ 20. *cessisse* etc] possibly a *se* should be inserted before *illis;* anyhow it must be mentally supplied, and it may easily have fallen out after the last syllable of the preceding infinitive. But in 6 §§ 6, 26 we have similar omissions of the pronoun; so too in other writers, as Sallust Cat 31 § 7. 'He had given way to their fears of the Ganges and the numerous peoples beyond the river'. For *cedere*='to give way' compare X 7 § 18 (*precari*) *ut absisterent bello regique et pluribus cederent.*

§ 21. *iam...maris*] this high-flown stuff utterly spoils the picture and betrays the artificial nature of the whole paragraph. For *auram maris* see 9 § 3.

Herculis...terminos] Virgil Aen VI 801—805 *nec vero Alcides tantum telluris obivit, fixerit aeripedem cervam licet aut Erymanthi pacarit nemora et Lernam tremefecerit arcu, nec qui pampineis victor iuga flectit habenis Liber agens celso Nysae de vertice tigris.*

§ 22. *seditionis......maiora sunt*] we can render best by changing the metaphor slightly 'the means of quenching a mutiny are less important than the first sparks'. For the sense compare Ovid remedia amoris 91, 92 *principiis obsta: sero medicina paratur cum mala per longas convaluere moras.*

§ 23. *alacer*]=*alacritatis index* 2 § 30.

redditus] 'sent forth'.

quos]=*eos quos.* Hercules and father Liber are of course meant.

ad hostes] 'against the enemy'. This use of *ad* is found also in 1 §§ 19, 22, VIII 10 § 22. See also Livy I 5, 11, XXII 12 § 2, Terence hautont 545.

§ 24. *validissimae*] this refers to their numbers, and agrees with the account given by the other writers. See Arrian V 22.

ducem etc] Diodorus XVII 98 on the contrary says ἀλλὰ πάλιν στασιάσαντες ὑπὲρ τῆς ἡγεμονίας. In the following account of the campaign Curtius and Diodorus omit the important operations described by Arrian VI 5—8, in which the skill and judgment of Alexander were shewn to great advantage. See Thirlwall c 54 (vol VII pp 36—46). The siege of the town, which in these two authors constitutes the campaign, is in Arrian only the final operation. They speak mainly of the Sudrakae, Arrian represents the Malli as bearing the brunt of the war. The two accounts are so widely different in their general effect that we must consider them to have been gathered from different authorities. Arrian probably followed Ptolemy, so the reference to him by Curtius (5 § 21) is most likely no more than an indication that he consulted that book when describing the siege, and found that Ptolemy did not profess to have been present. Had Curtius read Ptolemy's account of the campaign, it is hard to see how he could have dismissed it so summarily. The town, which Arrian VI 8 § 4 speaks of as τὴν μεγίστην τῶν Μαλλῶν πόλιν, is generally placed (as has been mentioned) at Multan. See below on § 26.

identidem] with *conatus*.

§ 25. *metune...ipsos*] the leading notion is contained in these words; on which stress must accordingly be laid, and not in the chief verb of the clause *profugerint*.

certe] at all events, 'anyhow'.

occupaverunt] escaped in time to (the hills). Arrian VI 6 § 6 speaks of Perdiccas chasing some who had fled and putting to the sword ὅσοι γε μὴ ἔφθασαν ἐς τὰ ἕλη ξυμφυγόντες. But this is quite a different operation, and there seems to be nothing in Arrian corresponding to the present affair. Diodorus is also silent.

§ 26. *Sudracarum*] the siege of this town is one of Alexander's most famous exploits. Plutarch also speaks of the Oxydrakae, but Arrian VI 11 § 3 says αὐτίκα ἐν Ὀξυδράκαις τὸ πάθημα τοῦτο γενέσθαι Ἀλεξάνδρῳ ὁ πᾶς λόγος κατέχει· τὸ δὲ ἐν Μαλλοῖς ἔθνει αὐτονόμῳ Ἰνδικῷ ξυνέβη, καὶ ἥ τε πόλις Μαλλῶν ἦν καὶ οἱ βαλόντες Ἀλέξανδρον Μαλλοί, and Strabo XV 1 § 33 Μαλλοὶ μὲν παρ' οἷς ἀποθανεῖν ἐκινδύνευσεν Ἀλέξανδρος τρωθεὶς ἐν ἁλώσει πολίχνης τινός.

§ 27. *admovebat*] compare VIII 9 § 1 *movit*.

ne committeret etc] we have retained the old reading in preference to the conjecture of Jeep adopted by Hedicke *ni omitteret, at certe*....... The expression *committere obsidionem* is strange, but it is to be noted that the substantive is put with *differret*. Perhaps then we should rather supply some such notion as *pugnam* from *obsidionem* to go with *committeret*. *committere proelium* or *pugnam* are common enough. In VIII 2 § 6 we have *caede commissa*.

differret] we must supply an *ut* from the preceding *ne*. See Madvig § 462 b.

§ 28. *Demophontem*] Diodorus tells much the same story and gives this soothsayer the same name.

si quis etc] for a trenchant criticism of this story see Thirlwall c 54 (vol VII p 40). In place of the testy speeches which Curtius affects to report, Diodorus only says ὁ δὲ βασιλεὺς τούτῳ μὲν ἐπέπληξεν ὡς ἐμποδίζοντι τὴν ἀρετὴν τῶν ἀγωνιζομένων, and the more sober Arrian says nothing of the affair.

§ 30. *diutius quam respondit*] Vogel remarks that the construction is formed on the analogy of that with *prius...quam*. Compare 5 § 30.

cunctantibus etc] Arrian VI 9 § 3 Ἀλέξανδρος δέ, ὡς βλακεύειν αὐτῷ ἐδόκουν τῶν Μακεδόνων οἱ φέροντες τὰς κλίμακας, ἁρπάσας κλίμακα etc. But he says that this was against the citadel wall, the town having been carried at the first assault. So too Diodorus. Plutarch Alex 63 seems to make it the town wall, as Curtius does.

angusta] the narrowness was in the top of the parapet running round the wall, which was not marked out along its upper edge with battlements (*pinnae*), but was built in an unbroken line of breastwork (*perpetua lorica*) which was in the way of assailants (*obducta*), preventing their getting over (*transitum*).

muri] see on § 19.

corona] the use of this word to signify the defensive parapet of a wall is very strange. Arrian VI 9 § 4 calls it ἡ ἔπαλξις.

§ 31. *itaque rex* etc] 'the king then was rather clinging to than standing up on the edge (of the parapet) warding off with his shield the darts that fell upon him from every side: for on all sides he was now made a mark for shot from the towers'. Curtius seems here to picture him at the moment when, having climbed on to the edge of the *corona* and having both his feet on it, he would at the same time be obliged to rest his right hand also on the edge, in order to gain the steadiness necessary for the manipulation of his shield as a protection from the shower of missiles with which he was assailed. Arrian VI 9 § 4 seems to speak of him at an earlier stage, just before he took his feet from the ladder. His words are ἤδη τε πρὸς τῇ ἐπάλξει τοῦ τείχους ὁ βασιλεὺς ἦν, καὶ ἐρείσας ἐπ' αὐτῇ τὴν ἀσπίδα τοὺς μὲν ὤθει εἴσω τοῦ τείχους τῶν Ἰνδῶν, τοὺς δὲ καὶ αὐτοῦ τῷ ξίφει ἀποκτείνας γεγυμνώκει τὸ ταύτῃ τεῖχος.

eminus] merely shews that the weapons with which he was being assailed were of a missile character.

§ 32. *nec subire......obruebantur*] probably a piece of gratuitous padding put in by Curtius to heighten the effect of his picture. Nothing of the kind is found in Arrian or Diodorus.

subire] to mount the wall.

magnitudinem periculi] = (their fear of) the great danger. Vogel well compares VIII 2 § 34 (of a severe march) *et rarius subinde agmen fiebat, pudorem, ut fere fit, inmodico labore vincente.*

§ 33. *auxilia*] nominative to *morabantur*, plural because denoting the help that many were ready to bring. 'But their help was delayed by their hurry'.

nam dum etc] this agrees with Arrian and Diodorus.

spem fefellerunt) 'baulked his hope'.

in solitudine] in strong opposition to *in conspectu* above.

CHAPTER V.

§ 1. *ad ictus*] to meet the blows.

circumferebat] was shifting about. Compare VI 1 § 4 *undique nunc comminus nunc eminus petebatur, diuque arma circumferens alia tela clipeo excipiebat corpore alia vitabat.*

stabantque excepturi] the change of construction here is very remarkable. Having begun with *clamantibus = et clamabant*, he could not well have gone on *stantibusque excepturis*, and so changed the construction in the second clause.

cum ille etc] Arrian makes him think of only two alternatives, staying where he was or jumping into the citadel. Diodorus says XVII 99 ὁ δὲ βασιλεὺς ἐρημωθεὶς πάσης βοηθείας ἐτόλμησεν ἐπιτελέσαι πρᾶξιν παράδοξον καὶ μνήμης ἀξίαν. τὸ γὰρ ἀπὸ τοῦ τείχους ἀπελθεῖν ἄπρακτον πρὸς τοὺς ἰδίους ἀνάξιον κρίνας ὑπάρχειν τῆς ἰδίας εὐπραξίας καθήλατο μετὰ τῶν ὅπλων μόνος εἰς τὴν πόλιν, a much less imaginative way of telling the tale than that of Curtius.

ad famam......insignem] 'notable rather as conferring a rash reputation than a glorious one'. We make shift to render it thus, but think it scarce possible to translate the words satisfactorily. For the construction with *ad* compare Cic pro Mur §§ 29, 38, Lucretius III 214 with Munro's note. See also Kennedy § 70.

famam] here 'repute' in a neutral sense. It is common in a good sense = 'renown', and also occurs in a bad one = 'evil repute', 'notoriety'. See Cic pro Mur § 8.

gloriae] for a definition of *gloria* see on 10 § 24 where we again have *gloria* and *fama* distinguished.

§ 2. *cum vix* etc] Arrian VI 9 § 5 (of Alexander's thoughts) εἰ δὲ μή, καὶ κινδυνεύειν δέοι, μεγάλα ἔργα καὶ τοῖς ἔπειτα πυθέσθαι ἄξια ἐργασάμενος οὐκ ἀσπουδεὶ ἀποθανεῖται.

non inultum] that is, not without having first slain some of the enemy. Compare Virgil Aen II 670 *numquam omnes hodie moriemur inulti*, and in illustration of the sense generally XI 166—168.

§ 3. *libraverat*] had flung with nice poise. Compare IV 14 § 5 *funda saxa librare.*

§ 4. *arbor*] Diodorus mentions this, Arrian does not.

adplicuit] Diodorus makes him keep the tree on his right, the wall on his left.

§ 7. *adflueret*] came pouring on. Compare Livy XXXIX 31 *dimicantibus eis legio quinta supervenit, deinde ut quaeque potuerant copiae adfluebant.*

perfregerant] Diodorus only says πολλὰς μὲν γὰρ εἰς τὸ κράνος ἐλάμβανε πληγάς.

succiderant] so Lucretius III 156 *succidere artus* (*videmus*).

§ 8. *itaque* etc] Arrian VI 9 § 6 ἔνθα δὴ ἐρεισθεὶς πρὸς τῷ τείχει τοὺς μέν τινας εἰς χεῖρας ἐλθόντας καὶ τόν γε ἡγεμόνα τῶν Ἰνδῶν προσφερόμενόν οἱ θρασύτερον παίσας τῷ ξίφει ἀποκτείνει· ἄλλον δὲ πελάζοντα λίθῳ βαλὼν ἔσχε, καὶ ἄλλον λίθῳ, τὸν δὲ ἐγγυτέρω προσάγοντα τῷ ξίφει αὖθις. οἱ δὲ βάρβαροι πελάζειν μὲν αὐτῷ οὐκέτι ἤθελον, ἔβαλλον δὲ πάντοθεν περιεστηκότες ὅτι τις ἔχων βέλος ἐτύγχανεν ἢ ἐν τῷ τότε ἔλαβεν.

§ 9. *diximus*] in VIII 9 § 28.

super latus] Arrian VI 10 § 1 Ἀλέξανδρος δὲ βάλλεται καὶ αὐτὸς διὰ τοῦ θώρακος ἐς τὸ στῆθος τοξεύματι ὑπὲρ τὸν μαστόν, ὥστε λέγει Πτολεμαῖος ὅτι καὶ πνεῦμα ὁμοῦ τῷ αἵματι ἐκ τοῦ τραύματος ἐξεπνεῖτο, Diodorus XVII 99 says ὑπὸ τὸν μαστόν.

§ 10. *quo vulnere* etc] Arrian goes on § 2 ὁ δὲ ἔστε μὲν ἔτι θερμὸν ἦν αὐτῷ τὸ αἷμα καίπερ κακῶς ἔχων ἠμύνετο· πολλοῦ δὲ δὴ τοῦ αἵματος καὶ ἀθρόου, οἷα δὴ ξὺν πνεύματι, ἐκρυέντος ἴλιγγός τε αὐτὸν καὶ λιποψυχία κάτεσχε καὶ πίπτει αὐτοῦ ἐπὶ τὴν ἀσπίδα ξυννεύσας.

emicante] Lucretius II 194, 195 *quod genus e nostro quom missus corpore sanguis emicat exultans alte spargitque cruorem.*

itaque etc] Diodorus says εὐθὺς δ' ὁ μὲν τοξεύσας Ἰνδὸς καταφρονήσας προσέδραμε, καὶ καταφέροντος αὐτοῦ πληγὴν ὁ Ἀλέξανδρος ὑπέθηκε τῇ λαγόνι τὸ ξίφος καὶ καιρίου γενομένου τοῦ τραύματος ὁ μὲν βάρβαρος ἔπεσεν.

§ 11. *linquentem*] his 'swooning' spirit. Compare VII 9 § 14 *iamque linquente animo*, and see below § 28.

nudum] 'exposed' by raising his arms for a blow (as Diodorus says).

subiecto] 'with an upward thrust' of his sword. So Diodorus says ὑπέθηκε.

hausit] 'pierced'. Compare VII 2 § 27 *tum latus eius gladio haurit Cleander*, Virgil georg III 105, Aen II 600 with Conington's notes.

§ 12. *dimicans iam extingueretur*] 'that he might die sword in hand before his last breath failed him'. The *iam* affects the whole expression *dimicans extingueretur*, and cannot be rendered in English, as its function is to lead up to *antequam*.

§ 13. *postquam...virium*] 'finding that he had no strength left for the effort'. Compare III 1 § 8 *postquam nihil inde praesidi mittebatur, ad praestitutam diem permisere se regi*, 12 § 1 *postquam et nox adpetebat et consequendi spes non erat, in castra paulo ante a suis capta pervenit.*

ramos etc] Diodorus goes on ὁ δὲ βασιλεὺς ἐπιλαβόμενος τοῦ πλησίον κλάδου καὶ διαναστὰς προεκαλεῖτο τῶν Ἰνδῶν τοὺς βουλομένους διαγωνίσασθαι.

§ 14. *muri*] to be taken with *propugnatoribus*.

vestigia] that is, *regis*. We must not with Zumpt press too strongly the words *per aliam oppidi partem*, and so force *vestigia* to go with *muri*, but remember that Curtius is all the while stupidly thinking of the town wall, not that of the citadel. Diodorus says of Peucestes δι' *ἑτέρας κλίμακος προσαναβὰς πρῶτος ὑπερήσπισε τὸν βασιλέα*, and Arrian VI 9 § 3 makes him mount directly after the king and by the same ladder. Clearly then Curtius writing loosely and starting with an inaccurate conception has merely written *oppidi* when according to his authorities he should have said *muri*, for he only means what Diodorus says, viz that the man mounted by another ladder.

§ 15. *solacium*] the meaning has to be stretched a little in order to fit it to *vitae*. There is in fact a sort of zeugma here. 'Not to succour him in life but to comfort him in his death'.

clipeo...excepit] that is, he gave way and fell over on his shield.

Timaeus] Plutarch Alex 63 speaks of one *Λιμναῖος*, Arrian speaks of *'Αβρέας*, and there was altogether a great diversity in the accounts as to the names of those who fought so well on this day. See § 21 below and Arrian VI 11 §§ 7, 8.

Leonnatus] according to Arrian he mounted next after Peucestes by the same ladder.

Aristonus] Arrian VI 28 § 4 mentions *'Αριστόνους* as one of the original seven *σωματοφύλακες* of Alexander, the addition of Peucestes to whom (*Πευκέστας* in Arrian) made the number eight. But Curtius alone mentions him on this occasion.

§ 16. *edita*] compare VIII 14 § 37, and VII 7 § 37 *in medios hostes se inmisit et memorabili edita pugna obrutus telis est*, VIII 2 § 37 *nobilem edidit pugnam regemque comminus cum hoste dimicantem protexit*. Render 'after a gallant struggle'.

§ 18. *clipeum*] from Arrian VI 9 § 3, 10 § 2 (compared with I 11 §§ 7, 8) we learn that this was the sacred shield taken down by Alexander from the temple of Athena at Ilium, which was borne before him in fight by his immediate body-guards.

§ 19. *perfregere*] the wall was earthen according to Arrian VI 10 § 3 'some driving pegs into the wall (which was of earth), hung on by them and were with difficulty crawling up'.

moliti] where they had formed an entrance (by breaking the wall). See on VIII 10 § 30, and for *moliri aditum* compare VI 6 § 28 *multam materiam ceciderat miles, aditum per saxa molitus*.

§ 20. *parentatum est*] 'they satisfied their righteous anger'. *parentare* strictly means to avenge A by the destruction of B. Compare V 6 § 1 (of the contemplated burning of Persepolis) *excidio illius parentandum esse maioribus*, VII 2 § 29 *omniumque sanguine duci parentaturos*, Caesar bell Gall VII 17 etc. What is specially remarkable in our present passage is that we have the word metaphorically used, not of satisfying by vengeance the spirit of a dead person, but of glutting the wrath of the soldiers at the wounding of their king who was not dead.

§ 21. *Ptolomaeum* etc] Arrian VI 11 § 8 *τὸ δὲ δὴ μέγιστον πλημμέλημα τῶν ξυγγραψάντων τὰ ἀμφὶ 'Αλέξανδρον ἐκεῖνο τίθεμαι ἔγωγε. Πτολεμαῖον γὰρ τὸν Λάγου ἔστιν οἳ ἀνέγραψαν ξυναναβῆναί τε 'Αλεξάνδρῳ κατὰ τὴν κλίμακα ὁμοῦ Πευκέστᾳ καὶ ὑπερασπίσαι κειμένου καὶ ἐπὶ τῷδε*

Σωτῆρα ἐπικληθῆναι τὸν Πτολεμαῖον· καίτοι αὐτὸς Πτολεμαῖος ἀναγέγραφεν οὐδὲ παραγενέσθαι τούτῳ τῷ ἔργῳ· ἀλλὰ στρατιᾶς γὰρ αὐτὸς ἡγούμενος ἄλλας μάχεσθαι μάχας καὶ πρὸς ἄλλους βαρβάρους, where Sintenis refers to Pausanias I 8 § 6.

regnavit] 'became a king', ἐβασίλευσε. He founded the great dynasty of the Egyptian Ptolemies.

auctor est] Timagenes is regarded as a mere echo of Clitarchus, so that the singular verb is particularly appropriate. Compare Cic II in Verrem III § 42 *dixit hoc apud vos Zosippus et Ismenias.* See Madvig § 213 a obs.

scilicet] 'one may be sure', 'of course'. There is no strong irony conveyed by this word here, and the original form *scire licet* explains its force best.

refragatus] the word is used in its proper sense of 'gainsay'. So Cic pro Mur § 46 *tota illa lex...petitioni refragata est*, Livy XLV 40.

monumenta] 'records'. Frequently of books, as in Livy praef § 10, Tacitus Agr 2. *rerum*='events'. The whole expression then=the old books of history.

securitas] 'carelessness'.

§ 22. *abscidunt ita ne moveretur*] such is the order of the sense 'They cut off the wood taking care not to stir the point'. For *ita ne* (=*ita ut ne*) see Madvig § 456 obs 4.

medici] Arrian says VI 11 § 1 that either Kritodemus a doctor or Perdiccas—for accounts differed—drew out the dart after enlarging the wound.

§ 23. *inesse* etc] that there were barbs on the dart. *telo* is dative. For *inesse* compare Ovid fasti IV 658 *nec digitis anulus ullus inest.*

§ 24. *occuparet*] be too quick for them, and so prevent their stanching it in time.

verebantur ne] Madvig § 376, Kennedy § 200.

ingens] Plutarch Alex 63 says of this arrow-head 'it is said to have been 3 fingers' breadth broad and 4 long'. Here *ingens* is in a way part of the predicate, 'the dart that had been driven home was a large one' or better 'was a large one and had been driven home'. For *adactum* compare Virgil Aen IX 431, 432 *sed viribus ensis adactus transabiit costas et candida pectora rumpit.*

viscera] probably the right lung is meant.

§ 25. *Critobulus*] Pliny speaks of a doctor of this name NH VII § 124 *magna et Critobulo fama est extracta Philippi regis oculo sagitta et citra deformitatem oris curata orbitate luminis.*

recideret] 'recoil'. Compare VII 7 § 15 *an soli sumus qui flumina transnare possumus? multa in nosmetipsos recident quibus adhuc vicimus. fortuna belli artem victos quoque docet.*

§ 26. *metuentem*]=*metuere se dicentem* or *metum prodentem.*

exanguem] 'deadly pale'. Compare Virgil Aen II 212 *diffugimus visu exangues.*

quid...expectas] 'for what or how long are you waiting?'

dolore] emphatic, hence *me* comes in and displaces *saltem*.

moriturum] 'if die I must'. The nervousness of the doctor had caught the eye of the patient. For *moriturum* compare Horace carm I 28 6, II 3 4.

ne reus sis] 'that you should be held to account', as though you were your king's keeper.

cum acceperim] 'for my having received'.

§ 27. *dum...evelleret*] 'while he (Critobulus) was pulling out the point'.

§ 28. *sicut praeceptum erat*] the clause refers to *sine motu*.

igitur] carries us back to the end of § 23. For the matter see Arrian VI 11 §§ 1, 2 ἐγκελευσαμένου Ἀλεξάνδρου τῷ ξίφει ἐπιτεμεῖν τὴν πληγὴν καὶ κομίσασθαι τὸ βέλος. ἐν δὲ τῇ κομιδῇ φορὰ αἵματος πολλοῦ γίγνεται, ὥστε λιποψυχῆσαι αὖθις Ἀλέξανδρον καὶ οὕτω σχεθῆναι αὐτῷ τὸ αἷμα ὑπὸ τῇ λιποψυχίᾳ.

linqui animo] this is the stock phrase for fainting away. The ablative is of a locative nature and is of the kind usually called ablative of respect. Compare IV 6 § 20 *linqui deinde animo et submitti genu coepit*, Cic div in Caec § 41 *non solum commoveor animo, sed etiam toto corpore perhorresco*. See Kennedy § 149.

caligine] 'a mist came over his eyes'. The word is used of swooning and dizziness. Compare VII 6 § 22 *namque cervix eius saxo ita icta est ut oculis caligine offusa collaberetur ne mentis quidem compos*, Livy XXVI 45.

moribundus] Virgil Aen V 374 (*Buten*) *perculit et fulva moribundum extendit harena*.

§ 29. *medicamentis*] IV 6 § 19 *suppressus paulo ante sanguis medicamento*.

§ 30. *spiritu*] 'by the breath (=life) of one'. The ablative is nearly akin to that of cause and also to that of means. Compare VI 9 § 2 *deum providentia et misericordia vivo*, VII 10 § 7 *non inimici mihi, cuius beneficio victuri estis*.

CHAPTER VI.

§ 1. VII *diebus*] 'for the space of seven days'. The ablative is sometimes used in this construction, especially in the later writers. See Madvig § 235 obs 3, and compare Tacitus Agr 14 *Paulinus biennio prosperas res habuit*, ann I 53 *quattuordecim annis exilium toleravit*.

curato] kept under medical treatment (*curatio* θεραπεία).

obducta] that is *vulneri*, as we find it fully expressed in VIII 10 § 31.

in medium]=εἰς μέσον, a very common construction, ='into the middle' so as to be under the observation of all; thus leading up to the epithet *undique conspicuum*.

§ 2. *amne*] what river is here meant is not easy to say. We have pointed out Curtius' confusion on 4 § 8. Arrian VI 13 § 1 describing this incident says that it was the Hydraotes.

aliquantum] a definite portion, hence a considerable portion, large quantity. Compare 8 § 1 and see Holden on Cic de off I §§ 33, 108.

praecipiens] taking in advance, that is, as a start. Compare 10 § 14, Livy XXXVI 19 *aliquantum viae praeceperat rex*, and the Greek προλαμβάνειν in Thuc IV 33, VII 80, Herod III 105.

corpori] there is reason to suspect corruption in the MSS here, so we have not hesitated to follow Zumpt and others in accepting this correction of Junius. Compare VII 9 § 13 *vexationem invalidi corporis pati non poterat.*

adhuc] 'still'. This sense is common in silver-age Latin.

§ 4. *ante praetorium*] 'before the general's tent', a Roman expression. In VIII 6 § 3 he says *excubabant...proximi foribus eius aedis in qua rex adquiescebat.*

hoc...servato] this statement as to the observance of the custom on this occasion also (*servato* being in past time) is brought in here to account for the presence of the friends and body-guards of the king. Thus *universi......intrant* follows naturally.

§ 5. *ne quid novi* etc] 'lest they might be the bearers of some ill tidings'. *novus*, like the Greek νέος and νεώτερος, is euphemistically used to express the notion 'bad'. So *res novare*, as in 10 § 21.

§ 6. *sollicitos esse*] *nos* is left to be understood, as *se* often is when the speech is in the third person (*oratio obliqua*). See on 4 § 20. *esse* ='should be being'='should be'. Vogel remarks that it corresponds to εἶναι ἄν.

ut nunc est] this expression is to be taken closely with *tibi vilis*, 'by which as it seems you set little store'. The words occur again V 5 § 10 in a slightly different sense.

§ 7. *consternat* etc] for this exaggerated talk of covering the sea with ships see Livy XXXV 49 (*rex*) *consternit maria classibus suis*, and below 8 § 5. Juvenal X 175.

beluas] refers of course to the employment of elephants in war.

§ 8. *columen*] compare Horace carm II 17 4.

sidus] compare Horace carm I 12 47.

trahere in casum] are drawing into peril, endangering. Compare VIII 3 § 2 *quam......in omne discrimen comitem trahebat.* The force of the plea is that all depends on Alexander, hence when he risks his own life he also risks those of his men.

§ 9. *reduce*]=*reducente*, a rare poetical sense and used especially in speaking of guiding divinities, as when in Ovid heroid XIII 50 Laodamia says *et sua det reduci vir meus arma Jovi.* The ordinary sense of 'returning' is illustrated by 2 § 34 above.

penates] their gods of hearth and home, hence their homes. Common in Latin writers, but sounds oddly in treating of a Greek subject. See Virgil Aen VIII 679.

§ 10. *ne admirari quidem*] the implied antithesis is, as Vogel remarks, *nedum indignari*, 'could not even think it strange [much less find fault with it]'.

paria] 'matched': the one as great as the other.

§ 11. *tuo capite*] the ablative denoting the price at which the thing is bought. See Madvig § 258, Kennedy § 147.

§ 12. *rei*] the deadly peril of Alexander, described in the last chapter.

inertissimas] the hands of the greatest laggards or cowards. In 2 § 26 we had *inertia* in the sense of 'want of enterprize'. Here *iners* is a trifle stronger. Both shades of meaning are common in other writers. The original meaning appears in Lucilius frag XIII 12 *ut perhibetur iners, ars in quo non erit ulla.*

fuisse infecturas] 'would have polluted' the spoils of an Alexander.

misericors in nos] 'looking with pity on us'.

persequi] to 'keep up with' you, when you ran into such danger.

§ 13. *ignominia notes*] these words are Roman and technical. When the Roman Censors in virtue of their office affixed a mark to the name of a citizen on the roll, that citizen lost certain political and social privileges, and was said to suffer *ignominia*. The mark itself was called *nota*, and we find frequent reference to it in Roman writers, both directly and (as here) metaphorically. See Cic pro Cluentio § 117.

luere] to pay the price for, give satisfaction for. Compare VII 5 § 35 *nunc culpam maiorum posteri luere*, Horace carm III 6 1 *delicta maiorum inmeritus lues.*

id quod etc] that from the guilt of which he could not secure himself.

admitteret] this verb is used with such words as *maleficium*, *dedecus*, *facinus* etc almost in the sense of 'commit'. Compare VI 7 § 32 *faventem habes iudicem, si quod admitti non oportuit saltem purgari potest*, Cic de off III § 95. A common construction is *admittere in se* 'to bring upon oneself', which well shews how the notion of guilt came to be implied. See Cic phil II § 47.

praestare] from the sense of 'to secure' or 'guarantee' we have the force of the word extended so as to imply precaution, like *cavere* or *providere.*

alio modo] these are the emphatic words in the sentence. If, says Craterus, you must needs shew in some way how cheap you hold us, let it be done in some other way than by exposing your own person so as to endanger the safety of us all.

§ 14. *quocumque* etc] compare Juvenal III 78 of the versatile Greek *in caelum, iusseris, ibit*, and Horace epist II 2 40, Lucan I 367—386.

capiunt] 'contain', that is, can contain, give scope for, your greatness. *capere* used thus = χωρεῖν is common, but the present passage is a somewhat remarkable one. We may compare VI 1 § 17 *maiores res erant quam quas praefecti modus caperet* 'the affairs were too great to suit the capacity of a mere subordinate'.

gloria] glory won.

obsolescit] grows mean or common. Compare Horace carm II 10 6, 7 *caret obsoleti sordibus tecti*. See on 1 § 2 above.

in sordidis hostibus] in (a contest with) mean or worthless foes.

§ 15. *exsatiatus*] compare § 23 *laudis satietas*.

id est publicae] Curtius strangely says this in his own person, though it is clear that he is expressing the feelings of Ptolemy and the rest.

§ 16. *grata* etc] Arrian VI 13 § 4 says on the contrary (reporting the account of Nearchus) that Alexander was irritated and vexed at this remonstrance of his friends, knowing well (so thinks Arrian himself) that he had deserved the blame implied in their words.

pietas] affectionate loyalty, as often. See Conington on Virgil Aen I 10.

familiarius] with more warmth than usual. So 7 § 2 *neglegentius*, 8 § 26, 9 § 1 and often.

§ 17. *altius*] that is, he went far back and reviewed his whole career in justification of his ambition and rashness. Compare Virgil georg IV 285—6 *altius omnem expediam prima repetens ab origine famam*.

piissimi] this form of the superlative is rejected by Cic phil XIII § 43, who declares that no such form is found in Latin. His stricture is however most likely in part the result of his hatred for Antony who had used it. Anyhow it soon found a place in the language. Thus Tacitus Agr 43 says *optimae uxori et piissimae filiae*. The forms *piissimus* and *pientissimus* both occur in inscriptions.

habeo] compare III 6 § 17 *pro se quisque dextram eius amplexi grates habebant velut praesenti deo*.

eo nomine] on that account, viz because....... Compare VII 4 § 10 *natura mortalium hoc quoque nomine prava et sinistra dici potest, quod in suo quisque negotio hebetior est quam in alieno*, Cic pro Mur § 82 *meo nomine* 'on my own account', div in Caec § 19 *quo nomine*, and many other places. *nomen* = a name or heading in an account-book, hence *eo nomine* 'under that head' almost = *ea de causa*. So we say in English 'on that account', 'on that score', and so on.

§ 18. *non eadem* etc] the sense is the same as if he had written *non idem cogitant ii...et ego*. 'Their notion is not the same as mine' means 'They do not look at the matter from my point of view'.

qui quidem] *qui* is the clever restoration of Junius, now generally accepted by editors. The sense is 'inasmuch as', like the Greek ὅς γε.

cupiatis] though the subjunctive may be justified as containing an assumption or admission (Madvig § 352), it is probably here influenced by *forsitan*, so far at least as the second clause is concerned.

ego me metior] 'but I measure myself not by the span of age but by that of glory'. The same sentiment is found in §§ 19, 22 with a slight difference of expression. There is no disjunctive particle after *ego*, and the contrast is effected by co-ordination, as often: see Mayor on Cic phil II § 110.

§ 19. *paternis*] that is, the kingdom of his father Philip.

per otium corporis] 'in a life of bodily ease'. Compare 8 § 26 *per quietem*. *per*='in a course of', a sense in which Tacitus is fond of using it. See Agricola 4 *per omnem honestarum artium cultum*, 6 *per mutuam caritatem*, hist V 10 *proximus annus civili bello intentus quantum ad Iudaeos per otium transiit*.

ne pigri quidem etc] for the sentiment compare Horace carm III 2 13—16.

occupat] takes them unawares.

bene] that is, rightly.

§ 20. *Maedis*] these were a Thracian tribe not far from the Triballi.

rubro mari] the Indian ocean, as usual.

subluitur] 'is washed below'. This may refer to the washing of the lower part of the coast-line by the sea, but more probably indicates that the *rubrum mare* formed the southern boundary of Asia. The ancients often speak of the north as above and the south as below. For the word compare Caesar bell Gall VII 69.

orbem] compare Juvenal X 168 of Alexander *unus Pellaeo iuveni non sufficit orbis*.

aperire] to open up. Tacitus Agr 22 *tertius expeditionum annus novas gentes aperuit*.

§ 21. *Europae*] this refers to the crossing of the Jaxartes to attack the Scythians. So in VII 7 §§ 2, 12, 13 we find the river mentioned as the boundary of Europe and Asia, and in § 13 Alexander is made to say *unus amnis interfluit, quem si traicimus, in Europam arma proferimus*. The river is there it is true called Tanais, but Arrian III 30 §§ 7, 8 well shews that there were two rivers of that name and that the Jaxartes is really meant. Indeed he quotes Aristobulus in support of his statements.

momento] compare Horace sat I 1 7—8 *horae momento cita mors venit aut victoria laeta*.

post] after, that is, on attaining. Instances will be found in Madvig § 276 obs 6.

nonum] this is one year, and *vicesimum atque octavum* two years too little. But a historian trained in rhetorical schools would think nothing of straining a point of chronology in order to make the more of his hero's exploits. So Tacitus Agr 33 has *octavus annus*, 34 *quinquaginta annis*, both rhetorical exaggerations.

excolenda] working up, completing. Compare Tacitus dial 22 (of Cicero) *primus enim excoluit orationem*.

ego vero] introduces the denial with emphasis. Madvig § 454 obs 1.

in theatro] that is, before the eyes of the world, with all mankind as spectators. Cic II in Verrem v § 35 has a similar passage, which may have suggested the expression to Curtius, but it is probably of Greek origin.

§ 22. *submoverat*] had (hitherto) kept far away. Such is the force of the tense. For the word compare Horace carm II 10 17.

feret] for this word meaning 'lead' 'guide', especially in speaking of the tendency or course of destiny, see Conington on Virgil Aen II 34 *seu iam Troiae sic fata ferebant.*

longam] it is worth noticing that in a similar context (Agr 44) Tacitus employs this adjective to aid in expressing what Curtius here renders by *multam:* (of Agricola) *et ipse quidem, quamquam medio in spatio integrae aetatis ereptus, quantum ad gloriam, longissimum aevum peregit.*

§ 23. *quibus*] to which—that is, in the sight of which—the name of a woman is most famed for valour.

Samiramis] the admiration entertained by Alexander for this great Assyrian queen is spoken of above VII 6 § 20. She was said (V 1 § 24) to have founded Babylon, and to have made great conquests in the East.

molita est] undertook, planned. So *moliri bellum* IV 1 § 39 and other phrases.

et iam etc] 'and have we already had our fill of glory?' For *et* compare Virgil Aen VI 806 *et dubitamus adhuc virtutem extendere factis?*

§ 24. *maiora*] in X 1 §§ 17, 18 Curtius says that he meant to make an expedition along the north of Africa, conquering Carthage on the way, and then over to Spain and so home by way of Italy.

ita...si] 'only on condition that'. So in other writers, as Cic ad fam XV 20 § 2, Livy XXI 21.

nihil parvum etc] this is in answer to what Craterus said in §§ 11, 12, 14.

domesticorum] 'those of my household'. The reference is to the plot of the pages headed by Hermolaus, and to the real or supposed treachery of Philotas.

subibo] will submit myself to, hence 'face'.

§ 25. *in theatro*] Philip was assassinated by one Pausanias in the theatre at Aegae, in the year 336.

§ 26. *olim*] goes with *agitatae in animo meo*, and means 'for a long time', a sense which it often bears in silver-age Latin. See Mayor on Juvenal IV 96, X 173.

inmortalitati etc] that is, deified. In X 5 § 30 Curtius speaks of the *pietas* of Alexander towards his parents, *quorum Olympiada inmortalitati consecrare decreverat*, and VIII 5 § 17 he makes Kallisthenes speak of Hercules and Liber as *consecratae inmortalitatis exempla.* Hence the words seem to imply the making a mortal into an immortal.

quandoque] =*quandocumque*, as often in Livy.

praeceperit] anticipate, (like *occupo*). Compare Virgil ecl III 98 *si lac praeceperit aestus.*

mandasse] that is, *me.*

CHAPTER VII.

§ 1. *colonias*] referring generally to the settlements made by Alexander in central Asia, and in particular to those of Baktra and Alexandria on the Tanais (Jaxartes). Diodorus in his brief reference to the incident XVII 99 speaks of *οἱ κατὰ τὴν Βακτριανὴν καὶ Σογδιανὴν κατοικισθέντες Ἕλληνες.* The story of Biton Boxus and Athenodorus has come down to us in the version of Curtius only.

ipsos] as opposed to disagreements between them and the barbarians.

§ 2. *popularium*] 'their countrymen', that is, the leaders who remained loyal to Alexander.

§ 3. *regis nomen*] the name 'king'. Genitive of further definition, like *vox voluptatis, nomen Catonis* and many other phrases. See Madvig § 286.

auctoritatem] his advice or guidance, his 'lead' as we say.

§ 4. *nationis*] the general word meaning 'nation' is *gens*, the smaller bodies or tribes are commonly denoted by *natio.* Here the meaning probably is that they were citizens of the same Greek state, both Arcadians, both Boeotians or so forth.

per] denotes the agency, as often.

§ 5. *ultro*] of his own accord, unprovoked. So VII 7 § 11 *Scythas ultro arma inferentes*, Virgil Aen II 193, XI 286 *ultro Inachias venisset ad urbes Dardanus*, Cic de off III § 86.

fraus Bitonis] 'foul play on Biton's part'.

manare] trickle, spread about. Compare Livy II 49 *manat tota urbe rumor.*

suspitio] we have ventured to restore the spelling here. See Kennedy § 12 note, and appendix 17, Mayor on Cic phil II § 114.

§ 8. *admovebantur*] 'were on the point of being applied'.

§ 9. *tumultuantium vociferatione*] literally 'by the shouting of the rioters'. But their shouting would not be any serious hindrance to the application of torture to Biton, and we are not here concerned with the extracting information by torture. It seems then that we must take this for an instance of the common use of abstract for concrete, so as to be equivalent to *a tumultuantibus qui vociferabantur* = 'by the rioters whom they had heard shouting'.

§ 10. *sicut nudatus erat*] 'stripped as he was'. Compare X 4 § 2 *sicut vincti erant.* The Greek would be *ὥσπερ ἐγεγύμνωτο* or *ὥσπερ ἦν γεγυμνωμένος.*

in diversum] to the other direction, *εἰς τοὐναντίον.* That is, caused a strong revulsion of feeling.

§ 11. *a rege*] *Alexandro.*

revertit] Diodorus XVII 99 says that they never reached their homes, but after suffering great hardships on the way were cut to pieces by the Macedonians after the death of Alexander.

§ 12. *duarum*] the Sudrakae and Malli are meant.

magnitudine] ablative of quality or description.

lineae] see on VIII 9 § 15.

§ 13. *libertatem*] Arrian VI 14 §§ 1—3 in speaking of this episode says that they claimed to have been free since the time of the eastern conquests of Dionysus (*Liber pater* in Curtius).

§ 14. *pensitabat*] as they were a free people, this cannot mean that they had been and were in the habit of paying tribute to any other power, and must be a remark of Curtius' own, stating that they used to pay it at one time; 'and laid on them the tribute which the two tribes actually paid to (the satrap of) the Arachosians'. Perhaps however the text is corrupt, and we should rather read *pensitaret*. Arrian only says that they submitted to Alexander and offered to pay tribute, and that Alexander set Philippus over them as satrap.

pensitabat] paid in instalments.

imperat] Arrian says that he demanded 1000 of their chief men as hostages. If Curtius means these (which is very doubtful) then *equites* must be taken to denote men of high standing, a Roman notion derived from the Roman *ordo equester*. But Arrian further says that they sent him besides of their own accord 500 war-chariots with their complement of men. It is probable therefore that Curtius has confused two parts of the account given in his authorities, unless indeed they had done the same before him. See below 8 § 1.

§ 15. *modicis*] = 'small', as usual. The close packing of the couches shews the great number of guests.

aulaea] tapestry curtains. So in VIII 5 § 21 of Alexander overhearing the speech of Kallisthenes *nec quicquam eorum quae invicem iactata erant rex ignorabat, cum post aulaea quae lectis obduxerat staret.*

nova inmutatione] 'by their new-fangled change (of manners)'. That is, their adoption of Oriental customs and dress.

corruptum] 'tainted'. Compare V 1 § 36 *nihil urbis eius corruptius moribus*, and below IX 9 § 6 of the sea-water.

§ 16. *virtutem virium*] 'excellence of his strength' = his excellent strength. As *virtus* like ἀρετὴ can be used for any sort of excellence, there is no need to find fault with this strange phrase.

iam] so the MSS, and it is surely as good as the correction *etiam*. We can hardly find in the latter an allusion to Alexander's dislike of athletes in general (Plut Alex 4). Some editors omit the word altogether.

increpabant] used to carp at him, saying....

saginati corporis] genitive of quality or description, here part of the predicate and parallel to *inutilem*. 'That they had a full-fed good-for-nothing beast in their company'. See on VIII 10 § 24 *obiecta est*. *sagina* is particularly applied to the plumpness produced by the high feeding of athletes. See Mayor on Quintil X 1 § 33.

oleo] the oil employed by athletes for anointing themselves.

praeparare etc] getting up an appetite by exercise.

§ 17. *in convivio*] at this particular banquet; opposed to the imperfect *increpabant* above.

Horratas] Diodorus XVII 100 gives an account of this affair almost word for word the same as that of Curtius, but gives the same Macedonian the name Κόραγος.

exprobrare] used absolutely, as we say 'to upbraid'.

postero die] Diodorus says that the king appointed a day for the duel.

tandem] at last, that is, after the duel.

vel...vel] in the proper sense, as connected with the root of *volo*. The logical order of the sentence is obscured by the necessary repetition of *de*, for the sense is *de* (*vel sua temeritate vel illius ignavia*) = in direct speech 'on (call it my rashness or your cowardice)'.

ignavia] so Virgil Aen XI 733 *quae tanta animis ignavia venit*.

§ 18. *eludente*] 'setting at nought', 'making fun of'. Compare III 1 § 18 *oraculi sortem vel elusit vel implevit* (in cutting the Gordian knot), VIII 1 § 42 *oraculum eludens*, Livy I 36, 48, Cic div in Caec § 24.

condicio] 'the (terms of the) challenge'.

deterrere] Diodorus says that Alexander backed up Koragus, and gives no hint of any attempt to stop the duel.

§ 19. *ingens hic* etc] the MSS here are confessedly corrupt, and the insertion of *qui* between *quos* and *erant* is necessary to the sense. *hic* is the MSS reading, for which Hedicke accepts Jeep's conjecture *vis*. [The emendation *conventus erat* for *convenerat* found in 2 MSS is my own. I believe the word *multitudo* found in the same MSS to have arisen from a comment on *conventus*. For the latter word in the simple sense of 'meeting' compare IV 5 § 11 *isdem fere diebus solemne erat ludicrum Isthmiorum, quod conventu totius Graeciae celebratur*, Cic II in Verrem IV § 107 *festos dies anniversarios agunt celeberrimo virorum mulierumque conventu*, Horace sat I 7 23. W. E. H.]

studebant] = *favebant*, were backing. Diodorus says τῶν δὲ Ἑλλήνων τῷ Διωξίππῳ συναγωνιώντων.

iusta] 'proper'. The 'regulation arms', as we say now.

sarisam] this spear was over 20 feet long, and suited only to the heavy charging formation of the Macedonian phalanx.

§ 20. *laeva*] probably the scarlet cloak was wrapped round his left fore-arm.

suspenderat] kept awhile in suspense. Compare Quintil IX 2 § 22 *cum diu suspendisset iudicum animos*, Ovid met VII 308. Diodorus tells us that those present likened the scene to a conflict between Ares (Koragus) and Herakles (Dioxippus).

§ 21. *interfici posse*] that is, *eum*.

vitasset] IV 6 § 16 *exigua corporis declinatione evitato ictu*, Virgil Aen V 444—5 *ille ictum venientem a vertice velox praevidit celerique elapsus corpore cessit*. Diodorus here says βραχὺ παρεγκλίνας τὴν ἐπιφερομένην πληγὴν ἐξένευσεν.

antequam...dextram] Diodorus makes him advance with levelled sarisa.

§ 22. *occupatum conplexu*] grappled him before he was ready. Diodorus says μέλλοντος δ' αὐτοῦ σπᾶσθαι τὴν μάχαιραν, ἔφθασε προπηδήσας, καὶ τῇ μὲν εὐωνύμῳ κατέλαβε τὴν ἕλκουσαν τὸ ξίφος χεῖρα, τῇ δ' ἄλλῃ κινήσας ἐκ τῆς βάσεως τὸν ἀντίπαλον ὑπέσυρε τὰ σκέλη.

arietavit] knocked (here, knocked down) like a battering ram. For the word compare Plautus truc II ii 1 *quis illic est qui tam proterve nostras aedes arietat?* Virgil Aen XI 890.

iacenti] the general dative of relation, closely related to the *dativus commodi et incommodi*. Compare Virgil Aen IX 347—8 *pectore in adverso totum cui comminus ensem condidit adsurgenti*.

elisurus] meaning to brain him. Compare Plaut Poen II 46 *iam elidam caput nisi auscultas*. Diodorus says that having got his enemy down he looked up to the spectators, who cheered and made a great noise, but adds nothing as to the intentions of the conqueror. Curtius is probably striving to make the most of his story by little effective touches.

§ 23. *tristis* etc] Diodorus XVII 101 says ὁ μὲν βασιλεὺς προσέταξεν ἀφεῖναι, καὶ τὴν θέαν διαλύσας ἀπηλλάγη δυσφορῶν ἐπὶ τῇ τοῦ Μακεδόνος ἥττῃ.

verebatur] the use of this word in the sense of seeing with grief and vexation, taking an accusative and infinitive after it, is rare. Compare Ovid heroid XVI 75, 76 *vincere erant omnes dignae, iudexque verebar non omnes causam vincere posse suam*. See Madvig § 376 obs.

§ 24. *ex conposito*] by private arrangement. The expression is common.

subducitur] Diodorus says that they took the cup, and hid it beneath Dioxippus' pillow, then charged him with theft, and made pretence to find it there.

§ 25. *constantiae*] 'firmness', here applied to the power of sitting unmoved under an imputation. So Nepos Att 22 § 1 says of the words of the dying Atticus *hac oratione habita tanta constantia vocis atque voltus*, that is, without faltering in speech or moving a muscle of his face. 'Constancy' in this sense is common in Shakespeare.

rubore] abstract for concrete. The sense is 'often those who blush at a false insinuation are less able to bear the glance of reproach than those who are really guilty'.

coniectum etc] Diodorus says ὁ δὲ θεωρῶν τὴν ἐπ' αὐτὸν συνδρομὴν τῶν Μακεδόνων τότε μὲν ἐξῆλθεν ἐκ τοῦ πότου.

§ 26. *graviter* etc] Diodorus says that he was vexed at the man's death and longed for him when it was too late, and ἔγνω τὴν καλοκαγαθίαν τἀνδρὸς ἐκ τῆς τῶν διαβαλόντων κακίας.

CHAPTER VIII.

§ 1. *cum donis*] the account here following seems to be an entirely different one from that of Arrian cited on 7 § 14 above.

vestis] 'raiment', clothing material; that is, cloth. See 10 § 25, Virgil Aen IX 26 *dives pictai vestis et auri.*

ferri candidi] probably steel is meant. For the famous Indian steel see Colonel Yule's learned and interesting note on Marco Polo bk I c 17.

§ 2. *domitum*] Strabo XV 1 §§ 37, 69 speaks of tame lions in India, and Marco Polo bk II c 16 tells of a tame lion taught to lie down before the great Kaan, and in bk II c 18 of tamed lions (tigers) leopards and wolves used for hunting purposes like dogs by the Great Kaan. See Colonel Yule on the passage.

lacertarum] probably the hides of crocodiles are meant. Aelian hist anim XVI 6 speaks of an animal which M'Crindle p 163 makes out to be the scaly ant-eater.

dorsa] the backs, that is shells, of tortoises. See Aelian hist anim XVI 14, 18.

§ 3. *Cratero*] Arrian VI 15 § 4 says that he took Craterus and his force over to the left bank of the Indus, and sent him along that side.

Mallorum] Curtius, it is to be remembered, has made the affair related in chapter 5 take place among the Sudrakae. See above on 4 § 24. We see here that he conceived the Malli to have lived further down the river, whereas Arrian puts the Malli above and the Oxydrakae (Sudrakae) below.

§ 4. *Sabarcas*] Diodorus XVII 102 says κατῆρεν εἰς τὴν χώραν τῶν ὀνομαζομένων Σαμβαστῶν, and the same may be meant by Arrian VI 15 § 1 τὸ τῶν 'Αβαστανῶν ἔθνος αὐτόνομον.

populi imperio] in Arrian we find frequent mention of independent tribes. See V 20 § 6, 22 § 1, 24 § 8, VI 14 § 2 etc. So also in his Indica 11 § 9, 12 §§ 5, 6. Diodorus II 38, 39, 41 mentions states governed democratically, and Plutarch Alex 59 speaks of τοὺς ἐλευθέρους δήμους. Diodorus here says of the Sambastae οἰκοῦντες δὲ τὰς πόλεις δημοκρατουμένας. For these independent communities observed by the Greeks in India see Elphinstone appendix III p 261.

LX milia etc] these numbers are the same as those given by Diodorus.

§ 5. *maxime in ripa*] no doubt for the convenience of being near the water.

arma fulgentia etc] Virgil Aen VI 489—491 is very like this, and perhaps suggested it.

nova] strange, unusual. So 10 § 13.

§ 6. *hinc...hinc*] does not mean that these were on different sides of them.

hortantium] used absolutely as in IV 13 § 38 *hortantem exercitus exaudire non poterat.*

impleverant] filled for the time. Compare IV 12 § 20 *fremitusque tot milium etiam procul stantium aures impleverat.*

§ 7. *legatos* etc] Diodorus says that the elder men advised them not to attempt resistance, and so ambassadors were sent.

§ 8. *alias gentes*] called by Diodorus *Σόδρας καὶ Μασσανούς.*

oppido] Diodorus gives precisely the same account. Arrian VI 15 § 2 speaks of Alexander's ordering a town to be built at the confluence of the Acesines and Indus. If this (as is probable) be the same as is meant by Curtius, we have here another instance of the latter's confused geographical notions. The place is now occupied by the town of Mithan Kot.

Musicani] see on VIII 12 § 14 *sequente nomine.*

§ 9. *Teriolte*] Arrian VI 15 § 3 says that he was deposed, and gives him the name *Τιρυάσπης.* Diodorus says nothing of the matter.

isdem] that is his subjects the Parapamisadae.

cognovit] 'held an enquiry'. A common legal word.

avare ac superbe] extortionately and tyrannically. Compare *Tarquinius superbus*=Tarquin the tyrant. Arrian's words are *οὐκ ἐν κόσμῳ ἐξηγεῖσθαι.*

convictum] for the use with following infinitive compare 10 § 21 *suspectus voluisse.* See Madvig § 400 c obs.

§ 10. *praetor*]=*σατράπης.*

absolutus] this probably refers to the revolt of the colonists in Bactria. See 7 §§ 1—11. Alexander acquitted him of complicity in the mutiny. Arrian says nothing of this.

iure amoris] Alexander had married his daughter Roxana.

amplioris imperii] Arrian says that he received the government of the Parapamisadae from which Tiryaspes had been deposed.

§ 11. *Praestos*] no other writer mentions this name, and it is very likely due to some corruption in the MSS.

et ipsam] has not some adjective such as *validam* or *magnam* fallen out here? Or *indigenam?*

Porticanus] so Diodorus. Arrian VI 16 §§ calls him *Ὀξυκανός.*

rex] Diodorus speaks of *τὴν Πορτικάνου δυναστείαν*, Arrian styles him *τὸν νομάρχην τῆς ταύτῃ γῆς.*

§ 12. *occiditur*] so Diodorus; Arrian says that he was taken prisoner.

§ 13. *cuniculo*] a mine or passage under ground. The name is probably derived from the resemblance to a rabbit's burrow. Livy IV 22, V 21, Caesar bell Gall III 21, VII 22.

§ 14. *simile monstri* etc] the passage closely resembles Livy V 21 § 10, and is very likely a reminiscence of it.

terra existebant] So Zumpt and Hedicke read in VII 4 § 19 *convivio prosiluit*, VIII 3 § 5 *abire conspectu iubet*, 6 § 26 *periculi quo evaserat*, X 2 § 4 *civitatibus quis pulsi erant*.

specus] the cave, hollow; that is the mine.

§ 15. *LXXX milia*] this number is corrected from Diodorus. The best MSS of Curtius give *DCCC Indorum*. Zumpt.

sub corona] this is a technical expression in Roman warfare for the selling of prisoners as slaves, with which view they were dressed out with garlands.

§ 16. *defecerunt* etc] the revolt and its suppression are related in much the same terms by Arrian VI 17 §§ 1, 2.

eundemque] 'who was also'. Madvig § 488.

in crucem sublato] κρεμάσαι, says Arrian, probably in the same sense.

§ 17. *oppidum*] this is evidently the same as that described by Diodorus XVII 103 as τῆς ἐσχάτης τῶν Βραχμάνων πόλεως, ἣν ὀνομάζουσιν Ἁρματήλια. It will be observed that he speaks of the Brahmans as a tribe, and this mistaken expression is found in other writers also. It is clear from comparison of the narratives of Arrian Diodorus and Plutarch (Alex 64) that it was the influence of the Brahman caste to which the resistance and subsequent revolts in these districts were due.

§ 18. *paucitate contempta*] compare Tacitus Agr 37.

D Agrianos] ὀλίγους τῶν ψιλῶν, says Diodorus.

§ 20. *eventu*] the 'sequel', final result.

veneno] Diodorus tells the same with more circumstance, both as to the effect of the wounds received, and the method of preparing the poison. For the use of poisoned weapons in India see Elphinstone I 2 (p 26) in abstract of Menu.

strenuae] strong, violent. Compare III 6 § 2 *non praeceps se sed strenuum remedium adferre*, Horace epist I 11 28 *strenua nos exercet inertia*. Diodorus says δεινοὺς θανάτους ἀπειργάζετο.

etiam leves plagae] so Diodorus καὶ τοῖς μικρὰν καὶ τὴν τυχοῦσαν ἀμυχὴν ἀναδεξαμένοις.

§ 21. *excipi*] 'met with', almost 'cut off', in a hostile sense. Compare 9 § 5, Virgil Aen III 332 *excipit incautum*.

et] 'and indeed'. Compare Virgil ecl II 44 *et faciet*.

forte] 'as it chanced'. That is, by good luck rather than caution he had escaped untouched.

§ 22. *praecipue*] Diodorus tells us that he did not trouble himself so much about the others who were wounded, but was extremely anxious about Ptolemy.

sanguine coniunctus] Arsinoe the mother of Ptolemy, observes Vogel, was of the Lyncestae. For the connexion of the Macedonian royal family with that of this Illyrian tribe through Eurydike the mother of Philip, see Strabo VII 7 § 8 (p 326).

eius] *Philippi*] The story occurs also in Pausanias I 6 § 2.

§ 23. *corporis custos*] here in the narrower sense of the two mentioned in note on VIII 11 § 11.

pacis artibus] 'civil pursuits', meaning probably statesmanship and diplomacy. Compare Tacitus hist I 8 *Cluvius Rufus, vir facundus et pacis artibus*. This side of Ptolemy's character shewed itself afterwards in his encouragement of learning and in the book of memoirs he himself wrote.

cultu] way of living. So Tacitus Agr 40 says of Agricola *cultu modicus, sermone facilis*.

liberalis] the generosity of Ptolemy is marked in his apophthegm quoted by Plutarch 'that it was more royal to make others rich than to be rich yourself', τοῦ πλουτεῖν τὸ πλουτίζειν εἶναι βασιλικώτερον.

aditu facili] ablative of description. Madvig § 272.

regiae] the 'court'.

§ 24. *ominati*] 'foreboded'. The word is more commonly used in an unfavourable sense as in 9 § 22 below, and Cic de off II § 74.

§ 25. *adsideret*] almost technical of watching by a sick-bed. See Horace sat I 1 82, Tacitus Agr 45.

§ 26. *per quietem*] 'in a vision'. So Justin XII 10 § 3, and Cic de divin II § 135 *secundum quietem*, speaking of this very matter. Compare Tacitus hist IV 83. The following story is told by Cicero (just referred to) Justin and Diodorus with very trifling discrepancies. Arrian says nothing of it, and Strabo XV 2 § 7 makes it happen among the Oritae.

§ 27. *adgniturum*] that is, the fortunate finder, the *si quis* following.

§ 28. *Pataliam*] this adjective seems to be formed from *Patala*. As to the forms of the name, Arrian speaks of τὰ Πάταλα and τῶν Παταλέων τῆς χώρας, Strabo of τὰ Πάταλα and ἡ Παταληνή, Pliny of *Patale Patala* (nom sing. it seems) and *Patalene*, Arrian in his Indica of Πάτταλα, and Diodorus has the apparently corrupt form Τάυαλα. It seems that *Patala* denotes the city. The place is now occupied by Haidarâbâd, the old name of which was Nirankot, also *Pâtalpur*, and is called *Patasila* by the Chinese traveller Hwen Thsang in the 7th century A D. Cunningham pp 279—287.

rex] Diodorus XVII 104 says that at Τάυαλα there were two royal houses and the general control of affairs was in the hands of a senate.

profugerat] Arrian VI 17 § 5 ἐξαγγέλλεται ὅτι ὁ τῶν Παταλέων ὕπαρχος *ξυλλαβὼν τῶν Παταλέων τοὺς πολλοὺς ἀποδεδρακὼς οἴχοιτο, ἀπολιπὼν τὴν χώραν ἔρημον.*

§ 30. *ducibus*] probably some of the men whose capture Arrian speaks of in VI 17 § 6.

insulam] see on VIII 9 § 7.

enatam] which had sprung up. For this curious half-personification we may compare the use of *ναιετάω* in Odyssey I 404, IX 23.

CHAPTER IX.

§ 1. *nec repertis*] *nec=et non*, but the negative only affects *repertis*. Compare III 13 § 2 *nec dubitare eum......adiecit.*

peritis] that is, *hominibus*. So § 6 *ignaris*.

coegit] this is one of the makeshifts proposed for filling up this lacuna. Others are *compulit* and *instigabat*.

§ 2. *colerent*] this is very strange, being used absolutely, leaving *terras loca* or *regionem* to be supplied mentally.

quam placidum] how quiet (or the reverse).

patiens] enduring, that is 'navigable by'. Compare Tacitus hist IV 21 *Rhenus incognita illi caelo siccitate vix navium patiens*, Livy XXI 31.

longarum] *μακρῶν*, war-vessels. See above 4 § 11.

anceps etc] compare VI 11 § 21 *anceps coniectura est.*

caeca] groping in the dark, baseless. Compare VIII 13 § 25, Caecina to Cicero (ad fam VI 7 § 4) *in hac calumnia timoris et caecae suspitionis tormento.*

§ 3. *ipsos*] either simply=*se*, or to be explained 'of themselves', that is, unaided by guides.

§ 4. *nauticos*] the mariners. An unusual word, used three times by Curtius in this chapter, here and §§ 7, 26.

incumberent] Virgil Aen V 15, X 294.

deesse] wanting to complete.

capi] so VII 8 § 19 *Lydiam cepisti.*

§ 5. *navigio*] in (on) a boat. Arrian VI 18 § 5 *τῶν ψιλῶν τοὺς κουφοτάτους ἐκπέμψας.*

§ 6. *dulcem*] 'fresh', as opposed to *amarus* or *salsus*. See Lucretius VI 890—4.

destinari] marked out, described, 'meant'.

§ 7. *leni adhuc*] 'still gentle'. That is, they were as yet only at the weaker or upper end of the tide-way.

§ 8. *evecti*] sailed out to or past. Compare § 27.

cursus] the stream of the river. Compare Lucan X 246—7 of the Nile *ille mora cursus adversique obice ponti aestuat in campos.*

adplicant] 'put in' to the lower end of the island mentioned, or to some other point along the shore. Compare *adpulsa* 10 § 1.

ignaris] being only acquainted with the practically tideless shores of the Mediterranean.

§ 9. *tertia*] by Roman reckoning = 9 a m with us.

stata] fixed, 'periodical'. Lucan X 240 of the west winds affecting the Nile *quorum stata tempora flatus*, and below § 27.

exaestuans] 'rising in flood-tide', 'flowing'. Arrian VI 19 §§ 1, 2, in his far more sober account of the incident, says that they were first troubled by the ebb and then yet more sorely by the floods, which sounds more likely than (see §§ 19, 20 below) the account of Curtius. Diodorus says nothing of it. Burnes vol III c 1 gives a description of the violent tides of the Indus estuary, shewing that all the main details of this account are quite in accordance with facts.

invehi] to assail, 'burst upon' them. Arrian says ἀθρόου ἐπελθόντος τοῦ κύματος.

coercitum] 'checked' in its course.

adversum] adjective of course, meaning 'up against its natural flow'.

torrentia] *flumina*, 'rivers in flood'.

§ 10. *identidem*] 'over and over again', hence 'continuously', 'every instant'. So § 21, 4 § 18, Catullus 49 (51) of the youth gazing upon his mistress *qui sedens adversus identidem te spectat et audit dulce ridentem*.

§ 11. *trepidi*] in a hurry.

§ 12. *festinatio* etc] 'more haste less speed', as we say.

tarda] cramping, hindering. For this transitive use compare Horace sat I 9 32 *tarda podagra*, II 2 88 *tarda senectus*.

aptari] fitted, 'shipped'. Compare Virgil Aen V 753 *aptant remosque rudentesque*.

consederant] until some support is found for the sense 'run aground', we feel bound to keep that of 'sit down', which has the further advantage of referring to the men, not the ships (which are not in question as subject of any verb till *aliae* § 13). Compare Virgil Aen III 289 *considere transtris*, IV 573, V 136 etc. The sense of the whole will then be 'some were pushing the vessels with poles, others had taken their seats [to row] but [in their crowding and scrambling] had meanwhile been preventing the orderly shipping of the oars'. The description of this scene of confusion is graphic, though at first sight somewhat difficult.

§ 13. *enavigare*] to sail out into the clear channel.

clauda] crippled, lame. The meaning is that more oars were manned on the one side than on the other, as in Virgil V 271 *ordine debilis uno*. For the word *claudus* see Lucretius IV 436, Livy XXXVII 24, Tacitus ann II 24.

moliebantur] were 'working' them feebly.

non receperant] had not taken on board, that is, had not been able (by reason of the hurry caused by the sudden rise of the tide) to do so. We must as Zumpt says understand *omnes*. The sense in general is that, seeing a vessel suddenly getting afloat, a number of men belonging to different vessels would try to crowd on board, but could not all do so before she drifted away with the stream.

§ 14. *hinc...hinc*] here the meaning is 'from one side'......'from another'.

tendentium] keeping in view, making an object. For this use with a pronoun see Livy XXXII 32 *quod summa vi ut tenderent amicis et propinquis mandaverat.*

§ 16. *abstergeri*] compare Livy XXXVII 24 (of the Rhodian naval tactics) *aut proram lacerabat aut remos detergebat.*

urgere] to press on them from behind, bump their sterns. Observe that three distinct sorts of collision are spoken of, this last being the same as that described in § 17.

§ 17. *ad manus*] that is, to violence. Cic II in Verrem V § 28 *nonnumquam etiam res ad pugnam atque ad manus vocabatur.*

§ 19. *subsederant*] had sunk or settled down, that is (as Vogel remarks) at the time of the formation of this land, and implying that the subsidence still shewed its effects. 'Where there were depressions in the ground'. For the word compare Ovid met I 43 *iussit et extendi campos, subsidere valles.*

fastigium] a raised point, elevation. See VIII 9 § 3.

occupaverant] had seized, that is 'covered'. For the sense of seizing a strong post compare 4 § 26, VIII 11 § 2.

§ 20. *reciprocari*] to run the other way, here to 'ebb'. Livy XXVIII 6 *fretum Euripi non septiens die, sicut fama fert, temporibus statis reciprocat*, where we have the active form.

tractu] 'suck', 'current'. So § 25 and often.

fretum] 'channel'. The proper sense, hence often a 'strait'.

reddebat] was restoring, rendering up, as it retired. Compare with this passage generally VI 4 § 19 of the Caspian *a septentrione ingens in litus mare incumbit longeque agit fluctus et magna parte exaestuans stagnat. idem alio caeli statu recipit in se fretum eodemque impetu quo effusum est relabens terram naturae suae reddit.*

destituta] 'left high and dry', 'stranded', as in § 22.

tabularum] planks. Virgil Aen I 118—9 *apparent rari nantes in gurgite vasto, arma virum tabulaeque et Troia gaza per undas* probably suggested the present passage.

§ 22. *beluae*] ? crocodiles. See Herodotus quoted on VIII 9 § 4.

§ 23. *non obruunt quin*] *obruunt* conveys the general notion of hindrance. For *quin*='that not' see Madvig § 440 a obs 3. We should say 'so as to prevent him from'.

persideret] from *persideo.*

in speculis] 'on the watch'. Compare Cic I in Verrem § 46 *nunc autem homines in speculis sunt, observant* etc, Ovid her XVIII 12 *in speculis omnis Abydos erat.*

equitesque etc] Arrian says nothing of this strange precaution.

praecederent] go before it and herald its approach.

§ 24. *paratosque esse* etc] that is *nauticos* or *milites nauticosque* according to § 26.

§ 25. *inpulit*] set in motion. Compare Virgil Aen x 246—7 *dextra discedens inpulit altam haud ignara modi puppim*, v 241—2 *et pater ipse manu magna Portunus euntem inpulit.*

§ 26. *eiusdem*] Vogel with some plausibility brackets the syllable *dem*. *clementi* is the generally accepted correction of MSS *mentis*.

modo......obnoxia] that is, it seemed so to them.

discors] that is, at first they thought it out of harmony (with natural laws) because (see §§ 8, 10, 22) this bore of the tide was beyond their own experience, but presently they found that it did obey certain laws in respect of time. For *discors* used of the tides see Pliny nat hist II § 218 who speaks of *diversi aestus tempore non ratione discordes.*

§ 27. *acciderat*] commonly used of evil. See Mayor on Cic phil II § 17.

occuparet] catch it in time, take advantage of it.

voti etc] see 2 § 26, 4 § 21, Arrian VI 19 § 5 says that he gave out that his object was to see whether any land appeared rising from the sea near at hand, adding ἐμοὶ δὲ δοκεῖ, οὐχ ἥκιστα ὡς πεπλευκέναι τὴν μεγάλην τὴν ἔξω Ἰνδῶν θάλασσαν.

sacrificio] Arrian VI 19 §§ 4, 5 and Diodorus XVII 104 relate this more in detail. See also Arrian Indica 20 § 10.

CHAPTER X.

§ 1. *adversum flumen subit*] 'goes up against the stream'. Literally 'ascends the opposing stream'. Compare Caesar [or Hirtius] bell Gall VIII 15 *barbari confisi loci natura quum dimicare non recusarent si forte Romani subire collem conarentur.* Curtius uses the construction with the ablative 'by' or 'along' in § 3 below.

lacu salso] Arrian VI § 20 says that Alexander went up to Patala again and then, having found his orders for the foundation of a strong station progressing satisfactorily, descended the other (left) branch of the river; in the course of which voyage he came upon a great lake in which sea-fish were seen.

alios] those who had not bathed. He means that the infection was communicated by contact with the sores.

§ 2. *Leonnato*] Arrian VI 20 § 3 mentions Leonnatus, but not § 5 where he is speaking of this well-digging. Strabo XV 2 § 3 speaks of the party as μεταλλευτὰς τῶν ὑδρείων. See also Justin XII 10 § 7.

sicca] so say Arrian Strabo Diodorus and Plutarch.

vernum tempus] Arrian VI 21 §§ 1, 2, Indica 21 § 1, Strabo XV 2 § 5 quoting Nearchus [with which XV 1 § 17, quoting Aristobulus, agrees] place the time of departure in the latter part of the summer, that of the fleet in the autumn. Mützell observes that Plutarch Alex 66 assigns seven, not ten months, as the time spent in sailing down the rivers, and so probably followed another account, which may have been the same as that followed by Curtius. Anyhow it would bring him to Patala in April, not (as Aristobulus says) in July.

urbes] Arrian speaks of the town and station at Patala and of sundry naval stations. Curtius is probably making the most of the statements of his authorities, whatever they were.

plerasque] simply 'a number', 'many'. So in Tacitus hist I 39, 86 we find *plerique* opposed to *plures*.

§ 3. *Nearcho*] he was the admiral (ναύαρχος) and Onesikritus the head pilot or sailing-master (ἀρχικυβερνήτης) of the fleet. We know that there was a jealousy between them (Strabo XV 2 § 4), for which the latter was probably to blame, as he proved himself in his account of Alexander's expedition a steady and enormous liar (see Strabo XV I *passim*) and in particular affirmed that he had himself been ναύαρχος of the fleet. The παράπλους of Nearchus was a work of considerable merit.

deducerent etc] Diodorus XVII 104 τὸν δὲ λοιπὸν στόλον παραδοὺς Νεάρχῳ καὶ τισιν ἄλλοις τῶν φίλων προσέταξε τὴν παραλίαν πᾶσαν παραπλεῦσαι δι' ὠκεανοῦ καὶ πάντα κατασκεψαμένους ἀπαντᾶν ἐπὶ τὰς ἐκβολὰς τοῦ Εὐφράτου ποταμοῦ. Arrian Indica 20 §§ 1—3 says (quoting Nearchus) that Alexander wanted to go on this voyage himself, but abandoned it from motives of prudence. When searching for a trusty admiral he received an offer from Nearchus to undertake the business.

§ 4. *crematis*] so says Diodorus.

exercitum] not the whole, for a part had been sent off under Kraterus through Karmania. For details see Arrian VI 17 § 3, Strabo XV 2 § 5.

§ 5. *Arabiton*] Diodorus calls them Ἀρβῖται, Strabo Ἄρβιες, Arrian Ἀραβῖται in his Anabasis, Ἀράβιες in his Indian history. Their further or western boundary was the river variously called Ἄρβις, Ἀράβιος, Ἀράβις and *Arabus*. Beyond this river lay the Oritae, and beyond them again the Gedrosii Gadrosii or Kedrosii. The words *inde......Cedrosiorum* are obviously wrong. But, as has been already observed by Vogel, they may very well for all that have been written by Curtius himself, for Diodorus speaks of the submission of τοὺς τὴν Κεδρωσίαν οἰκοῦντας immediately after that of the Arbitae, and then goes on to mention the Oritae, returning further on to the march through Κεδρωσία, as Curtius does below. They probably both followed the same authorities, in which there may have been some confusion to account for their strange muddle. It is remarkable that Arrian VI 22 § 1 mentions Gadrosian troops as having assisted the Oritae to oppose the entrance of Alexander into the territory of the latter. See on § 12 *iumenta* and § 18 *quiete*.

liber] Ἀραβῖται, ἔθνος καὶ τοῦτο αὐτόνομον, says Arrian VI 21 § 4.

dedidit se] Arrian and Diodorus agree with this statement.

§ 6. *ibi maiorem* etc] Diodorus and Arrian agree in substance with this account of the march and laying waste of the country of the Oritae.

§ 7. *urbem*] so says Diodorus and tells us that its name was Alexandria. Arrian VI 21 § 5 says only that he praised a certain spot as suited for the development of a great city.

Arachosii] this statement rests on Curtius' authority alone.

§ 8. *maritimos Indos*] these are clearly the same as those whom Diodorus XVII 105 calls **ἔθνος ἄξενον καὶ παντελῶς θηριῶδες**, and to whom other writers give the name Ichthyophagi. But it is remarkable that Arrian VI 28 § 5, Indica 24—29 *passim* speaks of their being visited by Nearchus, not by Alexander, and this is perhaps the more probable version of the story, unless we refer this passage of Curtius to the exploring party under Thoas, sent by Alexander to survey the coast district. See Arrian VI 23 §§ 2, 3. Pliny N H VI § 95.

commercii iure] 'intercourse', perhaps in the way of exchange. The word *ius* means 'right' or 'rightful relation', and the expression *ius commercii* is important in early Roman history. See note on VIII 9 § 19.

§ 9. *ipsa*] 'of itself', opposed to *natura quoque* 'even by nature'.

efferavit] 'has made savage'. Compare VIII 2 § 16 *tum ferocia ingenia non bellum modo sed etiam veniae desperatio efferaverat.*

ingenia] 'characters'. The following account of this loathsome tribe is in strict agreement with the other authorities.

§ 10. *tuguria*] these are the huts called by Arrian Ind 24 § 2 'stifling cabins' (**ἐν καλύβῃσι πνιγηρῇσι**). The following account of them corresponds with the more detailed descriptions in Strabo XV 2 § 2, Diodorus XVII 105, Arrian Ind 29 § 19, 30 §§ 8, 9, anab VI 23 § 3.

conchis] Arrian VI 23 § 3 **ξυνθέντας τὰς κόγχας**.

purgamentis] off-scourings, refuse. The other writers inform us that these were the bones of whales or other huge animals (**κήτη**) cast up by the sea.

pellibus] so Diodorus, **δορὰς θηρίων**. Arrian Ind 24 § 9 says that some wore thick fish hides.

sole duratis] Strabo and Arrian Ind 29 §§ 9—13 say that they catch fish in nets made of palm-bark, and then dry the larger ones in the sun and grind them when dried into meal and even bake the meal into loaves. From Pliny N H VII § 30 we learn that Klitarchus is his authority for this statement, and Curtius probably took it also from the same source. See Pomponius Mela III 8.

eiecit] so Diodorus **σιτοῦνται δὲ τὰ ἐκβαλλόμενα κήτη σαρκοφαγοῦντες**, and the rest agree.

§ 11. *igitur*] the country supplying no food.

ad ultimum] 'at last', 'in the end'. So *ad extremum*.

radices palmarum] Strabo XV 2 § 5, Arrian VI 23 § 6, Indica 26 § 6, 29 § 1 mention only the fruit (**βάλανοι** ?dates) and pith (**ἐγκέφαλος**) of the palms. Diodorus says nothing of the matter, which makes it probable that Curtius has not mistaken his authorities but followed different ones. Zumpt well refers to Cic. II in Verrem V §§ 87, 99 where we read of sailors compelled by hunger to eat *radices palmarum agrestium*, a non-fructiferous sort of palm.

gignitur] that is *ibi, in ea regione.*

§ 12. *iumenta* etc] so Arrian VI 25 § 1, who however (cc 24—26) places the scene of these terrible sufferings in the land of the Γαδρωσοὶ proper, which is the more probable account. See on § 18 *quiete.*

cremabant incendio] 'set fire to and burnt', as we say.

§ 13. *pestilentia*] Arrian VI 25 §§ 2, 3 speaks of their suffering from a νόσος, but does not attach such importance to it as Curtius seems to have done, probably following different authorities.

ad hoc] on the top of this, 'besides'.

§ 14. *strati* etc] Arrian substantially agrees with all this, and likens those who lay down in the sandy desert to men lost at sea.

agmen etc] Arrian says *σπουδῇ γὰρ πολλῇ ἐγίγνετο ὁ στόλος, καὶ ἐν τῷ ὑπὲρ τοῦ παντὸς προθύμῳ τὸ καθ' ἑκάστους ξὺν ἀνάγκῃ ἠμελεῖτο.*

proficere ad] make advance towards. Compare Cic Brutus § 92 *nulla enim res tantum ad dicendum proficit quantum scriptio.*

praeciperent] so IV 1 § 3 of the retreat of Darius in haste, *id demum credens fore ipsius, quod celeritate praecipere potuisset.*

§ 15. *orabant*] with all this compare the pathetic passage of Thucydides VII 75 §§ 3, 4.

nec...et] there were not...and. So *οὔτε...τε* often in Greek. Madvig § 458 c.

iumenta] *ἀπορίᾳ τῶν ὑποζυγίων*, says Arrian.

excipi] be picked up. See *excepturi* 5 § 1 above.

portabat] =*portare poterat.*

et ipsis] 'themselves also'.

ante oculos erat] =*obversabatur.*

saepius] too often, that is, so often that they ceased to take heed.

sustinebant] bear, endure.

misericordia] for others, *formidinem* for themselves.

§ 16. *sacra communia*] the rites of their common religion.

ipsis] themselves, that is the persons addressed, those hurrying on.

§ 17. *quia...esset*] because (as he felt) he was, 'feeling himself to be'. This subjunctive of the assumed reason is common enough. See Madvig § 357 a. Arrian VI 24 §§ 2, 3 tells us that Alexander well knew what he had to expect when he undertook this march; but the legends of the journeys of Semiramis and Cyrus through the same district, how the former lost all her army but 20 men, and the latter all but 7, roused him to attempt to succeed where they had failed. So too Strabo XV 2 § 5.

misit etc] Diodorus XVII 105 gives substantially the same account of his messages to the satraps and their prompt attention to his orders.

finitimarum] Diodorus τὴν Παρθυαίαν καὶ Δραγγηνὴν καὶ Ἀρείαν.

§ 18. *fame*] it would be more natural to have *a fame* after *vindicatus*, but the present construction seems a possible one.

dumtaxat] here 'at least'.

in Cedrosiae etc] see on §§ 5, 12.

omnium rerum] 'all sorts of things'.

sola] that is, alone of all the districts round. So Mützell and Zumpt take it; and emendations are not wanted.

quiete] Arrian VI 27 § 1 makes him rest and refresh his army at the capital of the Gadrosi, which in 24 § 1 he calls Ποῦρα. Plutarch Alex 66, 67 says that he found himself in plenty on entering Gedrosia, and that he gave his men a second rest at the capital of that district. But, as he makes them march seven days through Karmania in the mean time, we cannot attach much weight to his statement. It is however clear that there were two accounts of Gedrosia; but, as Arrian and Strabo agree, we cannot have much hesitation in believing that the country (at least as far as Pura) was scorched and barren to the last degree.

§ 19. *Leonnati*] his victory is mentioned also by Arrian VII 5 § 5, Ind 23 §§ 5, 6. Diodorus gives a version less favourable to the Macedonians.

Cratero] see on § 4. This is the first hint we have had from Curtius as to the whereabouts of Kraterus.

Osinen] Arrian VI 27 § 3 speaks of Kraterus bringing one Ordanes a captured revolter to Alexander.

molientes] compare Virgil georg I 271 *insidias avibus moliri.*

§ 20. *Sibyrtio*] Arrian VI 27 § 1 says that he succeeded one Thoas (successor of Apollophanes) as satrap of Gadrosia, and that he was also satrap of Karmania.

morbo] so Thoas in Arrian.

§ 21. *Aspastes*] mentioned only by Curtius.

suspectus voluisse] so Tacitus hist I 46 *suspectus consilia eius fovisse.*

dum] used here with its favourite present indicative, though in the dependent clause after *voluisse*. See Madvig § 369 obs 3.

§ 22. *dum*] until such time as. See Madvig § 360 obs 2.

quae delata erant] the informations laid against them. Arrian VI 27 §§ 4, 5 speaks of three satraps Kleander Sitalkes and Herakon whom the king punished after enquiry into their conduct. See also Diodorus XVII 106.

cum inde] the order of the sense is *inde cum*. So we might have *cum igitur* or the reverse. For *inde*=after that, 'next', compare I § 33.

equorum etc] Arrian VI 27 § 6 gives much the same account.

sub imperio] 'under their rule'.

quibus] =*iis quibus* as often.

inpedimenta] =*iumenta* 'horses and carts'. Mützell compares Livy XXVIII 41 for this military expression.

§ 23. *cultum*] see 3 §§ 10, 11.

§ 24. *igitur*] having now reached a land of plenty.

supra] see VIII 10 §§ 17, 18. Diodorus XVII 106 and Plutarch Alex 67 give just the same account of this seven days' revel. Arrian VI 28 §§ 1, 2, following Ptolemy and Aristobulus, denies the truth of the story, and he is probably right.

gloriam] his 'glory' or 'renown' won by his great exploits as a conqueror in the east: *famam*, his 'repute' as the founder of the Bacchic revels. For the opposition of the words see 5 § 1. Cicero Tusc III §§ 3, 4 *est enim gloria solida quaedam res et expressa, non adumbrata; ea est consentiens laus bonorum, incorrupta vox bene iudicantium de excellente virtute; ea virtuti resonat tanquam imago. quae quia recte factorum plerumque comes est, non est bonis viris repudianda. illa autem quae se eius imitatricem esse vult, temeraria atque inconsiderata et plerumque peccatorum vitiorumque laudatrix, fama popularis, simulatione honestatis formam eius pulchritudinemque corrumpit.* But *fama*, we must remember, is in itself a neutral word.

sive...lusus] is a parenthetic remark by way of comment on *statuit imitari*.

illud] 'that'=what he did. So Virgil Aen III 173 *nec sopor illud erat*, where *illud*=what I saw and heard. See *quod* § 28 below.

triumphus] Arrian says καὶ Θρίαμβόν τε αὐτὸν ἐπικληθῆναι τὸν Διόνυσον καὶ τὰς ἐπὶ ταῖς νίκαις ταῖς ἐκ πολέμου πομπὰς ἐπὶ τῷ αὐτῷ τούτῳ θριάμβους. Greek writers always render the Roman *triumphus* by θρίαμβος.

§ 25. *aedium*] temples: or can it be that he means houses?

crateras] from nominative *cratera*.

constrata] with carpets or rugs, according to Plutarch.

velis] hangings, curtains, awnings.

§ 26. *cohors regia*] see on VIII 11 § 11.

redimita] a common word in the poets.

vehiculis] that is, *ibant*, 'rode'.

comissabundus] so Livy IX 17 says loosely of Alexander, *Indiae, per quam temulento agmine comissabundus incessit.*

poculis] 'cups', as distinct from *craterae* 'mixing-bowls'.

§ 27. *saltem*] goes closely with *adversus comissantes*.

viri modo] =*dummodo viri fuissent*.

§ 28. *fortuna* etc] compare Sallust Cat 8 § 1 *sed profecto fortuna in omni re dominatur; ea res cunctas ex lubidine magis quam ex vero celebrat obscuratque.*

praesens] that is, the contemporaries of Alexander. Curtius uses these very words in precisely the same sense VIII 5 § 11, where he has just put the same notion in the words *secum viventium*.

deinde] 'after them'. So Greek *ἔπειτα*.

§ 30. Curtius appropriately closes the book with one of the moral sentences dear to all rhetoricians.

APPENDICES.

A. The first *suasoria* of Seneca the rhetorician, from the text of Kiessling (Leipzig, Teubner, 1872), to be compared with Curtius IX 2 §§ 8—11, 3 §§ 1—15, 4 §§ 16—21, 9 §§ 20—22. For these declamations on themes see Mayor on Juvenal I 16, VII 162. Seneca's work is a collection of specimens, reported from his own notes or from memory, of the manner in which some of the greatest masters of the period had handled certain topics. The beginning of the present one is unfortunately lost. They are interesting as shewing the spirit of the rhetorical schools, their laboured striving after antithesis and tendency to wear a sentiment threadbare.

1 ...sinunt. cuicumque rei magnitudinem natura dederat dedit et modum: nihil infinitum est nisi Oceanus. aiunt fertiles in Oceano iacere terras ultraque Oceanum rursus alia litora, alium nasci orbem, nec usquam rerum naturam desinere, sed semper inde ubi desisse uideatur nouam exsurgere. facile ista finguntur quia Oceanus nauigari non potest. satis sit hactenus Alexandro uicisse qua mundo lucere satis est. intra has terras caelum Hercules meruit. stat immotum mare et quasi deficientis in suo fine naturae pigra moles: nouae ac terribiles figurae, magna etiam Oceano portenta quae profunda ista uastitas nutrit, confusa lux alta caligine et interceptus tenebris dies, ipsum uero graue et defixum mare et aut nulla aut ignota sidera. ita est, Alexander, rerum natura: post omnia Oceanus, post Oceanum nihil. 2 ARGENTARI. resiste, orbis te tuus reuocat: uicimus qua licet. nihil tantum est, quod ego Alexandri periculo petam. POMPEI SILONIS. uenit ille dies, Alexander, exoptatus, quo tibi opera desset: idem sunt termini et regni tui et mundi. OSCI. tempus est Alexandrum cum orbe et cum sole *desinere*. quod noueram uici: nunc concupisco quod nescio. quae tam

ferae gentes fuerunt quae non Alexandrum posito genu adorarint? qui tam horridi montes quorum non iuga uictor miles calcauerit? ultra Liberi patris tropaea constitimus. non quaerimus orbem, sed amittimus. inmensum et humanae intemptatum experientiae pelagus, totius orbis uinculum terrarumque custodia, inagitata remigio uastitas, litora modo saeuiente fluctu inquieta, modo fugiente deserta: tetra caligo fluctus premit et nescio qui quod humanis natura subduxit oculis aeterna nox obruit. MVSAE. foeda beluarum magnitudo et inmobile profundum testantur, Alexander, nihil ultra esse quod uincas: reuertere. 3 ALBVCI SILI. terrae quoque suum finem habent et ipsius mundi aliquis occasus est; nihil infinitum est: modum magnitudini facere debes, quoniam fortuna non facit. magni pectoris est inter secunda moderatio. eundem fortuna uictoriae tuae quem naturae finem facit: imperium tuum cludit Oceanus. o quantum magnitudo tua rerum quoque naturam supergressa est! Alexander orbi magnus est, Alexandro orbis angustus est. aliquis etiam magnitudini modus est: non procedit ultra spatia sua caelum, maria intra terminos suos agitantur. quidquid ad summum peruenit incremento non reliquit locum. non magis quidquam ultra Alexandrum nouimus quam ultra Oceanum. MARILLI. maria sequimur, terras cui tradimus? orbem quem non noui quaero, quem uici relinquo. 4 FABIANI. quid? ista toto pelago infusa caligo nauigantem tibi uidetur admittere, quae prospicientem quoque excludit? non haec India est nec ferarum terribilis ille conuentus. inmanes propone beluas, aspice quibus procellis fluctibusque saeuiat, quas ad litora undas agat. tantus uentorum concursus, tanta conuulsi funditus maris insania est; nulla praesens nauigantibus statio est, nihil salutare, nihil notum: rudis et inperfecta natura penitus recessit. ista maria ne illi quidem petierunt qui fugiebant Alexandrum. sacrum quidem terris natura circumfudit Oceanum. illi qui etiam siderum collegerunt metas et annuas hiemis atque aestatis uices ad certam legem redegerunt, quibus nulla pars ignota mundi est, de Oceano tamen dubitant utrumne terras uelut uinculum circumfluat, an in suum colligatur orbem et in hos per quos nauigatur sinus quasi spiramenta quaedam magnitudinis exaestuet; ignem post se cuius augmentum ipse sit habeat, an spiritum. quid agitis, conmilitones? domitoremne generis humani, magnum Alexandrum, eo dimittitis quod adhuc quid sit disputatur? memento Alexander: matrem in orbe uicto adhuc magis quam pacato relinquis.

5 DIVISIO. aiebat CESTIVS hoc genus suasoriarum aliter declamandum esse quam suadendum. non eodem modo in libera ciuitate dicendam sententiam quo apud reges, quibus etiam quae prosunt ita

tamen ut delectent suadenda sunt. et inter reges ipsos esse discrimen: quosdam minus aut magis osos ueritatem; facile Alexandrum exisse quos superbissimos et supra mortalis animi modum inflatos accepimus. denique ut alia dimittantur argumenta, ipsa suasoria insolentiam eius coarguit; orbis illum suus non capit: itaque nihil dicendum aiebat nisi cum summa ueneratione regis, ne accideret idem quod praeceptori eius amitino Aristotelis accidit, quem occidit propter intempestiue liberos sales: nam cum (deum) se uellet uideri et uulneratus esset, uiso sanguine eius philosophus mirari se dixerat, quod non esset *ἰχὼρ οἷός πέρ τε ῥέει μακάρεσσι θεοῖσιν*. ille se ab hac urbanitate lancea uindicauit. eleganter in C. Cassi epistola quadam ad M. Ciceronem missa positum: multum iocatur de stultitia Cn. Pompei adulescentis qui in Hispania contraxit exercitum et ad Mundam acie uictus est; deinde ait: 'nos quidem illum deridemus, sed timeo ne ille nos gladio *ἀντιμυκτηρίσῃ*'. in omnibus regibus haec urbanitas extimescenda est. 6 aiebat itaque apud Alexandrum esse dicendam sententiam ut multa adulatione animus eius permulceretur, seruandum tamen aliquem modum, ne conrueret ratio et accideret tale aliquid quale accidit Atheniensibus, cum publicae eorum blanditiae non tantum deprehensae set castigatae sunt. nam cum Antonius uellet se Liberum patrem dici et hoc nomen statuis subscribi iuberet, habitu quoque et comitatu Liberum imitaretur, occurrerunt uenienti ei Athenienses cum coniugibus et liberis et *Διόνυσον* salutauerunt. belle illis cesserat, si nasus Atticus ibi substitisset; (set) dixerunt despondere ipsos in matrimonium illi Mineruam suam et rogauerunt ut duceret. Antonius ait ducturum, sed dotis nomine imperare se illis mille talenta. tum ex Graeculis quidam ait: *κύριε, ὁ Ζεὺς τὴν μητέρα σου Σεμέλην ἄπροικον εἶχεν*. huic quidem inpune fuit, sed Atheniensium sponsalia mille talentis aestimata sunt. quae cum exigerentur conplures contumeliosi libelli proponebantur, quidam etiam ipsi Antonio tradebantur: sicut ille qui subscriptus statuae eius fuit, cum eodem tempore et Octauiam uxorem haberet et Cleopatram: *Ὀκταουία καὶ Ἀθηνᾶ Ἀντωνίῳ·* res tuas tibi habe. 7 bellissimam tamen rem DELLIVS dixit, quem Messala Coruinus desultorem bellorum ciuilium uocat, quia ab Dolabella ad Cassium transiturus salutem sibi pactus est, si Dolabellam occidisset: a Cassio deinde transiit ad Antonium, nouissime ab Antonio transfugit ad Caesarem. hic est Dellius cuius epistulae ad Cleopatram lasciuae feruntur. cum Athenienses tempus peterent ad pecuniam conferendam nec exorarent, Dellius ait: et tamen dicito illos tibi annua, bienni, *trienni die* debere. longius me fabellarum dulcedo produxit: itaque ad-

propositum reuertar. 8 aiebat CESTIVS magnis cum laudibus Alexandri hanc suasoriam esse dicendam, quam sic diuisit, ut primum diceret, etiamsi nauigari posset Oceanus, nauigandum non esse; satis gloriae quaesitum; regenda esse et disponenda quae in transitu uicisset; consulendum militi tot eius uictoriis lasso; de matre illi cogitandum: et alias causas complures subiecit. deinde illam quaestionem subiecit, ne nauigari quidem Oceanum posse. 9 FABIANVS philosophus primam fecit quaestionem eandem: etiam si nauigari posset Oceanus nauigandum non esse. at rationem aliam primam fecit: modum inponendum esse rebus secundis. hic dixit sententiam: illa demum est magna felicitas quae arbitrio suo constitit. dixit deinde locum de uarietate fortunae et cum descripsisset nihil esse stabile, omnia fluitare et incertis motibus modo adtolli, modo deprimi, absorberi terras et maria siccari, montes subsidere, deinde exempla regum e fastigio suo deuolutorum, adiecit: sine potius rerum naturam quam fortunam tuam deficere. 10 secundam quoque quaestionem aliter tractauit: diuisit enim illam sic, ut primum negaret ullas in Oceano aut trans Oceanum esse terras habitabiles. deinde si essent, perueniri tamen ad illas non posse; hic difficultatem nauigationis, ignoti maris naturam non patientem nauigationis. nouissime ut posset perueniri, tanti tamen non esse. hic dixit incerta peti, certa deseri; descituras gentes, si Alexandrum rerum naturae terminos supergressum enotuisset; hic matrem de qua dixit: quomodo illa trepidauit etiam quom Granicum transiturus esses. 11 GLYCONIS celebris sententia est: *τοῦτο οὐκ ἔστι Σιμόεις οὐδὲ Γράνικος· τοῦτο εἰ μή τι κακὸν ἦν, οὐκ ἂν νέατον ἔκειτο.* hoc omnes imitari uoluerunt. PLVTION dixit: *καὶ διὰ τοῦτο μέγιστόν ἐστιν, ὅτι αὐτὸ μὲν μετὰ πάντα, μετὰ δὲ αὐτὸ οὐθέν.* ARTEMON dixit: *βουλευτέον εἰ δεῖ ἄρα περαιοῦσθαι. οὐ ταῖς Ἑλλησποντίαις ᾐόσιν ἐφεστῶτες οὐδ' ἐπὶ τῷ Παμφυλίῳ πελάγει τὴν ἐμπρόθεσμον καραδοκοῦμεν ἄμπωσιν· οὐδὲ Εὐφράτης τοῦτ' ἐστιν, οὐδὲ Ἰνδός, ἀλλ' εἴτε γῆς τέρμα, εἴτε φύσεως ὅρος, εἴτε πρεσβύτατον στοιχεῖον, εἴτε γένεσις θεῶν, ἱερώτερόν ἐστιν ἢ κατὰ ναυς ὕδωρ.* APATVRIVS dixit: *ἐντεῦθεν ἡ ναῦς ἐκ μιᾶς φορᾶς εἰς ἀνατολάς, ἔνθα δὲ εἰς τὰς ἀοράτους δύσεις.* CESTIVS descripsit: sic fremit Oceanus, quasi indignetur quod terras relinquas. 12 Corruptissimam rem omnium quae umquam dictae sunt ex quo homines diserti insanire coeperunt, putabant Dorionis esse in metaphrasi dictam Homeri, cum excaecatus Cyclops saxum in mare reiecit... haec quomodo ex corruptis eo perueniant, ut et magna et tamen sana sint, aiebat Maecenas apud Vergilium intellegi posse. tumidum est: *ὄρεος ὄρος ἀποσπᾶται.* Vergilius quid ait? rapit haud partem exiguam montis.

ita (a) magnitudine discedit, ut non inprudenter discedat a fide. est inflatum:

καὶ καίρια βάλλεται νῆσοι.

Vergilius quid ait? qui de nauibus:

credas innare reuolsas
Cycladas.

non dicit hoc fieri, sed uideri. propitiis auribus accipitur, quamuis incredibile est, quod excusatur antequam dicitur. 13 multo corruptiorem sententiam MENESTRATI cuiusdam declamatoris non abiecti suis temporibus nactus sum in hac ipsa suasoria, cum describeret beluarum in Oceano nascentium magnitudinem... efficit haec sententia, ut ignoscamus ei qui dixit ipsis Charybdi et Scylla maius portentum: 'Charybdis ipsius maris naufragium', et ne in una re semel insaniret: 'quid ibi potest esse salui ubi ipsum mare perit?' DAMAS ethicos induxit matrem loquentem, cum describeret adsidue prioribus periculis noua superuenisse:...... BARBARVS dixit, cum introduxisset excusantem se exercitum Macedonum, hunc sensum: ... 14 FVSCVS ARELLIVS dixit: testor ante orbem tibi tuum deesse quam militem. LATRO sedens hanc dixit; non excusauit militem, sed dixit: dum sequor, quis mihi promittit hostem, quis terram, quis diem, quis mare? da ubi castra ponam, ubi signa ponam. reliqui parentes, reliqui liberos, commeatum peto: numquid inmature ab Oceano? 15 Latini declamatores in descriptione Oceani non nimis uiguerunt; nam aut minus descripserunt, aut (nimis) curiose. nemo illorum potuit tanto spiritu dicere quanto Pedo, qui nauigante Germanico dicit:

iam pridem pos terga diem solemque relinquunt,
iam pridem notis extorres finibus orbis
per non concessas audaces ire tenebras
ad rerum metas extremaque litora mundi;
nunc illum pigris immania monstra sub undis
qui ferat Oceanum, qui saeuas undique pistris
aequoreosque canes, ratibus consurgere prensis.
accumulat fragor ipse metus. iam sidere limo
nauigia et rapido desertam flamine classem
seque feris credunt per inertia fata marinis
tam non felici laniandos sorte relinqui.
atque aliquis prora caecum sublimis ab alta
aëra pugnaci luctatus rumpere uisu,

ut nihil erepto ualuit dinoscere mundo,
obstructa in talis effundit pectora uoces:
quo ferimur? fugit ipse dies orbemque relictum
ultima perpetuis claudit natura tenebris.
anne alio positas ultra sub cardine gentes
atque alium flabris intactum quaerimus orbem?
di reuocant rerumque uetant cognoscere finem
mortales oculos: aliena quid aequora remis
et sacras uiolamus aquas diuumque quietas
turbamus sedes?

ex Graecis declamatoribus nulli melius haec suasoria processit quam Glyconi; sed non minus multa magnifice dixit quam corrupte: utrorumque faciam uobis potestatem. et uolebam uos experiri non adiciendo iudicium meum nec separando a corruptis sana—potuisset enim fieri ut uos magis illa laudaretis quae insaniunt—et nihilominus poterit fieri, quamuis distinxerim. illa belle dixit:...sed fecit quod solebat, ut sententiam adiectione superuacua atque tumida perderet; adiecit enim: ...illud quosdam dubios iudici sui habet—ego non dubito contra sententiam ferre—: ὑγίαινε γῆ, ὑγίαινε ἥλιε· Μακεδόνες γὰρ χάος εἰσπλέουσι.

B. *A specimen of the translation of John Brende*, 1553.

[From IX 3 §§ 1—11].

Notwithstanding all that he had sayde, there was not one souldier that would open his mouth to speake, but stode wayting that some of the princes and great capitaynes shoulde declare unto the kynge their estates, and howe that there remayned not in them any obstinat refusall of the warres, but that they were so exhausted with woundes and weried with continuall travaill that they were not able to endure any lenger. As they stode thus astonied and afrayed, keping silence and lookyng upon the ground, there beganne first a whisperyng and a rumor and afterwardes a lamentacion amonges them, and by lyttle and little thei beganne more manifestly to shewe their dolour, the teares fallyng frō their eyes. The kynges anger was then so turned into compassion, that he was not able to keape hym selfe from weapyng. At length the whole assemble brast out into an excessive weapyng. And when all the rest were at a stay to speake Cenus toke upon hym to presse forwarde towardes the judgement seate where Alexander stoode, signifieng that he had somewhat to saye. When the souldiers saw he pulled his helmet from his head (for so it was the custome to speake unto the kyng) they began to require hym that he woulde utter the cause of the whole army. Then Cenus beganne in this wyse: The Goddes defende our myndes from all wicked thoughtes (as I doubt not but they wyll) there is none of your souldiers but be of the same mynde towardes you that they have bene in tymes past. Whether it be your pleasure to commaunde them to go forwardes, to fyght, to hasarde them selves, or with their bloud commend your name unto the posteritie. And if you will nedes persever in your opinion, though we be unarmed naked and without bloud, we will either come after you or go before, as you shall thynke expedient. But if you wyll be content to heare the griefes and complayntes of your souldiers that be not fayned but expressed by force of very necessitie, I humblie beseche you then that ye woulde vouchesave favourably to heare them, that constantly have folowed your authoritie and fortune, and are yet redy to folow wheresoever you wil appoynte. O Alexander, with the greatnes of your actes ye have not overcome only your enemies, but also your owne souldiers. Whatsoever mans mortalitie is able to fulfyll, that is perfourmed by us, having passed over so manye Seas and countreys better knowen to us then to the very inhabiters, nowe remayning in maner in the uttermoste ende of the worlde. And yet for all this, your purpose is to passe into an other worlde and seke out an Inde unknowen to the Indians. Ye covet to plucke out the wilde beastes and serpentes out of their dennes & lurking places, minding to serche further with your victory then the sonne hath visited wt her beames, which truly is an imaginaciõ mete for your harte, but farre exceding our capacitie and power. Your manhode and courage is alwayes an encrease, but our force groweth in declinacion. Behold our bodies destitute of bloud, perced with so many woundes, and rotted with so many scarres. Our weapons nowe be dulled, and our armour is wasted & consumed, we weare our apparell after the Perciãs maner, because our countrey garmentes do faill us. We are degenerate out of our own fasshion, & growen into a straũge habite. What is he that hath his corselet or horse particuler to himself? Cause it to be enquired how many servaũtes do folowe their maisters and what remaineth to every mã of the spoyle. Being the victorers of al mẽ, of all men we are the poorest.

C. Some extracts from the *Alexandreis* of Bishop Philippus Gualterus (12th or 13th century). These interesting passages are taken from Mützell's introduction: he quotes them to illustrate certain views as to the history of the MSS of Curtius, from whom the matter of the poem, and even much of the phraseology, was taken.

(1) *intercipit in mare Ganges*
decursurum Achesim: magnus occurrit uterque*
motibus et rapido inter eos colliditur aestu.

* Probably a misprint for *magnis*.

This comes from VIII 9 § 8 where the old reading was *Acesines eum auget. Ganges decursurum in mare intercipit, magnoque motu amnis uterque colliditur.*

(2) *iamque Argiva phalanx medium proruperat agmen*
Indorum.

So the old reading in VIII 14 § 18 was *prorupit.*

(3) *ausa tamen fatis Macetumque resistere famae*
gens Sudracharum.

See note on the name of this tribe in IX 4 § 15.

(4) *obiice nos cuivis portento: ignobile bellum,*
degeneres pugnas, obscura pericula vita;
gloria quantalibet vili sordescit in hoste.

So in IX 6 § 14 *bella* was read, where *pericula* is now generally adopted.

D. An abstract of the remarks of Mr J Talboys Wheeler in his *History of India from the earliest ages* vol III c 4 on the campaigns of Alexander in that country and other matters connected with the same; with a few comments added in brackets.

(*a*) He accepts the stories of Alexander's drunkenness and the weakening of his character, and thinks that the Macedonian phalanx had already degenerated when the Indian campaigns began. [See above in the Introduction B 13 for doubts as to the full acceptance of this view, though of course it is partly true.]

(*b*) Alexander's original design was to penetrate to the Ganges and conquer the great empire then existing on its banks. To do this he must conquer the smaller kingdoms on his way. Of the three Punjab kingdoms that of the 'elder' Porus was the most important: and from the eminence assigned to him it appears that his authority extended, in name at least, over the others. Thus he would be a sort of suzerain of the Punjab, a view confirmed by the Hindu tradition of the empire of *Puru* in these parts. The so-called hostile sovereigns (Taxiles and the younger Porus) were originally nothing more than refractory vassal kings. Under the non-cohesive system of Asiatic monarchies such nominal supremacy is often retained long after the political ties have been virtually destroyed. Alexander deemed it politic to treat the refractory vassals as independent sovereigns.

(*c*) Alexander had learnt that in Asiatic warfare the chief danger lay in the rear, and accordingly was careful to secure the real submission of the tribes as he passed. Liberal to ready submission and to obstinate resistance, he sternly repressed revolts and punished deception. His message to the Indian princes, requiring their submission, was probably sent by him as Great King of Persia to whom the whole region (Cabul and the Punjab) had been tributary in a previous generation (Herodotus III 94, 95, 102). After subduing the Assacani and taking Aornos, he made the kingdom of Taxiles his base of operations for crossing the Jhelum. The battle is one of the most remarkable actions in ancient story, and the passage of the river a wonderful feat. The results of his victory were most important. He was able to form a fleet on the Jhelum, a measure due both to his soldierly instinct of precaution and to his imagination. He at first took the Indus for the Nile.

(*d*) After crossing the Chenab and Ravee without opposition, he was called back to reduce the rebellious Kathaei to obedience. These seem to have been Rajpoots: at least their customs were of a Rajpoot character. But his plans were frustrated by the sullen resistance of his Macedonian soldiers. "Their spirits had been broken, not so much by the toils of war, as by the wind and rain of the south-west monsoon; and by this time their love of ease and sensual gratification had blunted that passion for glory and dominion which had formerly animated the phalanx". So they would not advance beyond the Sutlej. So he turned back and proceeded along the Jhelum and Indus through Scinde and thence through Beloochistan to Susa.

(*e*) The surface-observations of the Greeks who accompanied him shew care and acuteness. Their descriptions of the country are accurate, but they did not penetrate into the inner life of the people. One thing we may gather from them, that distinctions of caste had not as yet appeared in the Punjab, and that in this point (as also in respect of the system of government) the civilisation of the Punjab was essentially different from that of the Gangetic empire as described a few years later by Megasthenes, when Sandrokottos was on the throne. This prince, known to the Hindus as Chandragupta, ruled over a great populous and wealthy country: there caste institutions had long prevailed; the court was of rather a Tartar than an Aryan type, with its intrigues and conspiracies, its pompous ceremonies, and its hosts of women and body-guards round the person of the Raja. Espionage was the chief engine of government. The religion of the people was Brahmanical, but the Buddhists had then made some progress, and there is reason to think that the Raja was himself a convert to Buddhism. [It is to be gathered that the later writers in borrowing from Megasthenes did not understand the variety of customs and institutions in India, and (as possibly Curtius VIII 9) applied what was meant for the Hindus of the Ganges valley to those of the Punjab.]

(*f*) [Mr Wheeler remarks that the story told in Curtius IX 2 §§ 6—7 is a scandal unworthy of credit. It is, he says, simply the oriental form of abuse, which is directed not against the individual but against his mother and other female relatives. But he represents the tale as told to Alexander at Taxila by Sandrokottos[1]. On what authority he makes the two meet at all, and how he brings the latter to Taxila, I cannot discover. Mr McCrindle on the contrary makes the story to be told *of Sandrokottos;* at least he says that the Ξανδράμης of Diodorus XVII 93 and the Agrammes of Curtius are to be identified with him, and that the names are mere distortions of form. The last is a bold remark.]

[1] Is it possible that Sisikottos may have been meant here?

LIST OF NAMES.

Ammon] a god known to the Greeks by the name of Zeus Ammon. He had a temple and oracle in an oasis in the Libyan desert, which was visited by Alexander in person in the year 331 B C with the result that he was greeted by the oracle as the son of Zeus.

Antigenes] is mentioned by Curtius as having been present at the battle with Porus. After the death of Alexander Susiana fell to his share.

Aristonus] shewed great courage at the attack on the capital of the Malli when he helped to save the life of Alexander. He was a somatophylax and it was he who after Alexander's death proposed, probably according to arrangement, that the supreme power should be entrusted to Perdiccas. After Alexander's death he remained near Perdiccas and was subsequently put to death by the orders of Cassander.

Attalus] In VIII 13 § 21 we are told by Curtius that Attalus was of the same age as Alexander and that at the passage of the Hydaspes he was left, dressed in royal robes to deceive Porus, in command of the mercenaries while Alexander himself crossed higher up the river. He was one of the seven great officers at Alexander's death and subsequently joined Perdiccas, after whose assassination he made his escape only to be defeated and taken prisoner 317 B C.

Balacrus] was not a person of any great note. He was the son of Amyntas. After Issus he was appointed satrap of Cilicia and was subsequently employed in Egypt where after Alexander's departure he was left in command of an army. Later on we hear of him again at the siege of Aornus.

Barzaentes] satrap of the Arachosii and Drangae, accompanied the flight of Darius from Gaugamela and joined Bessus in murdering him. He was afterwards delivered up to Alexander who put him to death.

Cleitus] brother of Lanice the nurse of Alexander whose life he had the good fortune to save at the battle of the Granicus 334 B C. To this we may trace Alexander's great affection for him. At first he held the command of the royal squadron of the guard but after the death of Philotas he shared with Hephaestion the command of the horseguards. He was subsequently appointed satrap of Bactria in the room of Artabasus but before he set out to his government he was killed at a banquet in a fit of anger by Alexander himself whom he had enraged by sternly rebuking his flatterers.

Coenus] brother in law of Philotas, at whose trial he was one of the three presiding generals. Probably from a wish to save Philotas from being tortured he proposed the punishment of stoning. He commanded a division of the phalanx and was employed by Alexander on various occasions, as for instance against Spitamenes whom he defeated. Accompanying Alexander to India we find him in command of some cavalry at the battle with Porus. It was Coenus who in the name of the army strongly dissuaded Alexander from pushing on his conquests beyond the Hyphasis. He died not long afterwards.

Critobulus] a Greek surgeon in the service both of Philip, from whose eye he skilfully extracted an arrow, and of Alexander for whom as Curtius says he extracted the javelin from the wound received at the siege of the Mallian capital. Arrian however gives the credit of this operation to one Critodemus.

Craterus] one of the ablest of Alexander's officers but if we may judge from his conduct at the trial of Philotas not of a very scrupulous and upright character. Under Parmenio he commanded the infantry of the left wing at Issus and the cavalry at Gaugamela, and afterwards was entrusted with one of the divisions of the phalanx. Accompanying Alexander to India he was employed on numerous occasions where energy and ability were required. On the return from India he was sent back by the Bolan Pass to Carmania with the elephants the light troops and the disabled Macedonians, and arrived in safety. By Alexander's desire he married Amastris a niece of Darius and was then despatched with Polysperchon to conduct the discharged veterans back to Europe. After Alexander's death Greece and the countries to the north of it fell to the joint regency of Craterus and Antipater whose daughter he married. Craterus eventually fell in battle against Eumenes.

Eumenes] is only once mentioned in our period. He was a Greek of Cardia and a man of great ability. Having become secretary to Philip he held the same post under Alexander by whom he was employed not only in civil but also in military operations. On the death of Alexander he obtained Cappadocia Paphlagonia and Pontus and was established in his government by Perdiccas. He took a leading part in the subsequent wars.

Harpalus] who was about the same age as Alexander himself was banished for his share in the intrigue to bring about the marriage of Alexander with the daughter of Pixodarus. On Philip's death he was recalled and accompanied Alexander to Asia as his treasurer, but before Issus was guilty of peculation and fled to Greece. He was however recalled and pardoned and placed in charge of the treasury at Ecbatana with 6000 men. Again he grossly abused his trust and again fled to Greece on hearing of Alexander's safe return from India. He was eventually assassinated in Crete,

Hephaestion] was about Alexander's own age and his most intimate friend. He does not appear to have possessed any marked ability, and this perhaps was one reason for Alexander's affection towards him. We find him crowning the tomb of Patroclus in the Troad as Alexander did that of Achilles. In the Egyptian expedition he was in command of the fleet, and he received a wound at Gaugamela. At the trial of Philotas he was one of the three presidents and after the death of Philotas succeeded with Cleitus to the joint command of the horse-guards. He was subsequently employed in important operations in Sogdiana and Bactria and accompanied Alexander to India, where again we continually find him charged with the conduct of great operations. He shared with Perdiccas the task of preparing a bridge over the Indus, was sent to occupy the kingdom of the lesser Porus, led a division during the invasion of the territory of the Malli, and commanded half the army during the descent of the Indus. From this it would appear that he had acquired sufficient military experience to compensate for his want of striking ability. After this he was occupied with the building of several cities and when separated from the king it was on him that the command of the whole army devolved. On his return to Susa he married Drypetis a daughter of Darius and sister of Statira. Soon afterwards he was taken with a fever at Ecbatana and there died receiving after death the most extravagant honours from the affection of Alexander.

Leonnatus] was one of the ablest and most distinguished of Alexander's officers. He was a somatophylax and on several occasions shewed the greatest courage, notably at the siege of the Mallian town where with Peucestes he saved Alexander's life. On the march down the Indus he commanded the light troops and was left at the mouth of that river with most of the troops and the smaller vessels. On the return march from India he was left to overawe the Oritae and to wait for the arrival of Nearchus. For these services he was rewarded with a golden crown. After Alexander's death Lesser or Hellespontine Phrygia fell to his share.

Meleager] was present at Alexander's battles of the Granicus Issus and Gaugamela and took part in the operations in Bactria. At the passage of the Hydaspes he was in command of mercenaries. After Alexander's death he led the opposition against Perdiccas by whom he was put to death.

Memnon] was appointed governor of Syria and subsequently brought up reinforcements for Alexander from Thrace.

Nearchus] was in command of the fleet on the voyage down the Indus, from the mouth of which river he was sent round with a fleet on a voyage of survey to the Persian Gulf and arrived safe at Carmania after meeting with Leonnatus at Oritis, visiting the Persian Gulf, and finally landing near the island of Ormuz. From here he proceeded to explore the mouth of the river Tigris. At Susa he was married to a daughter of Mentor by Barsine, who had also had a son by Alexander (by name Hercules) whose claims to the throne were supported by *Nearchus* in the council held after the death of Alexander.

Onesicritus] was appointed pilot of the king's ship or chief pilot of the fleet built on the Hydaspes and accompanied Nearchus in that capacity on the voyage down the Indus and also to the Persian Gulf. At Susa he was rewarded for his services with a crown. He subsequently wrote a history of Alexander which, though he was to a large extent an eyewitness, is chiefly remarkable for its want of veracity.

Oxyartes] accompanied Bessus in his retreat across the Oxus after the murder of Darius, having left his family as he thought secure in a fortress of Sogdiana. Alexander however stormed the fortress and having taken them prisoners designed to marry Roxana his daughter. On hearing of this Oxyartes gave himself up and met with the kindest treatment and was appointed satrap of Parapamisus a post which he continued to hold after the death of Alexander probably until his own death.

Perdiccas] was one of the greatest of Alexander's generals and as after events proved one of the most unscrupulous. See Thirlwall chapter LVII (vol VIII p 221). He was one of the officers called somatophylakes and also commanded one of the divisions of the phalanx. At the siege of Thebes he was wounded and was present at all Alexander's great battles. He was subsequently employed both in the campaigns on the Oxus and in India where he was sent on with Hephæstion to prepare a bridge for the army over the Indus, distinguished himself in the battle with Porus, and was selected to lead the assault on the Mallian town where Alexander nearly lost his life. He married a daughter of the satrap Atropates and his favour with Alexander seems to have been continually on the increase and Alexander's last act (which was to hand his signet-ring to him) seems to have been intended to designate Perdiccas as his successor. He was chosen regent after Alexander's death in conjunction with Meleager and after many vicissitudes was finally assassinated in Egypt in a campaign against Ptolemy.

Peucestes] was appointed to carry the sacred shield which Alexander took down from the temple of Athena at Ilium, and in this capacity chiefly contributed to save Alexander's life among the Malli. As a reward for this he was made a somatophylax and appointed governor of Persia. At Susa he was rewarded with a golden crown. In 323 B C he joined Alexander with 20000 Persian soldiers and was in close attendance during the king's last illness. He further won Alexander's favour by adopting the Persian dress and manners. After the king's death he was continued in his government of Persia.

Pithon] the commander of the royal household was defeated wounded and taken prisoner by Spitamenes. He was employed in the Indian campaign and there received a province. Against the Malli he held a command and was also sent to put down the revolt of Musicanus. On the march down the Indus he had charge of a division with the duty of planting colonies and pacifying the country. After Alexander's death he retained his province and eventually fell in the battle between Demetrius and Ptolemy B C 312.

Polyperoon] or *Polysperchon*, one of the oldest veterans in the service of Alexander commanded a division of the phalanx. We find him mentioned as present at the passage of the Hydaspes and also in the descent of the Indus when he was under the command of Craterus with whom he was subsequently sent to conduct the discharged veterans back to Greece. Being absent at Alexander's death he was passed over and is not heard of again till sometime after that event.

Ptolemy] the reputed son of Lagus and thus of obscure origin, but also said to be an illegitimate son of Philip, was probably the ablest of Alexander's officers and was the author of an account of his conquests. He was banished from Macedonia on the discovery of Alexander's projected marriage with the daughter of Pixodarus, and this event was the beginning of his subsequent elevation. In conjunction with Asander he defeated Orontobates and captured Halicarnassus and other strong places in Caria. At the forcing of the Persian Gates he was in command of a division of 3000 men and was made a somatophylax in the room of Demetrius. He was sent to arrest Bessus and commanded a column in the operations across the Oxus and was engaged at the siege of the fortress of Chorienes. It was he who gained information of the plot of Hermolaus and the pages and reported it to Alexander, thereby in all probability saving the king's life. In the campaign against the Aspasians he killed their chief with his own hand. In the operations against the Malli he commanded one of the three corps of invasion and in the district of Oritis (or in the kingdom of Sambus) he received a wound which was healed by the application of a herb discovered by Alexander himself, who was thus enabled to requite his friend for saving his own life as above mentioned. On the return from India he was married to a daughter of Artabanus. After Alexander's death Egypt fell to his share and there he maintained himself and founded a dynasty.

Sisocostus] or *Sisicottus*, an Indian leader of mercenaries who, when Bessus fell into Alexander's hands, submitted and became attached to the conqueror. It was he who gave Alexander accounts of the country beyond the Indus. To him was committed the charge of the important rock-fortress of Aornis or Aornus.

INDEX TO THE NOTES.

a meridie viii 10 § 24
ab Oriente viii 9 § 5
Abisares viii 12 § 13
ablative ix 5 § 30, 10 §§ 12, 18
ablative of description ix 8 § 23
,, instrument viii 13 § 18
,, origin viii 10 § 1
,, price ix 6 § 11
,, time ix 6 § 1
,, without preposition after verbs ix 8 § 14
abstergere ix 9 § 16
abstinere viii 10 § 10
abstract for concrete viii 13 § 18, ix 7 § 8
Acadira viii 10 § 19
acceptus viii 12 § 11
accidere ix 9 § 27
Acesines viii 9 § 8, ix 1 § 8, 4 § 8
acrius quam cautius viii 11 § 15
ad = against viii 10 § 22, ix 4 § 23
ad hoc = praeterea ix 2 § 4, 10 § 13
ad ictus ix 5 § 1
ad manum viii 11 § 8
ad manus ix 9 § 17
ad omnia viii 14 § 23
ad speciem viii 9 § 22
ad ultimum ix 10 § 11
ad vocem viii 14 § 36
adactus ix 5 § 24
adeo and non adeo viii 9 §§ 11, 13, ix 4 § 7
adfinitas ix 3 § 22
adfirmare ix 1 § 34
adfluere ix 5 § 7
adgressi with infinitive ix 1 § 4
adhuc ix 2 § 4, 6 § 2
admittere ix 6 § 13
admovere ix 4 § 27
adplicare ix 9 § 8
adsidere ix 8 § 25
adsum viii 11 § 23
adventare viii 9 § 16
adversum flumen ix 10 § 1
adversus ix 9 § 9
advertere viii 13 § 19
aedes ix 10 § 25
aegris mortalibus viii 10 § 29
aegrum curare viii 14 § 45
aestimare viii 14 § 46, ix 1 § 26
Afghans viii 10 § 22
agger viii 10 § 27
agmen = acies viii 12 § 7
ago and dego viii 9 § 33
agrestis viii 10 § 14
Agriani viii 11 § 9
agricultores viii 12 § 12
alere viii 9 § 16
aliquantum ix 6 § 2
aliter viii 10 § 27
alitus viii 10 § 8
alter viii 13 § 2
altius repetere ix 6 § 16
amarus = salsus ix 9 § 6
amplius viii 10 § 2
anceps viii 14 §§ 7, 16, ix 9 § 2
animus est ire ix 3 § 5
antequam viii 10 § 30

Aornis viii 11 § 2
aperire viii 13 § 8, ix 6 § 20
appellata regina viii 10 § 35
aptare ix 9 § 12
apte ix 13 § 6
Aquilo viii 9 § 12
Arbela ix 2 § 23
Arabitae ix 10 § 5
arbores viii 9 § 34
ardua, niti per viii 11 § 9
arietare ix 7 § 22
arma)(tela ix 3 § 10
armentum (aro) ix 2 § 16
Arsinoe ix 8 § 22
artes pacis ix 8 § 23
at enim ix 2 § 22
attraction viii 9 §§ 10, 33, 10 § 36
avare facere ix 8 § 9
avaritia gloriae ix 2 § 9
auctor viii 12 § 4
auctoritas ix 7 § 3
aversus in viii 13 § 23
aves, talking birds viii 9 §§ 16, 25
aula ix 7 § 15
aura maris ix 4 § 21
aures fatigare viii 13 § 10
— pulsare ix 2 § 30
aureus ix 1 § 6
auro caelata viii 9 § 26
aurum viii 9 § 18
auspicium ix 3 § 6
autem ix 2 § 31
auxilium ix 1 § 16

baccar viii 10 § 14
Beira viii 10 § 22
beluae, crocodiles (?) ix 9 § 22
binum = binorum viii 9 § 28
Biton ix 7 § 9
brachia)(lacerti viii 9 § 21
Brahmans viii 9 §§ 31—33
Bucephala ix 1 § 6, 3 § 23

caecus ix 9 § 2
caligo ix 4 § 8, 5 § 28
candor ix 1 § 30
capere = χωρεῖν ix 3 § 7, 6 § 14
capital (archaic form) viii 9 § 34
carbasa viii 9 § 24
carbasus viii 9 § 21
carpere viii 9 § 10
castella viii 12 § 7
castra viii 12 § 4
Caucasus viii 9 § 3
cedere ix 4 § 20
Cedrosii ix 10 § 5
cedrus viii 10 § 8
celebratus ix 1 § 2
celeritas ix 4 § 10, viii 14 § 19
certamen ix 4 § 13
certe viii 10 § 36
ceterum viii 9 § 12
ceterum = sed viii 10 § 2
charta viii 9 § 15
Choaspes viii 10 § 22
circuitus viii 11 § 5
circumferre ix 5 § 1
claudus = debilis ix 9 § 13
climate, effect of viii 9 § 20
coetus ix 4 § 9
cognoscere ix 8 § 9
cohors regia viii 11 § 9, ix 10 § 26
colere viii 9 §§ 21, 34, ix 9 § 2
columen ix 6 § 8
comissabundus ix 10 § 26
comitatus viii 14 § 15
commendare ix 3 § 5
commercium viii 9 § 19
committere obsidionem ix 4 § 27
committi ix 4 § 1
comparative double viii 11 § 15
concursatio viii 14 § 24
condere viii 10 § 11
condere lucem viii 13 § 24
condicio ix 7 § 18
confirmatus viii 14 § 45
confundi ix 4 § 8
coniunctus ix 1 § 26
conserere viii 12 § 9
considerare viii 10 § 26
considere ix 7 § 12
constanter viii 14 § 25
constantia ix 7 § 25
consternere ix 6 § 7
constituere viii 9 § 19, 11 § 4
contentus with infinitive viii 11 § 18
contio ix 1 § 1
convictus with infinitive ix 8 § 9
convocare ix 1 § 23
co-ordination of clauses ix 6 § 18

copis viii 14 § 29
corona ix 1 § 14, 8 § 15
corona = a parapet ix 4 § 30
corrumpere ix 7 § 15
cratera ix 10 § 25
cremare incendio ix 10 § 12
crocodiles viii 9 § 9, ix 9 § 22
crudus later viii 10 § 25
crux ix 8 § 16
cultus ix 3 § 11, 8 § 23
cum viii 9 § 27
cum fide viii 11 § 25
cum potest viii 9 § 27
cum ramis viii 10 § 30, 11 § 8
curare, curatio ix 6 § 1
currus viii 9 § 29
cursus ix 9 § 8
curvare se ix 1 § 10
custodes corporis viii 11 § 11
custos ix 8 § 23

Daedala viii 10 § 19
Dahae viii 14 § 5
dative, ethic ix 2 § 25
dative of gerund or gerundive viii 10 § 30
dative of predication viii 9 § 37
dative of relation ix 7 § 22
declinare ix 2 § 20
decurrere ix 3 § 13
dedicare ix 3 § 23
deinde = ἔπειτα ix 10 § 28
deficere ix 4 § 18
degenerare ix 3 § 10
dego and ago viii 9 § 33
delphinus viii 9 § 9
dependent clause of oratio obliqua in Indicative ix 2 § 7
deprecari ix 1 § 20
derelinquere ix 4 § 8
destinata viii 10 § 28
destinare ix 9 § 6
destituere viii 14 § 31, ix 9 § 20
destruere viii 14 § 46
deurere viii 9 § 12
dies fati viii 9 § 32
dirigere viii 9 § 36
discors ix 9 § 26
distinguere viii 9 § 24
diversa regio ix 1 § 35
diversus viii 13 § 20
diutius quam ix 4 § 30
documentum ut viii 14 § 26
dogs ix 1 § 31
dorsum ix 8 § 2
dulcis (of water) ix 9 § 6
dum with present indicative ix 10 § 21
dum = until such time as ix 10 § 22
dumtaxat ix 10 § 18
Dyardenes viii 9 § 9

Ecbolima viii 12 § 1
edere viii 14 § 37, ix 5 § 16
elephants viii 9 §§ 17, 29, 14 §§ 26—40
efferare ix 10 § 9
effluere viii 14 § 36
effusus viii 14 § 34
elidere ix 2 § 21, 7 § 22
elisus viii 13 § 9
eludere ix 7 § 18
eluvies viii 11 § 7
emicare ix 5 § 10
eminere viii 12 § 13
emittere viii 14 § 5
enare viii 13 § 15
enatus ix 8 § 30
enavigare ix 9 § 13
equites equester ordo ix 7 § 14
ergo ix 2 § 12
erigere viii 11 § 6, ix 1 § 10, 3 § 2
eruere ix 2 § 9
Erythrus rex viii 9 § 14
et viii 10 § 11, ix 6 § 23, 8 § 21
et = καὶ = and in particular ix 1 § 8
Ethimantus viii 9 § 10
evehi ix 9 § 8
eventus viii 13 § 12, ix 8 § 20
everberare ix 4 § 13
ex solido ix 2 § 14
exacti viii 14 §§ 9, 30
exaestuare ix 9 § 9
exanguis ix 3 § 5, 5 § 26
excedere viii 9 § 3, 14 § 13
excipere ix 2 § 2, 8 § 21, 10 § 15
excolere ix 6 § 21
excusatio ix 3 § 17
eximius with genitive viii 9 § 5
existere ix 4 § 18
expectare ut ix 3 § 1

expelli viii 13 § 26
experiri viii 12 § 6
expertus se viii 13 § 11
expetere with infinitive ix 3 § 8
exponere viii 14 § 31, ix 3 § 24
exprobrare ix 7 § 17
expugnare ix 4 § 5
extendi ix 3 § 19
extra sidera ix 4 § 18

facere copiam etc viii 14 § 42
faciendo aggeri viii 10 § 30
facies viii 14 § 27
facturus viii 10 § 1
fallax miraculum ix 3 § 19
fallere ix 4 § 33
fama ix 5 § 1, 10 § 24
fastigium viii 9 § 3, 10 § 31, ix 2 § 28, 9 § 19
fati dies viii 9 § 32
fatigare aures viii 13 § 10
fauces ix 2 § 13
felicitas viii 10 § 18, 13 § 13
felix temeritas viii 13 § 15
ferox ix 4 § 16
ferre ix 6 § 22
ferrum candidum ix 8 § 1
fides viii 12 § 6, 11 § 25, ix 1 § 23
fingere=putare ix 2 § 13
flagitium viii 14 § 11
fluere viii 14 § 33
forma viii 14 § 13
fossa viii 13 § 17
fraus ix 7 § 5
frequens viii 13 § 14, ix 1 § 13
frequentative force lost in verbs viii 9 § 16
fretum ix 9 § 20
frigescens viii 10 § 29
frigus viii 10 § 7
fruges viii 10 § 14

Ganges viii 9 § 5
gemmae viii 9 § 19
gender, change of, implying change of subject viii 13 § 8
generare viii 9 § 16
genitive ix 1 § 26, 2 § 1
genitive, objective viii 9 § 32
genitive of definition viii 10 § 7, ix 7 § 3
" of further definition viii 14 § 41
" of quality with verb viii 10 § 24, ix 3 § 22, 7 § 6
genitive of distributive numerals viii 9 § 28
gerundive viii 10 § 30
gloria ix 5 § 1, 10 § 24
Great Kaan viii 9 § 29
Greek construction viii 10 § 3

habere viii 10 § 17
habitus ix 1 § 25
Hages viii 14 § 2
hasta viii 14 § 16
haud sane viii 9 § 37, 14 § 3
haud secus quam viii 14 § 45
haurire ix 5 § 11
hedera viii 10 § 13
hendiadys ix 1 § 26, 3 § 23
Hercules)(Vishnu viii 14 § 11, ix 3 § 2
Hesudrus ix 2 § 1
hinc...hinc viii 13 § 11, ix 4 § 10, 8 § 6
Hindoos viii 9 § 15
hortari ix 8 § 6
Hydaspes viii 13 § 8, ix 4 § 8
Hyphasis viii 9 § 8, ix 1 § 35, 2 § 1

iacere viii 10 § 24
Iaxartes ix 6 § 21
idem ix 8 § 16
idem animi, iuris ix 2 § 11
identidem ix 9 § 10
igitur viii 10 § 1
ignavia ix 7 § 17
ignis viii 10 § 7
ignobilis ix 2 § 6
ignominia notare ix 6 § 13
illud=*ἐκεῖνο* used of what follows viii 14 § 6, ix 10 § 24
imperium populi ix 8 § 4
impersonal use of verbs in passive viii 10 § 5
in artius viii 11 § 6
in crucem tollere ix 8 § 16
in diversum ix 7 § 10

in fidem accipere ix 1 § 23
in incremento esse ix 3 § 9
in medium viii 14 § 9
in multum diei viii 14 § 28
in obsidione viii 10 § 22
in oculis ix 4 § 10
in regionem viii 13 § 23
in solido ix 2 § 14
in speculis ix 9 § 23
incedere viii 11 § 16
incitamentum viii 14 § 11
includere viii 9 § 28, ix 8 § 11
inconditus viii 11 § 1, ix 1 § 16
incubare ix 4 § 18
incumbere ix 9 § 4
inde, of time ix 1 § 33, 10 § 22
index viii 11 § 8
India, climate viii 9 § 20
,, reports and traditions about viii 10 § 1
Indian dress viii 9 § 21
,, jewels viii 9 § 19
,, trees, the banyan tree ix 1 §§ 9, 10
Indian ocean (rubrum mare) viii 9 § 5
Indian animals for riding viii 9 § 29
Indian bows and arrows viii 9 § 28
,, burning of dead viii 9 § 32
,, classes among viii 12 § 12
,, division of months viii 9 § 35
,, drunkenness viii 9 § 30
,, dyeing of beards viii 9 § 22
,, fire god viii 9 § 32
,, hair and hairdressers viii 9 §§ 22, 27
,, marriage, exposing or rearing of children ix 1 §§ 25, 26
,, tree-worship viii 9 § 34
,, tree-wool (cotton) viii 9 § 15
indicative in apodosis of conditional sentences viii 13 § 15
indicium ix 2 § 30
Indus boundary of India viii 10 § 1
,, derivation of viii 9 § 4
,, tides in viii 9 § 9
indutus viii 9 § 24
iners, inertia ix 6 § 12
inesse with dative ix 5 § 23
infinitive depending on 'he says' 'he thought' not expressed ix 2 § 10
infractus viii 14 § 44
ingemere morte and morti ix 3 § 20
ingenium viii 9 § 20, ix 10 § 9
inhabilis viii 13 § 11
inluvies viii 14 § 14
inminere ix 1 § 21
inmobilis ix 4 § 18
inmortalitas ix 6 § 26
inmutatio ix 7 § 15
innoxius ix 4 § 11
inpedimentum ix 10 § 22
inpellere ix 9 § 25
inpius, inpiae mentes, inpia arma ix 3 § 5
inplere ix 3 § 7
inponere viii 14 § 19
inprovisus ix 2 § 13
inpunitas viii 12 § 3
inquinare viii 9 § 32
insignis ix 1 § 25, 5 § 1
instar ix 1 § 10
instare ix 1 § 33
institutus viii 14 § 39
insula viii 9 § 7
integer ix 4 § 16
intendere viii 13 § 17
inter hæc=interea ix 3 § 21
inter ora viii 10 § 18
interfluere viii 9 § 11
interritus viii 9 § 33
intrepidus viii 11 § 18
invehi ix 9 § 9
invertere se viii 9 § 13
invidus viii 12 § 18
inusitatus / invisitatus } viii 9 § 16
inultus ix 5 § 2
inundare ix 2 § 28
Iomanes viii 9 § 8
Iovis filius viii 10 § 29
ipsos ix 9 § 3
ipsos=se viii 10 § 1
ita ix 9 § 12
ita ne=ita ut ne ix 5 § 22
ita si ix 6 § 24
iunctus flumini ix 1 § 13
iungere viii 10 § 3

iura reddere and petere viii 9 § 27
iura naturae, belli ix 4 § 7
ius commercii ix 10 § 8
iustus ix 7 § 19

Kaan, the Great, viii 9 § 29
Karduchan archers viii 14 § 19
Kathaei ix 1 § 24
kingly duties ix 8 §§ 25, 27
kings attended by women viii 9 § 30
,, forbidden to get drunk viii 9 § 30

labi viii 14 § 38
laborare ix 3 § 11
lacerta ix 8 § 2
lana viii 9 § 15
lapillus viii 9 § 21
lascivia viii 10 § 15
latitudo viii 9 § 2
laurus viii 10 § 14
lectica viii 9 § 24
legatio viii 9 § 27
liber viii 9 § 15
liberalis ix 8 § 23
liberius ix 3 § 2
libido viii 9 § 19
librare ix 5 § 2
limen, in limine ix 2 § 26
lineae vestes ix 7 § 12
linquere ix 5 § 11
linqui animo ix 5 § 28
linum viii 9 § 15
lintea viii 9 § 21
liquidus, ad liquidum viii 14 § 2, ix 2 § 14
locorum situs viii 9 § 20, 10 § 13, ix 2 § 8
locum invenire ix 2 § 34
longus ix 6 § 22
lubricus viii 14 § 19
luere ix 6 § 13
luxuria viii 9 § 23

machina viii 10 § 31
magnificentia viii 9 § 23
Malli ix 4 §§ 15, 24, 8 § 3
malum viii 14 § 41
manare ix 7 § 5
manus, ad manum viii 11 § 8, 14 § 27, ix 7 § 17
margaritae viii 9 § 19
materia ix 1 § 14
maxime = μάλιστα ix 2 § 12
Mazagae viii 10 § 22
mecum esse ix 2 § 33
mei ix 2 § 25
memor ix 2 § 7
mensis viii 9 §§ 35, 36
mente complecti ix 2 § 11
mentiri, mendax viii 10 § 12
mentum viii 9 § 22
meridies viii 10 § 24
meta viii 11 § 6
militans gloriae viii 12 § 10
milites viii 12 § 12
miserabilis viii 11 § 12
Mithan Kot ix 8 § 8
mitigare viii 14 § 10
modicus viii 12 § 7, ix 7 § 15
moles saxorum, corporum viii 10 § 30, 13 § 10
moliri viii 9 § 7, 10 § 30, 14 § 19, ix 5 § 19, 6 § 23
momentum ix 6 § 21
monumenta ix 8 § 21
moribundus ix 5 § 28
moriturus ix 5 § 26
movere viii 9 § 1
movere se viii 14 § 6
mulcari viii 11 § 23
mundus viii 9 § 13
munimentum ix 4 § 8
Musicanus and Musicani viii 12 § 14

natio and gens ix 7 § 4
natus viii 9 § 1
nauticus ix 9 § 4
ne viii 10 § 5
nec = yet not viii 13 § 9
nec = et non ix 9 § 1
nec...et ix 10 § 15
Nicaea ix 1 § 6
nisi viii 9 § 16
niti per ardua viii 11 § 9
noctes viii 9 § 30
nomen...opus = ὄνομα...ἔργον ix 2 § 14
nomen ix 6 § 17

nomen regis etc ix 7 § 3
nomina ix 2 § 33
Nora viii 11 § 1
novus, novare res viii 14 § 29, ix 6 § 5
nudus ix 5 § 11
nuptiae ix 1 § 25
Nysa viii 10 § 7

ob, force of in composition viii 10 § 28
obequitare viii 10 § 6
obligare viii 10 § 28
oblique petition ix 4 § 18
obruere quin ix 9 § 13
obsidere vias ix 2 § 3
obsolescere ix 6 § 14
obsoletus)(gloriosus ix 1 § 2
obstrepere viii 13 § 23
obstrinxerat, force of pluperfect viii 12 § 17
occasio sua viii 13 § 26
occulta saxa viii 13 § 9
occulti = λάθρα viii 13 § 15
occupare viii 9 § 32, 11 § 2, 14 § 19, ix 1 § 32, 4 § 10, 5 § 24, 9 § 19
occurrere viii 13 § 2
Oceanus ix 2 § 26
oleum ix 7 § 16
olim viii 14 § 10, ix 6 § 26
Olympias ix 6 § 26
ominari ix 8 § 24
omission of pronoun ix 4 § 20, 6 §§ 6, 26
omittere viii 14 § 29
omnis, ad omnia viii 10 § 20, 14 § 23
omnino ix 1 § 32
Omphis viii 12 § 4
operae est ix 9 § 37
operatus viii 10 § 17
opimus ix 1 § 2
opportunitas viii 13 § 18
oppressus viii 10 § 20
opulentia viii 9 § 19
opus viii 10 § 23, 24, ix 2 § 14
Oritae ix 10 § 6
os viii 9 § 8
Oxydracae ix 4 § 15

palmam frangere, infringere ix 2 § 29
papyrus, paper viii 9 § 15
παραιτεῖσθαι ix 1 § 20
parcitur viii 10 § 5
parentare ix 5 § 20
parrots and talking birds viii 9 § 16
parta (praeda), parto frui ix 2 § 10
pars viii 10 § 2
partes viii 13 § 13
participle future viii 10 § 1
,, past with present meaning viii 10 § 17
,, ablative of used absolutely viii 12 § 6
,, past of deponent verbs used passively viii 14 § 15
participle and verb = two verbs viii 10 § 3
Patalia, Patala, Pattala, etc ix 8 § 24
patera viii 10 § 34
pati viii 9 § 23
patiens ix 9 § 2
pavidus viii 14 § 23
pavo ix 1 § 13
pecora viii 12 § 11
Penates ix 6 § 9
pensitare ix 7 § 14
per of agency viii 12 § 2
per in adjurations ix 2 § 27
per otium, per quietem ix 6 § 19
per ardua niti viii 11 § 9
per herbas viii 10 § 17
per insidias ix 2 § 7
per modica intervalla viii 12 § 7
percutere viii 10 § 27
perferre = nuntiare viii 3 § 1
permisso viii 12 § 6
perpetuus viii 13 § 13, ix 4 § 18
Persica vestis viii 12 § 16
petra viii 11 § 2
phalanx viii 10 § 4
philosophers viii 9 § 31
pietas ix 6 § 16
pientissimus, piissimus ix 6 § 17
pinna, lorica ix 4 § 30
plerique, plures ix 10 § 2
pluperfect, force of viii 12 § 17

poculum, cratera ix 10 § 26
poetical expressions viii 10 §§ 1, 15, 17, 13 §§ 10, 24
poma viii 10 § 14
populares ix 7 § 2
populi imperium ix 8 § 4
porro ix 1 § 5
post ix 6 § 21
posteritas ix 3 § 5
postulare ix 2 § 31
praecipere viii 10 § 5, ix 6 § 26, 10 § 14
,, προλαμβάνειν ix 6 § 2
praecipito viii 11 § 3
praeparare ix 7 § 16
praes, vas ix 2 § 25
praesens ix 1 § 12, 2 § 19
praesidere viii 13 § 21
praestare viii 14 § 13, ix 6 § 13
praesto esse viii 13 § 2
praetorium ix 6 § 4
precario ix 2 § 34
pretium operae viii 11 § 3
primordium ix 2 § 11
pro=in proportion to viii 13 § 9
pro contione ix 1 § 1
procul viii 14 § 13
procul with ablative viii 13 § 18
proditor, prodere viii 14 § 36
profecto ix 1 § 18, 3 § 5
proficere ad ix 10 § 14
prohibere with ablative viii 13 § 5
proinde ix 1 § 2
pronoun omitted ix 4 § 20, 6 §§ 6, 26
promptus viii 11 § 9
propior ix 2 § 7
propius ix 3 § 3
propulsare ix 2 § 6
publicis moribus=in public viii 9 § 33
pulso ix 2 § 30
purgamentum viii 9 § 19, ix 10 § 10
putris ix 3 § 10

quandoque ix 6 § 26
quasi, tamquam viii 13 § 18
que=sed viii 11 § 11
que...et=τε...καί ix 3 § 22
qui=eos qui viii 10 §§ 2, 10
qui quidem=ὅς γε ix 6 § 18
qui unus viii 14 § 36
quin ix 2 § 28, 9 § 23
quippe viii 9 § 8
quo=ut eo with comparative ix 1 § 17
quod=so far as viii 12 § 9
quod ix 2 § 31
quoque viii 9 § 20
quoque=καί viii 10 § 18

ratio viii 10 § 20
recidere ix 5 § 25
recipere viii 9 § 32, ix 1 § 21
reciprocari ix 9 § 20
recta regione viii 9 § 2
recto alveo viii 9 § 5
recubare viii 9 § 24
reddere ix 1 § 12, 9 § 20
reddi viii 9 § 32, 11 § 25
redux=reducens ix 6 § 9
refragari ix 5 § 21
regere ix 1 § 24
reges viii 9 § 23
reges)(reguli viii 10 § 2
regia ix 8 § 23
regio viii 13 § 23
regnare ix 5 § 21
relative proposition expressing reason of leading proposition viii 9 § 36
relative not attracted viii 9 § 31
relegare ix 2 § 9
reliqua belli ix 1 § 1
repercussus viii 9 § 8, 13 § 9
repetere ix 3 § 20
repetere altius ix 6 § 16
repletum ire ix 1 § 2
rerum monumenta ix 5 § 21
retractare ix 3 § 22
reverberari viii 9 § 6
reus ix 5 § 26
rhinoceros viii 9 § 16, ix 1 § 5
rigare viii 9 § 10
rubor ix 7 § 25
Rubrum mare viii 9 § 6
rudis with genitive viii 10 § 32
rumpere ix 3 § 10

Sabarcae, Sambastae ix 8 § 4

sacrificium ix 4 § 14
sagina, saginatus ix 7 § 16
saltem ix 2 § 31
Samiramis ix 6 § 23, 10 § 17
sapientia viii 9 § 31, 13 § 7
sarisa viii 14 § 16, ix 7 § 19
scala ix 1 § 18
scilicet ix 5 § 21
Scythae viii 14 § 5
secundo amne ix 3 § 24
securitas ix 5 § 21
senes facti ix 2 § 10
septentrio, septentriones ix 4 § 8
sequi ix 1 § 31
serpens ix 1 § 4
Sibi ix 4 § 2
sicut ix 7 § 10
sicut...ita=μὲν...δὲ viii 12 § 17
siderum motus viii 9 § 33
sidus ix 6 § 8
signatus viii 12 § 15
simpliciter, simplicius viii 14 § 46
simulacrum)(statua viii 14 § 11
situs locorum viii 9 § 20, 10 § 13, ix 2 § 8
sol ix 1 § 1
solea viii 9 § 21
solidus ix 2 § 14
solitudo ix 2 § 24
solutae vehi=solvi et vehi viii 10 § 3
Sopithes (Asvapati) ix 1 § 24
sopitus viii 9 § 30
sors ultima ix 2 § 6
spatium ix 2 § 10
spatia terrarum ix 4 § 19
species viii 9 § 22
spectare viii 9 § 2
spiritus ix 5 § 30
stadium genitive plural viii 10 § 25
stagnare viii 9 § 7
stagnum viii 13 § 9
stare in aqua ix 3 § 21
statuere viii 14 § 19
status viii 9 § 13, ix 9 §§ 9, 27
sternere ix 2 § 23
stipendium viii 13 § 2
strenuus, strenue viii 14 § 5, ix 8 § 20
stringere viii 9 § 5
studere ix 7 § 19
suasoria ix 3 § 5, appendix A
sub=ὑπὸ viii 10 § 10
subducere ix 1 § 34, 7 § 24
subducere vela ix 4 § 10
subject, change of viii 11 § 2, 10 § 10
subject, change of implied in change of gender viii 15 § 8
subicere ix 5 § 11
subinde viii 9 § 10, ix 1 § 33, 3 § 24
subire ix 4 § 32, 6 § 24
subjunctive imperfect second person singular ix 4 § 14
subjunctive of assumed reason ix 10 § 17
subluere viii 6 § 20
submovere ix 6 § 22
subsidere ix 9 § 19
subvehere ix 3 § 9
succedere viii 11 § 19
succidere ix 5 § 7
Sudracae ix 4 §§ 15, 24
suicide among Brahmans viii 9 §§ 32, 33
super with accusative viii 12 § 17
superbe ix 8 § 9
supervenire viii 13 § 15
supine with verbs of motion ix 1 § 2
supplementum ix 3 § 21
sura viii 10 § 28
Surena viii 12 § 14
suspectus with infinitive ix 10 § 21
suspendere ix 7 § 20
suspitio ix 7 § 5
sustinere viii 12 § 6
suus emphatic viii 13 § 2

tabula ix 9 § 20
tacere ix 2 § 31
tamquam and quasi viii 13 § 18
Tanais ix 6 § 21
tardus ix 9 § 12
Taxila and Taxiles viii 12 § 4
telum and arma ix 1 § 15
temeritas felix viii 13 § 15
temperare (oculis) ix 3 § 2
tendere ix 9 § 14
Terioltes, Tiryaspes ix 8 § 9
terra humore diluta=πηλὸς viii 10 § 25

theatrum ix 6 § 21
Timaeus ix 5 § 15
Timagenes ix 5 § 21
tollere ix 1 § 25
torrens viii 13 § 9
torrentia flumina ix 9 § 9
tractus ix 9 § 20
tradere ix 2 § 14
trahere in casum, discrimen ix 6 § 8
transcribere ix 1 § 34
transilire ix 1 § 15
transmittere ix 4 § 17
tree-worship viii 9 § 34
truncus viii 11 § 8
tugurium ix 10 § 10
turba ix 2 § 25
turbare ix 4 § 9
turris viii 14 § 13

vanitas ix 2 § 13
vas and praes ix 2 § 25
vastus viii 13 § 10
vel,..vel viii 12 § 8, ix 7 § 17
velum ix 10 § 25
venatus ix 8 § 28
venenum ix 8 § 20
verbs compounded governing the dative viii 10 § 6
verb singular with names of persons ix 5 § 21
vereri ix 7 § 23
vereri ne ix 5 § 24
vero ix 6 § 21
vestis viii 9 § 15, ix 8 § 1
vestis Persica viii 12 § 16
vices viii 9 § 13
victoria lustrare ix 3 § 8
vindicare ix 2 § 32, 10 § 18
vinum viii 9 § 30
virtus = ἀρετή ix 7 § 16
virus of snakes ix 1 § 12
vis ix 1 § 23
viscera ix 5 § 24
visurus = ἐποψόμενος ix 3 § 20
vitare ix 7 § 21
vitium viii 9 § 19, 10 § 29
vivarium viii 9 § 28
vivere with ablative ix 5 § 30
vix ullus viii 14 § 4
ullus, ullius, ulli as substantive viii 12 § 6
ultra = behind viii 13 § 6
ultro ix 7 § 5
universus viii 10 § 26
vorago viii 10 § 24, 14 § 4
usque preposition viii 9 § 21
usurpare viii 12 § 6
ut = ita ut viii 10 § 25
ut, concessive ix 3 § 12
ut, to be supplied from preceding ne ix 4 § 27
utcunque viii 10 § 36
utique viii 9 § 19
vultus viii 12 § 9

writing, on linen and skins viii 9 § 15

CAMBRIDGE: PRINTED BY C. J. CLAY, M.A. AT THE UNIVERSITY PRESS.